Discovering your Family History

Discovering your
Family History
by Don Steel

Edited by Bryn Brooks

British Broadcasting Corporation

This book is published in conjunction with
the BBC television series *Family History*,
first transmitted on BBC 2 from Wednesday 21 March 1979
and produced by Bryn Brooks

Published to accompany a series of programmes
prepared in consultation with the
BBC Continuing Education Advisory Council

First published 1980
Revised edition first published 1986
Published by the British Broadcasting Corporation
35 Marylebone High Street, London WIM 4AA

Typesetting by Tradespools Limited, Frome, Somerset
Printed in England by Spottiswoode Ballantyne Ltd.
Set in 10/11½ Ehrhardt Monophoto
ISBN 0 563 21222 5 (paperback)

Contents

Tables

Preface

When the BBC decided to produce five programmes on tracing ancestors, it was agreed that it must be a series on family history rather than genealogy. Although viewers would be introduced to basic genealogical procedures, the main emphasis would be placed not so much on these as on setting ancestors in their full social and local historical context.

Since Gordon Honeycombe, the author and former television news-reader, had long been an enthusiastic amateur genealogist, it was decided to invite him to present the series and to use his family as the example throughout all five programmes. He placed all his records at our disposal, and from then on the Family History series became inextricably linked with the story of the Honeycombes. However, unlike *Roots*, the series was not just the story of one family, but sought to use Gordon's researches to demonstrate general principles of family history research which could be applied to the viewer's own family.

This book uses a combination of two approaches – the case study and the guide to sources. The first part seeks to convey something of the thrill of the chase by following the genealogical and historical researches into the Honeycombes, and showing how different sources may be combined to yield meaningful results. The reference section gives more detailed information on the basic sources common to most families. In general, however, the aim has been not so much to achieve comprehensive coverage of genealogical sources as to strike a balance between the genealogical, biographical and historical aspects of researching a family history. Each period in the history of the Honeycombe family has been used to illustrate a particular aspect of the subject, such as proving a genealogy, setting the family in its physical and social environment, researching an occupation or looking at reasons for migration.

It may be felt that in selecting the Honeycombes as our example, we have chosen a family that is not really typical – that the amount of information we have obtained is much greater than the average family historian could reasonably expect to find. It is true that the possessor of an unusual name can contact or note down all bearers of that name he comes across, not by any means presuming that he is related to all of them, but confident that he will find many of his own relatives among them. Such a course of action is not open to Miss Smith or Mr Jones. However, although an unusual name gave Gordon Honeycombe something of an advantage, the bulk of the work of reconstructing the history of his family would have been almost exactly the same whatever his surname. Whether your name is Honeycombe or Smith, the golden rule is to proceed from the known to the unknown, proving each step of the way.

DON STEEL

Foreword to the Second Edition

Family history is a life sentence. However much you have done, there is always more to do. In 1980, shortly after the publication of the first edition, I took advantage of a visit to America to research immigration records and censuses and to track down some more of Gordon Honeycombe's distant relatives, including Florence Fones, the 86-year-old grand-daughter of the Jersey town crier (see p.84). Almost incredibly she was able to identify many photographs in albums Gordon had had copied, based on her recollections of a visit to Jersey in her childhood. Only a few weeks later, she died. Visiting relatives is definitely the one kind of family history research which cannot be delayed.

But my own efforts have been eclipsed by Gordon's. Since the book was first published, he has travelled widely, meeting many of his overseas kinsfolk and doing further research. The culmination of all this was the gathering in of the world's Honeycombes at what once was Honeycombe Hall, Calstock, in September 1984 – not to mention the first Honeycombe wedding in Calstock church for over 100 years. A fitting testimony to what can be achieved by a determined one-namer in generating interest among other bearers of the surname!

As far as official sources are concerned, there have been two major events in the Family History scene in recent years, the *Parochial Records Measure*, which has made parish records both safer and more accessible by ensuring that the vast majority are now in county or borough record offices, and the arrival of the Mormon *International Genealogical Index*, which has vastly speeded up searching and enabled it to become much more comprehensive. Both these events occurred before the first edition of this book was published, but their full impact has been felt since then, as more and more societies and libraries acquire copies and print-out facilities. Particular note should be taken of the substantial increase in Mormon branch libraries.

This progress in one area of sources has been balanced by a dispiriting lack of progress with regard to another. Despite protracted negotiations and an abortive parliamentary bill, the Registrar-General has still not disgorged his earlier records of births, marriages and deaths. When eventually these are deposited in the Public Record Office, this will produce a revolution in the subject comparable with the impact of the Mormon IGI and the Parochial Records Measure.

As I emphasised in the preface to the first edition, this is a guide only to the *basic* sources common to most families. The criterion for inclusion has usually been whether or not a source has been referred to in the Honeycombe story. 'Missing' sources like non-conformist, Irish or more advanced Scottish ones are ably covered by the works listed in the bibliography.

Because some sources have had to be omitted from the text, every effort has been made to make the bibliography as comprehensive as possible. Since the first edition was prepared six years ago, there has been a veritable explosion in listing, indexing and publishing in the field of family history. Note should be taken of the many invaluable census and marriage indexes produced by local family history societies, and of the excellent series of guides to records compiled by Jeremy Gibson and published by the Federation of Family History Societies. The Society of Genealogists and the Public Record Office have both produced useful series of leaflets and booklets, and the Society has brought out several more volumes of its *National Index of Parish Registers* and PCC wills series. Phillimore have produced new editions of many of the classic texts, have reprinted many old ones and have published some fine new books such as the *Phillimore Atlas and Index of Parish Registers*, edited by Cecil Humphery-Smith, and John West's *Town Records*, a useful companion to the long-awaited new edition of his *Village Records*.

This publishing explosion has necessitated the complete revision of the bibliography for this new edition and the opportunity has also been taken to expand several sections and introduce new ones. A development which was in its infancy in 1980, but which has exploded since, has been the application of the microcomputer to genealogy. Also, British family historians have established much closer links with foreign ones – there is now significant overseas membership of the Federation of Family History Societies, a two-way traffic in visits by leading family historians and some stout pioneering work has been done by members of the Guild of One-name Studies. (Formed in 1980, this Guild has 800 surnames listed in its most recent register – the first place to look for anyone with an unusual name.) Strangely, these two developments do not yet seem to have come together – American and British computer buffs seem to have been working in ignorance of each other's contributions. In the bibliography therefore I have sought to draw attention to American work in this area.

Essentially, however, the book remains a personal account of one man's quest not just to find his ancestors but to set them in their total historical context. Since 1980 this approach, as opposed to the more genealogical 'collecting' of ancestors, has gained much ground and I would imagine that the BBC *Family History* television series and book have made a major contribution towards this. However, 'ancestor collectors' still abound, and if the new edition of this book influences some of them to take a broader view of their hobby, I feel it will have done its job.   DON STEEL
September 1985

Acknowledgements

In writing this book, I have received considerable help from many people. I would like to thank Sheila Innes and John Radcliffe of the BBC Continuing Education Department for their support, John Robinson and Alan Jamieson of the Educational Broadcasting Councils for granting me a temporary attachment to work on the project, Lawrence Taylor and Michael Browning for reading through successive drafts of the entire manuscript and suggesting numerous improvements, Mary Beck, Lynne Browning and the late Cyril Richard for commenting on the first draft, and my secretary, Jane Nesbitt, for her patience in typing innumerable drafts and for her comments as a lay reader. The additions and amendments to the Second Edition were kindly read by Michael Browning, Jeremy Gibson, Derek and Pamela Palgrave, Pauline Saul and Cecil Humphery-Smith, as well as, of course, by Gordon. All made very useful suggestions.

Many people have helped with research. Particular mention must be made of Ann Chiswell (Devonport records), Sybil Bach (PRO), Brenda Hull (Cornwall Record Office), Mrs P. M. de Veulle and Mrs M. Backhurst (Jersey records) and Elizabeth McDowell for her considerable patience throughout and particularly for her assistance with so many of the last minute research projects.

I am also grateful to Canon Gordon Ruming, the Rev. William Smith and the Rev. Deryck Davey, Vicars of Calstock, St Cleer and Liskeard respectively, and the Very Rev. T. A. Goss, Dean of Jersey, for granting access to their records, to Peter Willis, Reference Librarian, Gravesend Public Library and P. L. Hull, Cornwall County Archivist and his staff for their help, to many members of the Honeycombe family for supplying information and photographs and to George Dicker, for permitting the inclusion of material from his booklet on Devonport Dockyard.

Above all, however, I am indebted to Gordon Honeycombe for allowing the use of his family history as an example, and for his interest throughout the project, and to Bryn Brooks, the Producer of the BBC series for his unfailing kindness, co-operation and encouragement.

DON STEEL

Illustrations

Acknowledgement is due to the following for permission to reproduce photographs: George Amy plate 86; BBC Hulton Picture Library plates 33, 34, 59, 60, 62; Church of Latter Day Saints plates 73, 103, 118; The Controller of H.M.S.O. for Crown Copyright records in the Public Record Office plates 12 (RG9/471), 54 (HO 107-153 Devonport), 64 (HO 107/181 & 182), 67 (PMG 25/13), 68 (RG9/4394), 71 (HO 107/153), 81 (HO 107 1461/14), 84 (RG9/1529), 98 & 99 (E306/2/1); County Record Office, Truro plates 92, 123, 124, 133, 134, 135; Devon Library Services plate 56; Devonport Dockyard plates 55, 57; Duchy of Cornwall plates 94, 95, 96, 97, 136; Francis Frith Collection plate 117; Gravesend and Dartford Reporter plates 28, 44; House of Lords Record Library plate 90; Gordon Honeycombe plates 1, 2, 4, 5, 6, 13–28, 38, 46, 48, 85, 105, 114, 115; Kent County Libraries, Gravesham Division, Local History Collection plates 32, 36, 37, 43; Lawn Road School, Gravesend plate 47; Mrs Mitchell plate 41; Morwhellam Quay Museum plate 116; Museum of English Rural Life plate 58; Parish of Calstock plates 93, 100; Parish of St. Andrew, Plymouth plate 51; Parish of St. Cleer plates 74–78, 87–89, 91, 126–130; Parish of St. Helier, Jersey plate 80; Parish of Stoke Damerel, Plymouth plates 50, 52, 53, 131; Plymouth Museum and Art Gallery plate 49; Register General for Scotland plates 10, 106, 108, 109; Registrar General of Births, Deaths and Marriage plates 7, 8, 9, 11, 31, 63, 69, 70, 82, 83, 107; Sexton of the Parish of St. Cleer plates 112, 113; Society of Genealogists plate 137; The Trustees of the Institute of Heraldic Studies plate 132.

1 In Search of Ancestors

Have you ever sat in your armchair with a thriller and seen yourself in the role of the super-sleuth, remorselessly tracking down the cunning murderer and nonchalantly explaining to the slow-witted police how you solved the apparently perfect crime? Few of us are able to put such fantasies into practice. However, if you trace your ancestors, you will need all the skills of a detective. The most obvious lines of enquiry so often take you nowhere, while the most unlikely clues may lead to an exciting discovery.

It is not surprising, therefore, that family history has become one of Britain's fastest growing hobbies. Some people are curious about the origin of an unusual surname; others have inherited a family legend of illustrious origins which they wish to confirm or disprove. In Gordon Honeycombe's case, it was a combination of both.

One day in 1955, when he was eighteen, a marriage announcement caught his eye in an Edinburgh newspaper:

HONEYCOMBE — VINESTOCK. — At St Matthew's Church, Morningside, Edinburgh, on Saturday, September 3, 1955, by the Rev. R. C. M. Mathers, ROY ALBERT HONEYCOMBE, of Richelieu Park, Jersey, Channel Islands, to EVELYN, youngest daughter of the late DAVID VINESTOCK and of Mrs BESSIE VINESTOCK, 8 Maxwell St., Edinburgh.

Gordon had no brothers; neither had his father, and his grandfather's only brother died unmarried. As far as he knew, he was the last of the Honeycombes. Yet here was a Honeycombe, living, apparently, in Jersey. The bride's mother supplied Gordon with her son-in-law's address. He wrote off and waited for a reply. None came.

Gordon had practically forgotten all about it, when a year later, out of the blue, a letter arrived from Roy Honeycombe. He knew relatively little about the family. His father had been a telephone linesman; his grandfather, Samuel, had been a mason in St Helier who later became the town crier.

Interesting though it was to learn about the Jersey Honeycombes, it was his enclosure which most intrigued Gordon. For Roy sent Gordon a copy of the family legend. When Gordon saw this, he suddenly recalled that his father had a copy of the very same document.

The family legend. Not every family has a legend, but it is surprising how many have. Usually it takes the form of descent from a titled family, or the right to vast sums in Chancery. In Gordon's case, the document which had apparently come down not only his family but Roy Honeycombe's as well, was a little printed booklet called *A brief abstract of the ancient Cornish surname of Honeycombe . . . together with some of its connections at a later period.* [2] It was written by a John Symons Honeycombe, of Newark, New Jersey, in 1907, and told how the family was founded by a companion of William the Conqueror, called Honi à Combat (meaning, John claimed, a 'bad man in a fight'), who was granted vast lands in Devon and Cornwall. In Elizabeth's reign, a Honicombe, as the spelling had become, built Honeycombe Hall, in Calstock, Cornwall, and intermarried with a neighbouring landowning family called Symons. In the eighteenth century, both families bought estates in the nearby parish of St Cleer, where John Symons Honeycombe (as the spelling finally became) was born in 1833, shortly after his father returned from a stay of some years in Jersey. In 1855 John's grandfather sold the manor house at St Cleer, and the whole family emigrated to America.

Gordon studied the details of the pedigree as given in the *Brief Abstract*. Honi à Combat seemed rather far-fetched, but the rest could well be true. For had not John Symons Honeycombe said that his father spent some years in Jersey? And here was a Roy Honeycombe still living there. Where did he fit in? Were both Gordon and Roy relatives of this American Honeycombe? Lastly, and most important of all, had Gordon's ancestors really been wealthy landowners who built a Honeycombe Hall in Calstock, Cornwall? Did the Hall still exist?

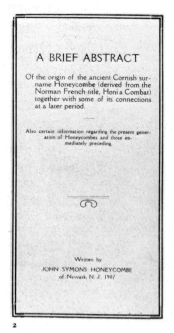

A BRIEF ABSTRACT

Of the origin of the ancient Cornish surname Honeycombe (derived from the
Norman French title, Honi a Combat)
together with some of its connections
at a later period.

Also certain information regarding the present generation of Honeycombes and those im-
mediately preceding.

Written by
JOHN SYMONS HONEYCOMBE
of Newark, N. J. 1907

2

3 *Gordon Honeycombe finds an ancestor.*

As Gordon was in Hong Kong doing his National Service when Roy's letter arrived, he was unable to follow it up. In fact it was not until 1959, when he was up at Oxford that his vague intentions were translated into positive action. Acting on a sudden impulse, he hired a car and drove down to Cornwall. There, near the village of Calstock, he found Honeycombe House, a building of uncertain age, rambling and derelict [4]. Excitedly, he made for a nearby parish church. The vicar produced the old parish registers of baptisms, marriages and burials, and near the start of the very first register, he found a Honicombe.

Turning over the pages, Gordon found more and more Honicombes. As time went on, the spelling changed to Honeycombe, just as John Symons Honeycombe had said. Were these the owners of Honeycombe Hall? The Symons family of Hatt, were, he discovered, a notable family in these parts. Moreover, it would seem that the Honeycombes had had other important relations. John Symons Honeycombe had said that his grandfather, John Honeycombe, married a Johanna Davey, a cousin of Sir Humphrey Davy. Gordon had heard that his own great-grandfather was called Samuel George *Davey* Honeycombe. How was he related to John Symons Honeycombe and to the people in the registers?

Gordon realised that at this stage the Cornish parish registers were not going to be of much help in finding out whether he was descended from the Honeycombes of Honeycombe Hall. True, they confirmed the presence of Honeycombes in the area, but he could find no mention of any known relatives. How could he find the connection? He decided that if he did not acquire more knowledge of the subject and set to work in a systematic way, he could waste a great deal of time with no guarantee of success.

A systematic approach. Before you start trying to find out about your ancestors, you should ask yourself why you are doing it and what you want to find out. Do you want, as Gordon did, to discover your relationship with others of the same surname, or to prove or disprove a family legend? Or, do you simply want to trace your ancestors back as far as you can? Many, like

4 *Honeycombe House in the early 1930s. (It was even more derelict when visited by Gordon in 1959.)*

Gordon, start with some such objective: only later does a broader aim emerge – the writing of a family history which might be of interest not only to members of the family, but to other people as well.

There are three aspects of a family history: the *genealogical*, the *biographical* and the *historical*. The first essential is a proven genealogy. Not every genealogist is a family historian, but every family historian must be a genealogist, for the genealogy is the foundation upon which all else rests. Unless this is proved every step of the way, the family historian may well find himself writing somebody else's family history. Whether your name is as rare as Honeycombe or as common as Smith, there is only one way to compile a family tree. You must start with yourself and work backwards. As genealogical data is assembled, some biographical data will be accumulated on the way. Later, you can concentrate upon the biographies and supplement this data from other sources. Finally, the biographies can be set in their full local and national social context. In practice, all three aspects of writing a family history may be undertaken simultaneously, for

the biographical and historical information you collect may provide clues which in turn help with the genealogy.

Whether you collect the genealogical information first and then seek to amplify it with biographical and historical data, or whether you work on all three aspects together, it is important not to postpone writing your family history until the research is complete, for that day will never come. Instead, you should write up your family history in stages, starting with your autobiography and working back, generation by generation. This does not necessarily mean that if you eventually produce a family history for distribution to relatives it will take this form – it may be necessary to recast it into a more conventional chronological framework. However, this method enables you to write the family history as you do the research. If you fail to do this, the odds are that it will not be written at all.

Help from others. Before commencing your researches, you would be wise to enrol for a course in genealogy or family history organised by a university extra-mural department, by an evening institute, or by

5 *Christchurch, Hants, 1951. Gordon is 15 and 6ft 4ins, Great-Aunt Emma is 88 and 4ft 11in.*

the WEA and to join at least one local family history society (see page 156). When Gordon did most of his research, he rarely met other genealogists and was often in doubt where to turn for help or advice. In the last few years, however, the situation has been transformed, and there are now both courses and family history societies in all parts of the country.

Tracing your ancestors. There are seven basic genealogical sources: information from relatives; family documents; civil registration; census returns; tombstones; wills and parish registers.

Information from relatives. Genealogists often start looking at records too soon, before they have obtained all the information they can from relatives. In Gordon's case, his Great-Aunt Emma lived to be 100 [5], yet when she died, in 1963, Gordon had not asked her about the family. She might well have been able to give him information which it has taken him years to find out or

which died with her. In fact it was only a year after Great-Aunt Emma's death that Gordon finally made a proper start. His father, Gordon Samuel Honeycombe (A15) had died in 1957, but his Aunt Dorothy (A17), his father's sister, was very helpful. She told Gordon that she and her brother were born in Edinburgh, he in 1898 and she in 1900. Their father, Henry Honeycombe (A9) supervised the catering in the restaurant cars on the London and North-Eastern Railway, and later became a hotel proprietor. Henry was born in 1861 at Gravesend, in Kent. He had an elder brother, William Thomas, who died unmarried at the age of thirty, and three sisters: Margaret (A6), who married a Richard Fox, Eleanor (A12), who became a Mrs Hoskins, and Emma (A11), who never married, and, as we have seen, died in 1963 at the age of 100.

Henry and his brothers and sisters were the children of Samuel George Davey Honeycombe (A3), a surveyor, who died about 1910. Aunt Dorothy thought that

Table A. Pedigree built up from oral evidence, Civil registration and census returns.

For ease of reference individuals have been numbered consecutively from left to right and these numbers are used in the text.

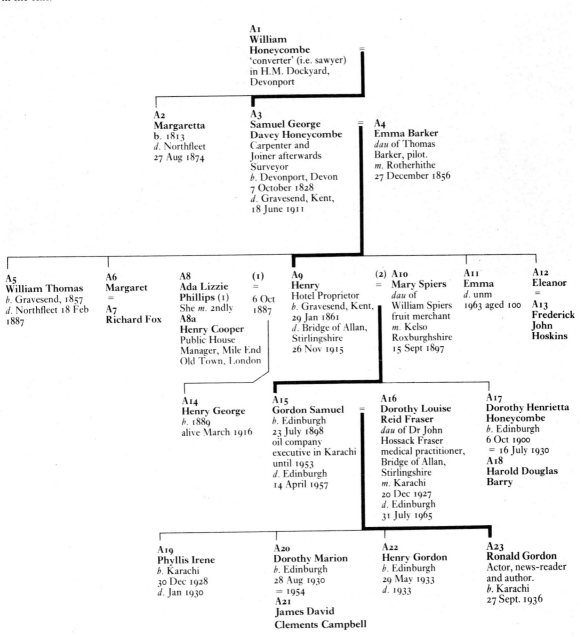

A1
William Honeycombe
'converter' (i.e. sawyer) in H.M. Dockyard, Devonport
=

A2
Margaretta
b. 1813
d. Northfleet 27 Aug 1874

A3
Samuel George Davey Honeycombe
Carpenter and Joiner afterwards Surveyor
b. Devonport, Devon 7 October 1828
d. Gravesend, Kent, 18 June 1911
=

A4
Emma Barker
dau of Thomas Barker, pilot.
m. Rotherhithe 27 December 1856

A5
William Thomas
b. Gravesend, 1857
d. Northfleet 18 Feb 1887

A6
Margaret
=
A7
Richard Fox

A8
Ada Lizzie Phillips (1)
She m. 2ndly
A8a
Henry Cooper
Public House Manager, Mile End Old Town, London
(1)
=
6 Oct 1887

A9
Henry
Hotel Proprietor
b. Gravesend, Kent, 29 Jan 1861
d. Bridge of Allan, Stirlingshire 26 Nov 1915
(2)
=

A10
Mary Spiers
dau of William Spiers fruit merchant
m. Kelso Roxburghshire 15 Sept 1897

A11
Emma
d. unm 1963 aged 100

A12
Eleanor
=
A13
Frederick John Hoskins

A14
Henry George
b. 1889
alive March 1916

A15
Gordon Samuel
b. Edinburgh 23 July 1898
oil company executive in Karachi until 1953
d. Edinburgh 14 April 1957
=

A16
Dorothy Louise Reid Fraser
dau of Dr John Hossack Fraser medical practitioner, Bridge of Allan, Stirlingshire
m. Karachi 20 Dec 1927
d. Edinburgh 31 July 1965

A17
Dorothy Henrietta Honeycombe
b. Edinburgh 6 Oct 1900
= 16 July 1930
A18
Harold Douglas Barry

A19
Phyllis Irene
b. Karachi 30 Dec 1928
d. Jan 1930

A20
Dorothy Marion
b. Edinburgh 28 Aug 1930
= 1954
A21
James David Clements Campbell

A22
Henry Gordon
b. Edinburgh 29 May 1933
d. 1933

A23
Ronald Gordon
Actor, news-reader and author.
b. Karachi 27 Sept. 1936

6

7

6. *Entries in the Honeycombe Family Bible. Note the different hands and the clues to the writers' identity.*

7. *Extract from the Index of Marriages at St Catherine's House for the December quarter of 1856. The reference number 1d 741 is the same as that shown elsewhere for Emma Barker, establishing that Gordon was applying for the correct marriage, a necessary check in the case of more common surnames and christian names. The Emma who appears immediately above Samuel George Davey is not, of course, Emma Barker, but an Emma Honeycombe belonging to a completely different branch of the family, who happened to marry in the same quarter.*

Samuel's ancestors had come from Cornwall. This made some kind of relationship with John Symons Honeycombe very likely but proving it was another matter.

Family documents. The most important family document Gordon was able to locate was the Family Bible [6], kept by his great-grandparents, Samuel George Davey Honeycombe and his wife.

From this he knew the exact dates of birth of his grandfather and other relatives and also the Christian name of his great-grandmother, Emma (A4).

Civil registration. Gordon's next step was to obtain birth, marriage and death certificates from Somerset House. That was in 1964; today he would have to go to nearby St Catherine's House. It is not possible to search the original registers, but access to the indexes is free [7]. From these you can note reference numbers and apply for appropriate certificates.

Research in civil registration proceeds by obtaining birth and marriage certificates alternately. Gordon knew the exact date of birth of his grandfather, Henry Honeycombe (A9), and so was easily able to locate his entry in the index to births for 1861 and apply for a certificate [8]. When this arrived, it showed that Henry was born at 21 Cutmore Street, Gravesend and that his mother's maiden name was Emma Barker (A4). It was interesting to see that Henry's father, Samuel George Davey Honeycombe (A3), whom Aunt Dorothy had said was a surveyor, was only a journeyman joiner, an occupation of much lower status.[1]

From the Family Bible, Gordon knew that Henry's eldest brother, William Thomas (A5), was born in October, 1857. Looking at the marriage indexes back

---

1. The word *journeyman*, originally meaning someone paid by the day, indicated that Samuel was not a master but an employee.

CERTIFIED COPY OF AN ENTRY OF BIRTH

The statutory fee for this certificate is 3s. 9d.
Where a search is necessary to find the entry,
a search fee is payable in addition.

GIVEN AT THE GENERAL REGISTER OFFICE,
SOMERSET HOUSE, LONDON

Application Number _827314_

REGISTRATION DISTRICT _Gravesend_

1861. BIRTH in the Sub-district of _Gravesend_ in the County of _Kent_

No.	When and where born	Name, if any	Sex	Name, and surname of father	Name, surname, and maiden surname of mother	Occupation of father	Signature, description, and residence of informant	When registered	Signature of registrar	Name entered after registration
352	Twenty ninth January 1861 21 Butmore Street Gravesend	Henry	Boy	Samuel George Davey Honeycombe	Emma Honeycombe formerly Barker	Joiner Journeyman	S.G.D. Honeycombe Father 21 Butmore St Gravesend	Twenty Sixth February 1861	Geo. S. Hammon Registrar	

8

Registration District _ROTHERHITHE_

1856. Marriage solemnized at the Parish Church
in the Parish of S. Mary Rotherhithe in the County of Surrey

No.	When married	Name and surname	Age	Condition	Rank or profession	Residence at the time of marriage	Father's name and surname	Rank or profession of father
55	December 27th 1856	Samuel George Davey Honeycombe / Emma Barker	Of full age Of Full age	Bachelor / Spinster	Joiner / ———	Rotherhithe / Rotherhithe	William Honeycombe / Thomas Barker	Converter in H. My's Dockyard Devonport Pilot

Married in the Parish Church according to the Rites and Ceremonies of the Established Church after Banns by me

This marriage was solemnized between us, { Samuel George Davey Honeycombe / Emma Barker } in the presence of us, { Robt. George Batt / Hannah Batt }

Edward Blick Rector

---

9 *Certificate obtained from the General Register office. Sometimes you are given a photocopy of the exact entry (8).*
Typescript or manuscript copies give considerable scope for transcription errors.

from then, Gordon was able to locate the entry of the marriage of Samuel and Emma (A3–4). The certificate [9] showed that they were married at St Mary Rotherhithe on 27 December 1856, both being described as resident in the parish. Samuel was again described as a joiner. More significantly, this certificate took Gordon back a generation further, for it showed that Samuel's father was William Honeycombe (A1), a 'converter' or sawyer in Her Majesty's Dockyard, Devonport.[2] Subsequent research showed that William was born in 1786. So although English Civil Registration did not begin until 1837, the information obtainable from

certificates will often get you back to someone born towards the end of the eighteenth century. However, what delighted Gordon even more was the mention of Devonport on the certificate, which proved the link with the West Country and brought him one stage nearer to John Symons Honeycombe and Honeycombe Hall.

Scottish registration. Gordon's researches were not confined to English records, for his father was born in Scotland which has its own registration system. Scottish registers are kept at New Register House, Princes Street, Edinburgh, and unlike England, you

---

2. When confronted with an unfamiliar occupation it is always worth looking up the meaning in the full multi-volumed *Oxford English Dictionary*. Smaller dictionaries may well give the correct meaning, but will usually not give the examples which may provide useful leads. One of the meanings of 'converter' given in the *Oxford English Dictionary*, is 'One whose business it is to convert rough

timber' and for the verb 'to convert' – 'to reduce from the rough state the pieces of nearly the required shape and size'. An 1811 reference from the *Naval Chronicle* is given to 'one of the timber converters of the dockyard'. So even if 'H.M. Dockyard, Devonport' had not been given, the word 'converter' might have suggested that William Honeycombe worked in a dockyard.

No	1 Name and surname / Rank or profession and whether single, married or widowed	2 When and where died	3 Sex	4 Age	5 Name, surname and rank or profession of father / Name and maiden surname of mother	6 Cause of death, duration of disease and medical attendant by whom certified	7 Signature and qualification of informant and residence, if out of the house in which the death occurred	8 When and where registered and signature of registrar
	1861–1965 — Extract of an entry in a REGISTER of DEATHS — Registration of Births, Deaths and Marriages (Scotland) Act 1965							
55	Henry Honeycombe, Hotel-keeper, married to (1) Ada Phillips (2) Mary Speirs	1915, November Twenty-sixth 3h. 30m. p.m. Queen's Hotel Bridge of Allan	M	54 yrs	Samuel Honeycombe Burgh Surveyor (Decd) — Emma Honeycombe M.S. Barker (Decd).	Carteries of the liver Chronic Interstitial Nephritis — Cerebral Haemorrhage Left Hemiplegia As cert by Jno. Henry Fraser M.B. C.M.	Gordon Honeycombe Son (present)	1915, At Bridge of Allan November 27th Richard Lawrie Asst. Registrar

	REGISTRATION DISTRICT Gravesend								
Columns:—	1 When and where died	2 Name and surname	3 Sex	4 Age	5 Occupation	6 Cause of death	7 Signature, description, and residence of informant	8 When registered	9 Signature of registrar
	1911. DEATH in the Sub-district of Gravesend in the County of Kent								
396	Eighteenth June, 1911. 458 Pelham Street Gravesend U.D.	Samuel Honeycombe	Male	82 years	a Consulting Surveyor (retired)	Enlarged Prostate Cystitis Exhaustion Certified by A. J. Sellor M.R.C.S.	M. Harrington present at death 2 Darnley Street Gravesend	Nineteenth June 1911	F. E. ... Hammond Registrar

11 *Scottish and English death certificates. The former name both parents which may enable a Scottish family to be traced almost to the '45 Rebellion from Civil Registration alone.*

can see the original records. Although civil registration started eighteen years later than in England, it is a much better system. For example, if you compare the Scottish death certificate [10] for Gordon's grandfather, Henry (A9), with that for Henry's father, Samuel George Davey Honeycombe (A3) [11], you will see that the former names both parents.

Census returns. Birth, marriage and death certificates should be used in conjunction with census returns. Censuses have been held every ten years since 1801. As the detailed enumerator's returns were not kept until 1841 and census returns for England and Wales may not be consulted until they are 100 years old, the only censuses currently available are those for 1841, 1851, 1861, 1871 and 1881. These may be consulted in London at the Portugal Street repository of the Public Record Office (p. 161). Most County Record Offices and some libraries have copies for their area. Those

indexed by family history societies are listed in Gibson's *Marriage, Census and Other Indexes* (see p. 164).

The 1841 Census [54] names each person in the household, gives ages (exact for children under fifteen, but rounded down to the nearest five for adults), occupations and whether or not born in the same county. From 1851, exact ages, status, relationship to the head of the household and county and parish of birth are given.

The birth certificate [8] of Gordon's grandfather, Henry (A9), provided us with the family's address in 1861 – 21 Cutmore St, Gravesend. When the census [12] was consulted, it told us that Samuel George Davey Honeycombe (A3) was then thirty-two (though ages in censuses are not always reliable) and was born in Devonport. It also confirmed the oral evidence regarding the names of the children and provided their approximate dates of birth. Rather surprisingly, although only a journeyman joiner, he employed a house servant.

10

The undermentioned Houses are situate within the Boundaries of the

Parish [or Township] of	City or Municipal Borough of	Municipal Ward of	Parliamentary Borough of	Town of	Hamlet or Tything, &c, of	Ecclesiastical District of
Gravesend	Gravesend	Gravesend				St James

No. of Schedule	Road, Street, &c., and No. or Name of House	HOUSES In-habited	HOUSES Un-inhabited (U), or Building (B)	Name and Surname of each Person	Relation to Head of Family	Condition	Age of Males	Age of Females	Rank, Profession, or Occupation	Where Born	Whether Blind, or Deaf-and-Dumb
186	21 Outmore St	1		Samuel Honeycombe	Head	Mar	32		Carpenter & Joiner	Devon Devonport	
				Emma Do	Wife	Do		32		Kent Gravesend	
				William Do	Son		3		Scholar	Do Do	
				Margaret Do	Daur			2		Do Do	
				Henry Do	Son		2 Mo			Do Northfleet	
				Sarah Roberts	Servt	Un		15	House Servant	Do Swanscombe	
187	22 Do	1		Eliza Chamberlain	Lodger	Mar		24	Wife of a Baker	Do Gravesend	
				Rebecca Do	Daur			1		Middx Bow	
188				Amelia Payne	Head	Un		50			
189	23 Do	1		Charles K. Creed	Do	Mar	30		Waterman	Essex Chadwell	
				Georgiana Do	Wife	Do		30		Kent Sittingbourne	
				Charles W. Do	Son		4			Do Gravesend	
				Miriam Do	Daur			10 Mo		Do Do	
190	24 Do	1		Frederick Wightman	Head	Mar	25		Clerk Railway	Surrey Putney	
				Annie Do	Wife	Do		25		Middx Hackney	
				Frederick Do	Son		10 Mo			Gravesend Kent	
				Amelia Basset	Sister in law			9	Scholar	Middx Stepney	
191	25 Do	1		Mary Masters	Head	Un		68	Proprietor of House	Somerset Bath	
				Elizabeth Shadwell	Boarder	Un		68	Do	Middx Knightsbridge	
				Anne Corner	Do	Un		74	Do	Kent Tenterden	
192	42 Do	1		George Bellingham	Head	Mar	46		Bricklayer	Do Southborough	
				Ann Do	Wife	Do		43		Do Gravesend	
				John Do	Son	Un	23		Bricklayer	Do Do	
				Annie E Do	Daur	Un		20		Do Do	
				Laura S Do	Do			15		Do Do	
7	Total of Houses... 6					Total of Males and Females...	9	16			

Eng.—Sheet D.

12 *1861 Census for Gravesend, Kent. The double lines demarcate different properties, the single line between 187 and 188 shows multiple occupancy.*

Monumental inscriptions. Oral evidence and entries from Civil Registration and census returns will almost certainly provide leads to monumental inscriptions – tombstones, memorial tablets and war memorials.

The Honeycombe family tombstone in Northfleet churchyard, records the deaths of Samuel (A3), his wife Emma (A4), his sister Margareta (A2), his son, William Thomas (A5), and, very surprisingly, his other son, Henry (A9), Gordon's grandfather, who died in Bridge of Allan, Stirlingshire, Scotland in 1915. In the case of the Honeycombes this stone was only of marginal help, though it supplied exact dates of death, which would otherwise have had to be obtained from St Catherine's House at great expense. In the case of a common name, such a tombstone could be invaluable, for knowing that a William Smith born in 1828 had a sister called Margareta, might well be the clinching piece of evidence which differentiated him from another William Smith born in the same year. Inscriptions often provide other kinds of useful information – places of origin, occupations or relationships.

Wills. Until 1858, most English and Welsh wills were proved[3] locally and the majority of these have ended up in County Record Offices. After 1858, all the wills for England and Wales are at Somerset House, Strand, London, WC2 1LP. The indexes to these may be consulted free and are very detailed, summarising the main contents of the will. Copies of these can also be consulted locally (see page 162). In addition to wills, there are sometimes letters of administration (known as 'admōns') when the deceased died intestate (i.e., leaving no will).

The Somerset House Index shows that Samuel George Davey Honeycombe's will was proved on 18

3. *Proved:* accepted as genuine and valid and registered. *Probate:* Instruction to the executor(s) to carry out the terms of the will.

This is my last will and testament of Samuel Honeycombe of No 45 Cobham Street Gravesend in the County of Kent Consulting Surveyor to the Northfleet District Council I hereby give devise and bequeath to my Daughter Emma Honeycombe her heirs executors and administrators for her and their own use and benefit absolutely and for ever all my estate and effects both real and personal whatsoever and wheresoever and of what nature and quality soever and I hereby appoint her the said Emma Honeycombe sole executrix of this my will In witness whereof I have hereunto set my hand this 9th day of July one thousand nine hundred and seven

Samuel Honeycombe

Signed by the said Samuel Honeycombe in the presence of us present at the same time who in his presence and in the presence of each other attest and subscribe our names as witnesses hereto

William Sheen 135 Dover Road Northfleet
James Abberley Mitchell Jnr 100 Dover Road Northfleet Kent.

13

Enrolled copy of will. Only one of the four living children is mentioned but James Mitchell was his son-in-law.

14

Samuel Honeycombe.

August 1911. He was described as 'of 45 Cobham St, Gravesend, Kent' and his date of death was given as the 18 June 1911. The will was proved in London, probate being granted to 'Emma Honeycombe spinster' (A11). His effects were valued at £236 12s 10d.

When the enrolled copy of the will was obtained [13, 14] it gave Samuel's occupation as 'Consulting Surveyor to the Northfleet District Council'. So Aunt Dorothy was right after all. Gordon's great-grandfather, Samuel (A3), had progressed from journeyman joiner in 1861 to consulting surveyor in 1911! Apart from this interesting piece of confirmation of family tradition, the fact that Samuel's will mentioned only one of his four surviving children served as a useful reminder

that there may often be other children of whose existence a will gives no clue.

Parish registers. Since English civil registration began only in 1837, Gordon had to continue his search for his ancestors in the old parish registers. However, the census had indicated the place and date where he should start looking for William's baptism, and Samuel's marriage certificate had given his father's name. This stage of Gordon's genealogical researches will be described in a later chapter.

Whatever happened to Henry George? Although we have dealt briefly with each kind of source material in turn – oral evidence, family documents, civil registration, census returns, monumental inscriptions and wills – it must not be thought that each represents a stage which you work through carefully and systematically and then move on to the next. It rarely works out that way. Not only are civil registration and census returns used together, passing from one to the other and back, but they often suggest more questions to ask relatives. Thus Henry's death certificate showed that he had been married twice. This was quite a surprise to Gordon, and he asked his Aunt Dorothy (A17) about it. Apparently, Henry's first marriage (A8) had ended in divorce. There was, however, a son, Henry George (A14), born in 1889. He was brought up by his mother, who, in 1895, married again. Henry George later went to America, coming to Bridge of Allan, Stirlingshire, Scotland 'for his inheritance' when his father died in 1915. When he left, he told his relatives he was sailing back to America from Liverpool and the family had no further contact with him. At the new Public Record Office at Kew, a search was made in passenger lists of all ships sailing from Liverpool, and Henry George was located, sailing on the *Tuscania* which left Liverpool for New York on 17 March 1916. He had come from Scotland, was twenty-six years old and an electrical engineer.

Immigration records in the United States archives supplied further details. The *Tuscania* sailed first from Glasgow to Liverpool, and Henry boarded the ship at Glasgow. She arrived in New York on 29 March. It was, as we know, Henry's second trip to America, the first having been five years previously. Henry was described as a 'non-immigrating alien' visiting a friend, R. G. Reid, 809 Maple, Turtle Creek, West Pittsburgh, Pennsylvania. The interesting thing is that Gordon has an R. G. Reid on his *mother's* family tree. His maternal grandmother, Christina Brown Reid was the daughter of the minister of Bridge of Allan and in 1889 married the doctor there, John Hossack Fraser. Their daughter Louie (A16) went out to India to marry Gordon's father in 1927. Mrs Fraser had a brother, Robert Gordon Reid, born in 1876 who became an assayer in Queensland. Whilst the identification is not yet certain, it does seem highly probable that when Henry visited his stepmother in Bridge of Allan, he was introduced to the Frasers, and Mrs Fraser gave him the address of her brother, who was at that time in Pittsburgh.

Henry's description as a 'non-immigrating alien' might suggest that he later returned to Britain, but he does not appear in either English or Scottish marriage or death indexes. Gordon has also circularised every Honeycombe in the American telephone directories without locating him or his descendants. It is strange that after tracing several hundred distant relatives, he has not found out what happened to his own uncle.

2 Times Remembered

It is strange how often family historians provide us with a great deal of information about their eighteenth-century ancestors but forget to say anything about themselves. Not only is your life an integral part of your family history, but you owe it to your descendants to leave them some record, for in the course of your researches, you will often regret that your own ancestors left so few letters, diaries, or autobiographies.

If you are like most people, you are rather modest and do not think your own life worth recording. You may not have been involved in momentous events or decisions or have done anything other than very ordinary jobs in offices or factories. Many of your friends and relatives may appear to have led much more interesting lives. Yet however undeserving of attention you may consider yourself, you are part of a historical process in which your own actions have contributed a part.

How to start. In writing your autobiography, it is best to start by making brief notes of the whole *outline* of your life – birth, education, marriage, children, changes of address, and the various jobs you have had. Thus:

I was born on 27 September 1936, in Karachi, (then in India) where my father was an oil-company executive. I came to Britain in 1946, and from 1946 to 1955, attended the Edinburgh Academy. This was followed by two years' National Service, mostly in Hong Kong with the Royal Artillery. From 1957 to 1961 I was at University College, Oxford, reading English. The three year course became four as I contracted TB in my second year and spent seven months in hospital. At Oxford I wrote, produced or acted in several student theatre shows. In 1962, I became an actor, and was with the Royal Shakespeare Company for two years. Like so many actors, I had difficulty getting continuous engagements; my height, – 6 feet 4 inches – was also a drawback. I was on the dole for a year before becoming an ITN newscaster, a post I held for twelve and a half years. I resigned in 1977 to concentrate on my writing career. So far, I have had four novels published – the fourth being a best-seller – as well as a stage play. Two other plays have been produced on TV and three on the radio and the stage.

Such an autobiography provides a framework from which to select one period in order to start writing it up in greater detail. Many people write most engagingly about their childhood – it lacks the bitterness that may creep in with the disappointments of later life and is often less overlaid with the protective covering we all use to shield ourselves from the adult world.

What are the main possibilities in Gordon's potted autobiography?

Child of the Raj. Perhaps the first point of interest, is that he was a child who grew up in the twilight of the British Raj. Here is an example of his memories in which he recreates the flavour of a way of life which seemed to him as a child so natural and normal, and yet which was very different from that led by most of his contemporaries in wartime Britain.

We lived on the edge of Karachi – in a first floor flat, one of four in a house. There was a fairly formal garden at the front and back of the house, and a verandah at the front of the flat. At the back, a spiral iron staircase led from the kitchen to the ground. We had three permanent servants – a bearer *(or butler), a* hamal *(houseboy) and a cook. All wore baggy white trousers and blousy white shirts with a waistcoat. The bearer had a black moustache, the hamal a moustache and beard which were grey, and the cook was darker skinned – he must have come from South India. They were kind and respectful towards the master's son, the* chota-sahib *(small master). We shared the* mali *(gardener) and the* dhobi *(washerman) with the families in the other four flats.*

Up to the age of five or six, I also had an ayah *(nanny), who escorted me when I visited other children, or went to fancy-dress parties, or with my mother to the Golf Club or Gymkhana. The ayah was very dark-faced and plump and was more use to my mother*

16

15

17

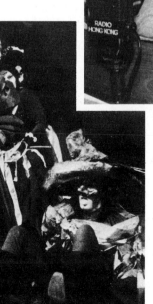

18

19

15. *Gordon at a Karachi gymkhana, 1940*

16. *Gordon at Oxford, 1961*

17. *Gordon during his National Service. The picture was taken at Aden on his way home from Hong Kong.*

18. *A part-time announcer, Radio Hong Kong, 1956.*

19. *Gordon with Diana Rigg in the* Comedy of Errors, *Royal Shakespeare Company, Stratford, 1962.*

20 *Gordon's parents' wedding reception. Karachi, 1927.*

21 *With his ayah, 1936.*

when I was a baby. Later on, my mother took over the task of bathing and dressing me. I was sorry when my ayah left, and created a rumpus, which must have reflected some of my annoyance at having to go to school. This happened when I was six.

In 1939, when War was declared, I was three. It hardly impinged on my childhood. Of course, servicemen visited the flat and were to be seen at clubs and beaches. But I never associated them with what was happening elsewhere; even on the fringes of India, in Burma. There was no television; I was too young to be interested in the wireless, though I liked its music. It was all meaningless grown-up talk. The only warlike excitement I recall was when a section of the Indian Navy mutinied, seized a cruiser in Karachi harbour, and fired blank shells over the town – at least, I was told they were blanks.

Otherwise, it was always sunshine – shirt, shorts, socks and sandals being worn all year. I was never aware of it being hot, although sometimes I got heated, uncomfortable and tired. It was just eternally sunny. There seemed to be no night, just day, and I was outside playing games all day and every day.

School was a sort of kindergarten in a private house. There were very few pupils and in between playing organised children's games, I learned to read and write and add and do the multiplication table. The lessons lasted only a couple of hours in the morning, but eventually I was bold enough to write some brief poems.

We children enjoyed a great deal of freedom, being allowed to roam in the gardens and roads and visit friends almost at will. My mother was apparently not too concerned about my coming to any harm from the natives. She fussed much more about sunstroke and tap-water and rabid dogs. Even when we were caught in a covered rickshaw in a riot in Naini Tal our lives never seemed in danger. We were British after all, invulnerable and not involved.

In this passage Gordon has given us very few facts, but has created an ambiance which a descendant a hundred years hence would be unlikely to recreate from the bare records of Gordon's presence in Karachi. What a host of assumptions are conveyed in that one phrase: 'We were British, after all, invulnerable and not involved'!

22 *Gordon and his mother, at the Country Club, Karachi, 1940.*

Oxford. Gordon went up to Oxford, at a time when, like the Indian Empire, the old order was changing:

Although grammar-school boys counted for about forty per cent of Oxford undergraduates, the tone was still set by the public-school boys. There was a strong urge to conform to traditional Oxbridge life-style, to learn when to drink sherry and when to pass round the port. and there was still a strong emphasis on games, particularly rowing. Oxford was a masculine club, on which the five women's colleges had made surprisingly little impact. There was good-humoured guerilla warfare with proctors and porters, both over the wearing of gowns (obligatory for lectures and after dark) and 'climbing in' after the gates clanged shut. Few undergraduates had cars; terms were eight weeks long, and the 'weekend', which today leaves Oxford almost denuded of undergraduates, had yet to be invented. Interest in politics tended to be in the traditional style of the Oxbridge Unions, where a witty speech and winning a point in debate were more respected than strongly held convictions. The majority of undergraduates were right of centre – the extreme left wing was regarded with some amusement as a lunatic fringe. However, for the observant, there were signs of change. Classics had already become just one possible choice of subject – the ambitious sixth former was more likely to choose natural sciences. Religion was losing its influence, the college chapels and religious societies competing for clients with all the other activities. The college servants, or 'scouts' complained that undergraduates no longer behaved like gentlemen.

Here we have a very different world from British India, although the insights we are seeking are not dissimilar. In this respect, the autobiography has certain advantages over the diary, for the 'ordinariness' of your life looks quite different twenty or thirty years later – it is only with hindsight that you can perceive the social changes through which you have lived. As you write up periods of your life which you find particularly interesting, the autobiography gradually builds up and you start filling in the gaps. An autobiography, of course, is never completed. You will always think of something important you have left out. The main thing is to make a start.

23 *Henry and Mary Honeycombe, Gordon Samuel (15) and Dorothy (12). Edinburgh 1913.*

Parents' biographies. The next stage in writing the family history is to work on your parents' biographies. Exactly the same principle applies. Write down an outline biography, and then develop different parts of it until they begin to link up. Your main source will probably be oral evidence or written memoirs. But even if your parents are living, you will need to supplement their memories with your own and with those of other living relatives.

Gordon encouraged his Aunt Dorothy (A17) to write her memoirs and from these he was able to write an outline biography for his father, Gordon Samuel Honeycombe (A15). This fell naturally into three sections – his *early life* spent in Wimbledon, Torquay, Edinburgh and Bridge of Allan, Stirlingshire, where *his* father, Henry Honeycombe (A9), managed various restaurants and hotels; the *First World War*, when he

fought in the Salonika campaign, and his *life in India* from 1919 to 1953, most of it as an oil company executive. Having completed the outline biography, Gordon then began to study each period in more detail.

Early life. Aunt Dorothy's memoirs gave Gordon a fascinating glimpse of the way of life and attitudes of a middle-class Edwardian family. She writes of when the Honeycombes were living in Edinburgh between 1900 and 1903:

It was usual for a nurse-maid to wheel me in a pram with my mother walking alongside, holding Gordon's hand – he was just a toddler – along Princes Street in the morning. My mother seldom pushed the pram herself – it would not have been considered correct, and my father wouldn't even walk alongside the pram – let alone push

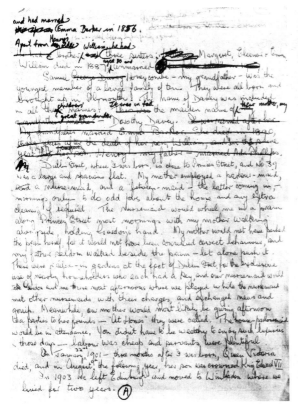

²⁴ *Draft of Aunt Dorothy's memoirs with Gordon's amendments.* ²⁵ *Aunt Dorothy on holiday in Rothesay, Bute. 1922.*

it! There were railed gardens where we played most afternoons while the nursemaid met other nursemaids with their charges, and exchanged news and gossip. Our mother would be giving afternoon tea parties to her friends – 'At homes' they were called. A house-parlourmaid would be in attendance – You didn't have to be wealthy to enjoy such luxuries in those days – labour was so cheap and servants were plentiful.

'Upstairs, Downstairs', even in a catering manager's household, with a nursemaid to look after the children, and a parlourmaid to serve afternoon tea!

The family historian is very much concerned with the family as a social unit and indeed, in this century few things have changed more than relationships between husband and wife, parents and children. Thus Dorothy's father, Henry Honeycombe (A9), was con-

cerned for the welfare of his family, but 'It was very much a case of children should be seen and not heard. I think my mother, who would not be very old herself, was a little afraid of him.'

Henry comes over in Dorothy's memoirs as a strict disciplinarian who rarely showed any warmth or affection for his children. Dorothy remembers her mother telling her how unhappy she was in London when Gordon's father, then only a small boy of five or so, was scolded and upbraided for not sitting upright at the table, and for not using his knife and fork correctly in the smart restaurant where they were lunching.

When economies had to be made, the daughters were the first to suffer. After her father's death in 1915, it was found that there were many outstanding debts. Dorothy, though a promising pupil, had to leave school at fifteen to help her mother in the hotel.

The First World War. Aunt Dorothy's memoirs give an interesting picture of what was happening on the Home Front during the First World War. When war broke out in August 1914, the hotel at Bridge of Allan was requisitioned by the Army. The troops were there throughout the war, and, says Aunt Dorothy, always behaved impeccably. Her memoirs record, almost unconsciously, the gradual change in the public mood from war-fever to war-weariness.

The enormous advantage of autobiography over a piece of history painstakingly recreated from documents, is that you really get to *know* the people. This is contributed partly by the revelation of their thoughts and feelings, and partly by anecdotes which are not only of considerable human interest, creating an instant rapport with a relative, but may also be of some historical significance. Thus Dorothy recounts a poignant story which reminds us forcibly of the way the war changed people.

During the war, she had a brief romance with an officer billeted at Bridge of Allan:

We used to meet most days when he was 'off duty' and would go for long walks – a favourite walk was 'up the Allan' to the salmon ladder where we used to watch the fish leaping and twisting in their endeavours to reach the top of the falls, and then continue to make their way up river. We used to laugh and wonder why the fish were so persistent in leaping and in being thrown back time after time when the stone ladder had been built alongside the falls especially to assist them.

When he went to the Front, they did not see each other for two years, and during that time the feelings of both had changed. But the change in him was also of another kind:

I was very nervous and felt I was meeting a stranger! He was wearing civilian clothes and looked so different out of uniform. He also looked years older and all the gay charm and merry laughter had gone. I felt sad and miserable and was glad my mother was there to keep the conversation going with her lively chatter. Not much was said that evening, but next day, being warm and sunny, we went for our favourite walk 'up the Allan' and sat by the river and talked and talked.
We both recognised the change in each other and tried

to be honest about it. He told me just a little of his life, or rather existence, in France, and of his terrible experiences, and I wasn't surprised when he said he wondered if he would ever be able to settle down to a normal life again . . . The war had been responsible for bringing us together, and the war, I think, was, at least partly responsible for bringing our little romance to an end.

This is not just a story of the First World War, but of any war; not just a story of Dorothy and a young officer, but a timeless tale of human relationships. In most fundamentals, life two generations ago was perhaps not as different from ours as people sometimes imagine.

As well as oral evidence, or – if you are fortunate – written memoirs, most elderly people have an assortment of family documents. The most important are probably letters and diaries, for these are essentially private documents, and therefore provide us with evidence about a person's feelings at the time. Despite the laconic nature of many diary entries, the writers often give themselves away through the odd comment or display of enthusiasm.

In Gordon's case, the most valuable document was his father's diary for the year 1918 [27]. While Dorothy was helping to look after the troops in Bridge of Allan, Stirlingshire, her brother, 2nd Lt Gordon Samuel Honeycombe [26], was fighting in the Salonika campaign against Germany's allies, the Bulgarians. He had his fair share of hardships – and not just in combat:

Tuesday 14 May: Weather very hot. Terrible perspiration.
Wed 22 May: Walked about 12 miles in a hot sun
Sat 8 June: A terrible march – dust and heat. About 15 men fell out (15 miles)
Sun 19 June: Weather hotter than ever. Altogether we walked 15 miles in a boiling hot sun.

However, despite the discomforts of marching in a Mediterranean summer, the diary provides a vivid contrast to the First World War diaries which record the horrors of trench warfare. It reminds us that there were other theatres of war which provided the time and opportunity for social activities and good food and drink:

26 *Gordon Samuel Honeycombe as an officer cadet, 1917.*

27 *2nd Lt Honeycombe's war diary.*

Friday 21 June: A Great Day. Visited Delphi and saw Temple of Apollo, Stadium, Theatre, Gymnasium. Home of the Oracle, and many wonderful things in the Museum. Left 7.00 am. Returned 5.00 pm. A lot of mountain climbing was done. Worth seeing. Lunch in hotel, wine and omelette.

Sunday 24 March: Palm Sunday. Church Parade. (Pres.) In the afternoon I visited Salonica again. Called on General Anderson GHQ. Dinner at the French Club in the evening and the Variety Show at White Tower. A box. Numerous French girls come in. Plenty of champagne. Terrible noise going on in Hall.

The war historian, in using the experiences of individuals, will inevitably select those which are either the most typical or the most dramatic. The family historian has a different function – he is interested in 2nd Lt Honeycombe's diary not because it throws fresh light on the conduct of the War, but because it contributes towards showing the impact of the War on a particular individual and family. Only to a very limited extent can the family historian choose what sources are the most 'important'. For him, the very scarcity of documentary material about his ancestors lends significance to almost every item. In fact, Gordon Samuel Honeycombe's diary for 1918 is a very human record of the phase of the War in which he was involved.

After Gordon's father's diary ends, his Aunt Dorothy's memoirs pick up the story. Her brother, after a week's leave in Bridge of Allan in September, returned to France, but was once again on leave at the end of October.

When Gordon arrived home looking tired and very thin, he told us that he had applied for a transfer to the Royal Flying Corps. He liked the idea of flying and thought that aerial combat would be preferable to foot-slogging and trench warfare. He went on to tell us that one day – after a rest period – his Battalion had been paraded to move forward to the front lines as a new offensive was about to begin, when his name was called out. He stepped forward and was told his transfer had come through and he was to report in London. Later, he learned that his Battalion had been heavily engaged in action, suffering severe losses in officers and men. It seemed a providential escape for Gordon.

So 2nd Lt Honeycombe escaped the appalling casualties and conditions of the Western Front, first by going to Salonika, and secondly by his transfer coming through at the right moment. Had the War continued, he might well have been killed in the newly formed RAF. However, when he reported to the War Office, he was sent home on leave to await further instructions. These duly arrived, recalling him to London and another interview at the War Office. So it happened that Gordon's father was in London on 11 November 1918 when the Armistice was signed.

This episode not only illustrates the interplay of general historical factors and personal decisions in a person's life, but also emphasises that the crucial factor may well be *chance*, a point we would do well to remember when trying to reconstruct the lives of more remote ancestors for whom the evidence is much more scanty.

Life in India. In 1919, shortly after his demobilisation, Gordon Samuel Honeycombe went out to India as manager for a company in Bombay. Three years later he became an executive with an oil company in Karachi. For background information on life in Karachi in the 1920s we turned to D. Kincaid's *British Social Life in India 1608–1937* (London, 1973).

There were diners dansants every night at the Carlton Hotel, opposite the station, and on warm evenings the dancers sat in the narrow garden where folding chairs were ranged round bamboo tables. There were picnics every holiday at Manora with hampers from Cumper's Café and in the evenings numbers of new American cars gathered at Clifton (which was already referred to by local patrons as 'The Brighton of Karachi') where a pier had been built, jutting out from the sandhills and, though not reaching as far as the water, affording a view over the sands and the sea, both a little grey with coal-dust from the harbour. There were breakfast and supper parties at the Boat Club, a tall, timbered building rising from the mud flats between Karachi and the port, with a terrace where one breakfasted on excellent cold-storage sausages and watched in an inlet of the sea below the evolutions of the swimming parties and, towards the opposite bank, native herdsmen washing their camels, and there was the Golf Club and the Country Club and the Gymkhana and the Karachi Club (but this was mainly for Indians who were not admitted to the other clubs) and the Sind Club, all flourishing in the post-war boom.

The historian is concerned not only with change, but also with continuity. The pace of change is not constant, even in the same environment. Physically, Karachi was greatly altered while Gordon's father lived there, but his way of life changed remarkably little until Indian independence in 1947. Except for points of detail, Kincaid's description of expatriate life in Karachi in the 1920s was probably valid enough for Gordon's childhood in the 1940s.

Social histories such as Kincaid's remind us that conventional genealogical and biographical sources tend to provide only the barest framework of the lives of our ancestors. In our background reading we should be concerned not so much with acquiring more facts as with seeking a greater understanding of the underlying environmental and social factors, and the ideas, beliefs and values of the time. Only then will our ancestors emerge as real people.

3 The Critical Historian

In the last chapter we emphasised one function of the family historian – to recreate the texture of life of his ancestors. Although he always hopes to gain an insight into their personality and motives, and is also alert to the part played by chance in human affairs, the picture he builds up will usually come in the main from an understanding of the total environment. The theme is continued in this chapter, but with more emphasis upon local history. However, it is concerned even more with the critical evaluation of evidence.

Gordon's great-grandfather, the father of Henry Honeycombe (A9), the Hotel proprietor, and the grandfather of 2nd Lt Gordon Samuel Honeycombe (A15) was *Samuel George Davey Honeycombe* (A3), who you will remember, was described in his will as Consulting Surveyor to the Northfleet Borough Council, Kent. If a person held local office, or was otherwise well-known, or if there were any unusual circumstances surrounding the death, it is always worth looking at the local press, and Gordon discovered that the *Gravesend and Dartford Reporter* for 24 June, 1911, [28] included an obituary for Samuel, the first few lines of which outlined his early life:

Death of Mr. S. Honeycombe.

It is with much regret we have to record the death of Mr. Samuel Honeycombe, which took place at his residence, 45, Cobham-street, Gravesend, on Sunday last, after a protracted illness borne with much fortitude. The deceased gentleman was well known both in Northfleet and Gravesend, and it is not too much to say that his general disposition made him much respected by all who knew him.

Born at Devonport on the 7th October, 1828, he had thus attained the advanced age of 83 years. Educated at one of the leading schools in Devonport, he was apprenticed in the Dockyard, afterwards joining the navy,

deceased tendered his resignation of the office of District Surveyor, and in the letter he said "I have been in the service of the parish for over a generation and it is a pleasant retrospect for me to consider that during the 31 years which have elapsed since my appointment as Surveyor and Inspector of Nuisances, at the Constitution of the old Local Board in 1874. I have always endeavoured to, and believe I have succeeded in maintaining amicable and friendly relations with the gentlemen who from time to time have been elected to look after the interests of the ratepayers." On his retirement from active service, the Council showed their

Born at Devonport on the 7th October, 1828, he had thus attained the advanced age of 83 years. Educated at one of the leading schools in Devonport, he was apprenticed in the dockyard, afterwards joining the Navy, and during his naval service he travelled round the world, and took part in the Crimean War. In 1860, having taken his discharge from the Navy, he came to the Northfleet Dockyard, where he was employed during the time of Mr. Pitcher. Subsequently he started on his own account as a builder and undertaker.

You may be tempted, on finding an account like this, to integrate it into your family history, thankful that you now have a fairly complete biography of your great-grandfather. The experienced family historian, however, like the detective, always seeks corroboration.

Northfleet Dockyard
A letter to the journal of the Kent Family History Society elicited a reply drawing attention to a useful article on Northfleet Dockyard [29].[4] Sited on the River Thames, near Gravesend, it was built by a Thomas Pitcher, and the first ship, an Indiaman, was launched

4. E.C. Watt 'Northfleet Dockyard' *East Coast Digest and Greenwich Times* vol. 1, no. 3 Autumn 1972, pp. 270–273.

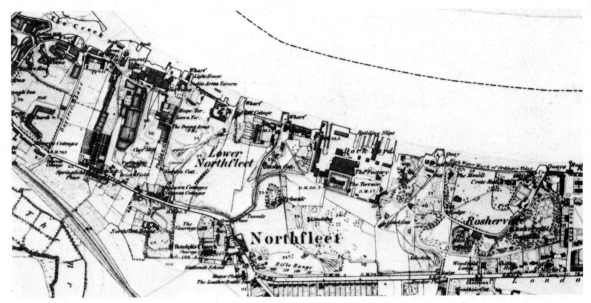

29 *Six-inch to the mile Ordnance Survey map of Northfleet, 1865, showing the dockyard.*

in 1789. It closed in 1825, but was reopened for repair work and shipbuilding by Pitcher's sons, William and Henry, in 1839, and became the largest yard on London's river, with the most extensive dry dock in the country. Brunel's *Great Western* was docked there in 1847 and 1851, and the latter year also saw the launching of the largest ship to date – the *Orinoco* [**30**]. The Crimean War brought an Admiralty order for fifty-four gunboats to be launched at the rate of one per week, and the yard was soon employing nearly 2,000 men. However, when the War ended, work dropped off, and the Pitchers went bankrupt. The yard was in the hands of the Official Receiver from 1857, and in 1860 it closed down completely, causing considerable distress and hardship.

Far from corroborating the obituary, this new evidence threw considerable doubt upon its accuracy. For if the yard closed in 1860, it was very unlikely that Samuel went there then, as the obituary stated. The only other evidence we had was Samuel's marriage certificate. As we have seen, he was married at Rotherhithe on 27 December 1856 to Emma Barker, the daughter of a pilot and was then described as a joiner of Rotherhithe. [**9**]

Historical method. When a detective has collected a certain amount of data, he formulates one or more theories to explain it, and then looks for further evidence. The historian proceeds in much the same way and is likely to find that evidence only by seeking to prove or disprove a particular theory.

Using the other information in the obituary, we advanced the theory that Samuel served in the Navy during the Crimean War, was discharged after the Peace of Paris in February 1856, at Rotherhithe, where he settled and married in December 1856, that he secured work in Northfleet dockyard in 1857, and was *discharged*, (not taken on as the obituary says) when the yard closed in 1860. We then looked for further evidence to test our theory. There were two main difficulties. Firstly the obituary stated that his early life was spent in Devonport, and this was confirmed both by the 1861 Census Return which gave Devonport as his place of birth, and by his marriage certificate, which described his father as a 'converter' or sawyer in Devonport Dockyard. The presumption was that if he joined the Navy and served in the Crimean War, he would sail in a *Plymouth* ship. Extensive searches were made to try to find him in Admiralty records at the

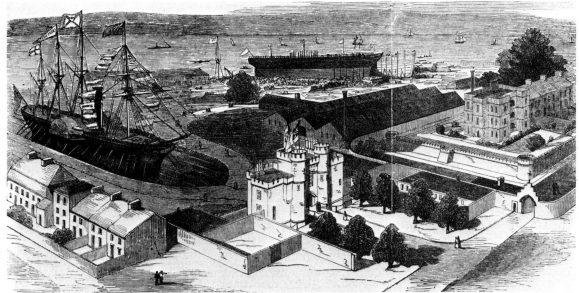

30 *Northfleet dockyard, 1851, showing the* Great Western *(left) and the launching of the* Orinoco *(right).*

Public Record Office at Kew without success. It now seemed improbable that he was in the Navy during the Crimean War – anyway not under his own name.[5]

Secondly, if Samuel went to Northfleet Dockyard *after* his marriage, he could not have done so until early in 1857. But this was the very time when the yard was in financial difficulties, and would have been reducing, not increasing, its labour force. It seemed much more likely, therefore, that Samuel worked in Northfleet Dockyard *before* his marriage, in December 1856. The evidence, therefore, strongly indicated that the obituary was incorrect, firstly in stating that Samuel was in the Navy, and secondly in giving 1860 as the date when he went to Northfleet Dockyard.

The Reliability of Evidence. The errors in Samuel Honeycombe's obituary provide an object lesson in the handling of evidence. Whatever piece of evidence the family historian has he must assess its reliability. The two key questions are 'Was the document written at

the time, or at a later date?', and 'Had the person writing the record personal knowledge of the events he describes?'. In this case, we can carry on to ask ourselves 'Who supplied the information for the obituary?'. There can be little doubt that most of the details included in the obituary were supplied by Samuel's daughter, Emma (A11).[6] In other words, a reporter wrote down what he thought Emma told him her father had told her. The obituary was, in fact, oral evidence twice removed.

Since Emma died in 1963, it is impossible now to identify the sources of the errors. Anyone who has had dealings with a local newspaper knows that in a report it usually gets something wrong. Emma may have told the reporter that her father *left* the Dockyard in 1860, and when he wrote up his hastily scribbled notes, this was misinterpreted as *came to* the Dockyard in 1860. More likely, 1860 might be a transcription or printing error for 1850. Alternatively, Emma may have mis-remembered what her father had said. Similarly, with

5. The musters in the Public Record Office of all ships sailing from Plymouth were searched without success, as were those for all ships in the Crimea. Nor was his name found among the artificers at Kazach Bay where there was a steam factory employing civilian shipwrights. Merchant Navy records were also searched unsuccessfully.

6. In the obituary, there are items such as the details of his last illness which would be known only to a close relative and it is known that he was living with his daughter, Emma, when he died.

No.	When and where born	Name, if any	Sex	Name, and surname of father	Name, surname, and maiden surname of mother	Occupation of father	Signature, description, and residence of informant	When registered	Signature of registrar	Name entered after registration

1850. BIRTH in the Sub-district of ____ Stoke ____ in the County of Devon

No.	When and where born	Name, if any	Sex	Name, and surname of father	Name, surname, and maiden surname of mother	Occupation of father	Signature, description, and residence of informant	When registered	Signature of registrar	Name entered after registration
184	Twenty fourth June 1850 3.15.a.m. 38 Keates Street Stoke Damerel	Ellen	Girl	Samuel Honeycombe	Elizabeth Frayne	Carpenter	x The mark of Elizabeth Frayne Mother 38 Keates Street Stoke Damerel	Fourth July 1850	W.M.Rickard Registrar	————————

31 *An illegitimate birth with the father's name given and no overt indication of bastardy.*

regard to the Crimean War, Samuel *may* have said only that he came to Northfleet 'because of the Crimean War', meaning that he was recruited with the expansion of the Yard – and this was later misinterpreted by Emma. He may have said he sailed round the world and Emma therefore assumed he was in the Navy. He may even have left the details of his past life vague for reasons of his own.

Fresh evidence. This does not always emerge by testing a theory. Sometimes solutions to problems turn up incidentally, when you are looking for something else. Because your attention is not on that problem, the significance of the evidence may be overlooked. This is nearly what happened in the case of Samuel George Davey Honeycombe.

The last positive evidence we have of Samuel being in Devonport was on 2 October 1849, when he was the informant on his mother's death certificate. He was not to be found anywhere in Devonport in the 1851 Census and so presumably had left there by 31 March, the day of the Census. Why did he leave? The answer is perhaps to be found on this certificate [31].

The interesting thing about this document is that it records beyond doubt the birth of an illegitimate daughter to Elizabeth Frayne. If the father and mother had been married, the normal form of words would have been *Elizabeth Honeycombe, formerly Frayne* – in conformity with the heading of column No. 5, and had the couple been married, the mother would have made her mark as Elizabeth *Honeycombe* in column No. 7. Although this certificate was among those Gordon obtained from Somerset House some years before, he had missed its significance – supposing that it referred

to a married couple – and had pencilled in a hypothetical Samuel on another branch. It is, in fact, quite unusual for the father's name to be entered on the birth certificate of an illegitimate child. We were extremely lucky to find this certificate – not only because the father's name was given, but because the child was indexed under Honeycombe. The original civil registration indexers made the same mistake as Gordon, and indexed Ellen as 'Honeycombe' rather than the Ellen Frayne she undoubtedly was.

There would seem to be two possible reasons for Samuel's name appearing. The first is that he openly acknowledged paternity. This would seem unlikely, for Ellen is quite unknown to his descendants, and his disappearance from the scene with such alacrity makes it much more likely that Elizabeth was determined either to shame him publicly, or to acquire some legal hold on him. The second explanation seems by far the more likely.

One possibility is that Samuel left Devonport Dockyard and started work at Northfleet Dockyard at the end of 1849 or the beginning of 1850. As we have seen, this was during the period when the yard was expanding rapidly. A booklet on Northfleet's history, produced by the local council[7] says 'such ship-building activity needed a big work force, not all of which could be found locally, and many workers moved in from other shipbuilding towns', which lends support to this possibility. However, the mention in the obituary of his going round the world is so specific that it is highly improbable that Samuel made it up. It therefore seems

7. *Northfleet, the story of the Borough and its emblem* 1973.

more likely that he was recruited in 1854, when the Crimean War brought the yard the order for the fifty-four gunboats.[8]

One theory which would fit all the facts is that when Samuel discovered that Elizabeth Frayne was pregnant, he left Plymouth on the first available ship – perhaps working his passage as a ship's carpenter – and sailed round the world, before finally returning to England some time later.

Whatever Samuel was doing between 1849 and 1856, one thing is clear. In later life, the worthy Borough Surveyor had a very good reason for not being too specific about his early life.

Rotherhithe. Whether Samuel went to Northfleet in 1850 or 1854, it seems likely that he left the Yard when work fell off after the Crimean War ended in February 1856. By December 1856, when he married, Samuel was a joiner in Rotherhithe. In all probability, he had left the dockyard for the building trade. Rotherhithe was twenty miles up river from Northfleet, and although various possible reasons can be advanced for his move,[9] no positive evidence can be found. We know that he was not there long, and as we shall see, his movements over the next few years are compatible with a building worker moving from one new development area to another.

At the time of their marriage Emma was also described as of Rotherhithe, although we know from the 1861 Census that she was born in Gravesend, about two miles from Northfleet. Whether she and Samuel met at Gravesend or Northfleet when they both lived there, or whether they met in Rotherhithe, we shall probably never know.

Gravesend. We next tried to discover when Samuel and Emma moved to Gravesend. At first sight, the answer was very straightforward, for we knew that Gordon's grandfather (A9), their second child, was born in Gravesend in 1861, and both Census Returns and Civil Registration had shown that the eldest child, William Thomas (A5), was born in Gravesend in 1857. This would suggest a move very soon after the marriage in December 1856. However, we could not be certain, for Emma herself was born at Gravesend and it was common for a young wife to go to her mother for her first confinement. A single source was not enough. What corroboration could we find?

Directories. We had now reached the point where it was necessary to visit Gravesend Public Library, which, we discovered, had a good collection of local directories. Samuel Honeycombe first appeared in 1858 – in Spencer St. The following year, however, he was at 21 Cutmore St, the house where he was at the time of Henry's birth and the 1861 Census. Since this street had not appeared previously in directories, it would seem to have been a new house. Maybe Samuel even helped to build it himself. He was there too in the 1860, 1861 and 1862 directories. We could therefore fairly safely assume that the stay at Rotherhithe was a very short one, and that the Honeycombes went to live in Gravesend immediately after their marriage.

Samuel's move to Gravesend was, perhaps a return, for he may well have lived there while working in Northfleet Dockyard. Since Emma was born in Gravesend, it also seems likely that her parents were still living there. Although both these factors may have influenced the young couple, the crucial one was probably the local opportunities for building workers. How could we find out what was happening in Gravesend in the 1850s?

8. Having put forward new theories we looked for further evidence, but alas, all efforts to locate the records of Northfleet Dockyard have failed. They are not held locally, nor in the Kent County Record Office. Enquiries at the National Register of Archives, the Business Archives Council and the National Maritime Museum have also proved fruitless. Since Northfleet Dockyard was privately owned, the Admiralty Records at the Public Record Office were not too helpful, although there were letters from Northfleet Dockyard to the Admiralty which repeatedly referred to the shortage of shipwrights.

9. Philip Banbury's *Shipbuilders of the Thames and Medway* (David and Charles, 1971) says that Northfleet Dockyard built only *wooden* ships and then sent them for copper bottoming and the installation of engines to dockyards *higher up the river*. Could Samuel have been sent up river from Northfleet in connection with this work? E. Walford's *Old and new London*, published in 6 vols. between 1873 and 1878, supplied another possible answer. The docks at Rotherhithe were the principal docks for the timber trade 'the timber remaining afloat in the dock until it is conveyed to the yards of the wholesale dealer and the builder'. Did builders come from far afield to buy timber straight from the docks and in turn supply employment to journeymen? A third possibility is that Samuel's bride lived or worked at Rotherhithe and the marriage took place there, Samuel's address being one of convenience. More likely than any of these explanations, however, is that Samuel went wherever new building was going on.

32. Rosherville Gardens, Gravesend in the early nineteenth century.

33–34. Two artists' impression of Victorian Gravesend.

Topographical dictionaries. To get a general picture of a place in the nineteenth century, one of the first places to look is the five-volumed Lewis' *Topographical Dictionary* of England, (there are separate volumes for Wales and Scotland) first published in 1831. Here we learned that:

Gravesend being within the jurisdiction of the port of London, all outward bound ships, until recently, were here obliged to undergo a second clearing; but this practice has long been disused. Outward bound vessels take in their pilots here, and all vessels entering the port of London take in pilots from this place for the navigation of the river.

This confirmed that Emma Barker's father, a pilot, lived at Gravesend where she was born, rather than at Rotherhithe, where she was married.

Guide books. The mid-nineteenth century also saw the publication of numerous guide books, which are now of considerable historical interest. In 1842, a guide book to *The Ports, Harbours, Watering Places and Coast Scenery of Great Britain* said of Gravesend:

The great facilities of communication with the metropolis, the salubrity of the air, the beauty of the surrounding scenery, and the public amusements, by which it is enlivened, have all contributed to render Gravesend the most frequented town on the River

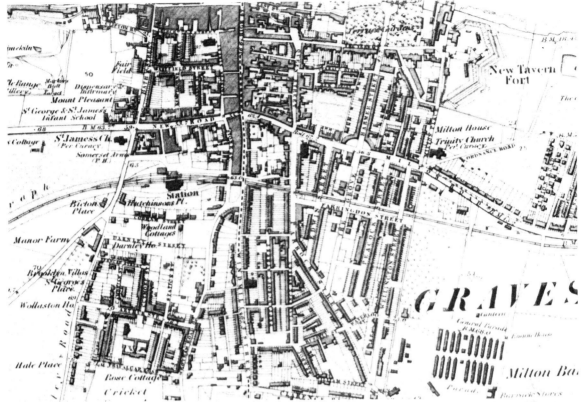

35 *Six-inch to the mile Ordnance Survey map of Gravesend, 1889.*

Thames. *The thousands of visitors who here keep holiday during 6 or 8 months of the year have insured resources to the inhabitants more to be depended on than the fluctuations of trade. New houses, new streets, hotels, reading rooms, public baths and pleasure gardens have all appeared in succession since the introduction of steam on the river.*[10]

By 1842, when that was written, over a million people were landing annually at the Town and Terrace

10. W. Finden and E.F. Finden *The Ports, Harbours, Watering Places and Coast Scenery of Great Britain, Illustrated by Views Taken on the Spot by W.H. Bartlett with Descriptions by William Beattie.* London, 1842.

Piers to enjoy amusements which included the piers and gardens, Tulley's Bazaar, outdoor concerts in the Tivoli or Victoria Gardens and donkey riding [32].

The quotation implies a substantial amount of new building. However, we must be careful. 1842 was not 1857. In 1849, the railway reached Gravesend and the river passage declined. By the 1860s, Gravesend was being displaced as a resort by Ramsgate, Margate and Broadstairs. It would seem that when Samuel and Emma went to Gravesend, the boom years were already over, though they probably did not realise this.

In using guide books as a historical source for what Gravesend was like at this time, we must once again assess their reliability as evidence. Since they were written for the benefit of visitors, they would tend to exaggerate the attractions and omit or play down the less salubrious parts. History is quite as much a question of assessing what the sources have left out as of making the best use of what they have put in.

Maps. The places where Samuel lived were plotted on the first edition six inch to the mile Ordnance Survey map of Gravesend published in 1865 [35]. Every effort should be made to obtain photocopies of such maps from local libraries or record offices. You can then mark on them not only your relatives' and ancestors' houses but their workplaces and the schools and churches they attended.

Local histories. As well as the various primary sources such as directories, guide books and maps, most county libraries also have a substantial collection of town and village histories though it is very much a matter of chance what has been written on the place in which you are interested. If you are lucky, you will find that a skilled historian has carefully explored the social structure and economic history of the area over many centuries. More probably, you will find that an enthusiastic amateur has collected a great deal of factual information, but has not really asked historical questions of the material. In either case, however, local histories repay careful study, for they may provide explanations for events in the family history and suggest further searches in primary sources.

Local History Societies. You would also be well advised to join not only the *family history* societies in the areas where your ancestors came from, but to make contact with the *local history* societies as well. These can prove a mine of information. Even if they are not particularly interested in genealogy or family history, through their work on particular topics members often have substantial information on local families, and local experts may well be able to suggest very plausible reasons for moves or other unexplained events.

Poplar. Samuel did not stay long in Gravesend – perhaps the amount of new building was dwindling. By October, 1862, when Emma was born, he had moved to Poplar, on the north bank of the Thames, opposite Rotherhithe. The stay there was also a short one, for in 1866, he was back in Northfleet. This move, however, was to prove a turning point in his career.

In this chapter, we have indicated a variety of sources for setting a family in its environment, – newspapers, guide books, maps and local histories. Such sources will not, however, yield meaningful answers unless the researcher not only asks the right questions in the first place, but also adopts a critical approach. For sources vary a great deal in their reliability – a newspaper account written long after the event cannot be depended upon, and guide-books may be very selective in their coverage. At times the family historian must admit frankly that the evidence is insufficient for him to come to a firm conclusion. Finally, research involves even more than asking the right questions, looking for answers and being critical of the evidence which is discovered. As we saw in the case of Ellen Frayne's birth certificate, it also involves being alert for the unexpected and in realising the significance of what turns up.

Postscript. Since the first edition of this book was published, another piece in the jigsaw has turned up. The 1851 census shows that Samuel was in Gravesend as a 22-year-old carpenter lodging at 22 Wrotham Road with the household of William Arnold, likewise a carpenter. Also lodging there were William Wood, a 34-year-old carpenter, his wife and infant daughter. Now we cannot be certain that Samuel was working in the dockyard, but the presence of three carpenters in the same house makes it very likely, and interesting in view of my hunch (see page 33) that Samuel lived in Gravesend earlier whilst working in the dockyard. The best route to new evidence is often formulating hypotheses based on what you have got. So it is looking more and more as if Samuel left Devonport shortly after completing his apprenticeship to get work as a carpenter in another dockyard, spurred on, no doubt by the desire to disentangle himself from Elizabeth Frayne.

4 The Surveyor of Northfleet

Samuel's return to Northfleet can be dated with some precision, for his youngest daughter, Eleanor, was born in Poplar in 1865, but he re-emerges in the 1866 Gravesend and Northfleet Directory, living at 1, Mount Street, Northfleet. Clearly, what attracted Samuel back was the expension of the town and the building opportunities this offered.

The Ordnance Survey six inch to the mile map of Northfleet Parish in 1865 [29] shows that it was a district with large areas of gardens – some styled as ornamental – arable land, pasture, osier beds, one claypit and one cement mill. In the 1871 Census, the population was 6,515; by 1891 it had grown to 11,717. That Northfleet continued to grow despite the closure of the dockyard, was largely due to the development of the cement industry in the area. The expansion of the town gave opportunities to an enterprising building worker. The directory shows that by 1869 Samuel was in business on his own account as a builder and undertaker at 36 The Hill. At the time of the 1871 Census he was forty-two. The Census, in which Samuel describes himself as 'carpenter and undertaker', shows his wife, Emma (forty-two), his children, William (thirteen), Margaret (eleven), Henry (nine) all born in Gravesend, and Emma (eight), and Eleanor (six), born in Poplar. With them also, was his sister Margaretta (fifty-five), a dressmaker.

The Local Board of Health.
As Northfleet grew from a village to a small town, urgent social needs arose, particularly with regard to public health. In this respect, Northfleet was typical of small towns all over the country. By an Act of 1848, ratepayers could petition for the setting up of *Local Boards of Health* to deal with water supplies, drainage, road maintenance and refuse disposal, a process accelerated by the setting up of a national *Local Government Board* in 1871. Northfleet duly set up its own Local Board of Health in 1874.

As the official history of Northfleet makes clear, the new Board faced a formidable task. Cesspools were seeping into wells, some inhabitants had to draw water from the Plough Pond, and the roads were dusty and badly maintained.[11] One of the first things the Board did was to appoint a *Surveyor and Inspector of Nuisances*. The man who got the job was Samuel Honeycombe – and he appears in the directory with that title from 1875.[12] Samuel's obituary notes that it was at his instigation that the streets were first paved and lit, and from his designs that the council offices were erected. Tramlines were laid down by the Gravesend and Northfleet Tramway Company [36, 37]. Under his surveyorship, says the obituary, Northfleet developed from a comparatively obscure village to an important town.

Whilst we may be sceptical as to how much the development of Northfleet may be directly attributed to Samuel and how much would have occurred whoever was Surveyor, the obituary is substantially confirmed by the official history which also refers to the efforts of the Local Board of Health to remedy the lack of a proper water supply by the purchase of a water cart in 1876 and the gradual extension of Water Company mains in 1878. Whether or not the initiative in these improvements came from Samuel, he seems to have carried out the job of Surveyor with energy and efficiency.

The Northfleet Fire Brigade.
It was March 1975 when Gordon discovered his great-grandfather's obituary. What interested him most was not that Samuel had played a major role in bringing paving, street lighting, trams and a mains water supply to Northfleet, but that he was 'first Captain of the Northfleet Fire Brigade'. The reason why this tantalisingly brief reference intrigued Gordon was that he had just started to write his fourth book, *Red Watch*, the true story of the worst fire in Central London in 1974.

11. *Northfleet, the story of the Borough and its emblem* 1973
12. Like most local government posts at this time, Samuel's appointment was – at least initially – a part-time one, for the Directory continues to list him as *Builder and Undertaker* until 1879. We know that his son, William Thomas, followed his father's occupation of undertaker. But as he was only seventeen in 1874, Samuel presumably carried on the business for some years until William could take over.

36 *The Hill, Northfleet, c. 1900. The Post Office kept by Margaret and Emma Honeycombe is beyond the Queen's Head and the Local Board behind the tree.*

Gordon therefore searched the files of the *Gravesend and Dartford Reporter* for contemporary accounts which would supply more information on why his great-grandfather, having been successively carpenter, builder and Surveyor for the Local Board should become a part-time fireman. He soon realised that to discover the whole story he would need to go to the official records, and at Northfleet he located the minutes of the Local Board and of its General Purposes Committee.

Reading between the lines. As we have seen, collecting raw material to build up the biography of an ancestor may be a slow and sometimes unrewarding business – births, marriages and deaths, Census Returns, perhaps some appearance in newspapers or directories, and a few casual references in other records. Sometimes,

however, we come across a rich vein of material which provides substantial information on a particular period of an ancestor's life. Here the problem is not so much making the most of very sparse data as being able to see the wood for the trees. In many family histories, such source material tends to be included almost verbatim with little attempt to assess its reliability. However, as with the Gravesend guide books, we must always think about what records leave out, as well as what they include. It is not always easy to unravel the full story. The story of the foundation of the Northfleet Fire Brigade is an excellent example, for we had a week by week – sometimes day by day – account of events in the minutes of the Local Board, in the minutes of the General Purposes Committee and in the columns of the local newspaper. What evidence could possibly be

37 *The Northfleet Tramway c. 1890. Tramlines can also be seen in* [36].

lacking in order to write a comprehensive historical account?

The problem was that just as guide books frequently leave out much of the important information about a place, so minutes cannot be taken as an accurate record of anything but the final decisions. Anyone who has served on a committee knows that they rarely convey the atmosphere of a meeting. 'After some discussion the proposal was agreed' may conceal fierce arguments in which the protagonists almost came to blows! A new committee member soon learns the vocabulary. 'Some disquiet was expressed' usually indicates a row. In using a source like this, we have to remember that it is an *official record*. Had Samuel kept a private diary, it might have given quite a different version of events. We had to try and read between the lines of the minutes.

Sometimes the newspaper reports helped us to do this; sometimes we had to resort to plausible guess-work.

A skilful tactician. The picture of Samuel that emerged from the rather dry minutes and newspaper accounts was of a skilful tactician who used every trick in the book to achieve his objective of getting Northfleet its own fire brigade.[13] Firstly, he employed Fabian tactics – starting with a modest proposal to increase the number of fire hydrants, then suggesting the purchase of a reel, hose and unions, and finally advocating the

13. Until 1865, fire brigades were organised entirely by the insurance companies, concerned with minimising their risks. In that year, the fire officers handed over to the Metropolitan Board of Works the fire protection of London, which for over thirty years they had carried on at their own expense. In the next twenty years, most cities and boroughs followed suit and formed their own brigades. Northfleet was served from Gravesend.

38 *The Northfleet Fire Brigade shortly after Samuel's resignation.*

formation of a voluntary force to use the new equipment. Secondly, he worked through sympathisers. The Councillor who proposed the purchase of the fire hydrants was a close friend, James Mitchell. The formation of a fire brigade was proposed in a letter from 'certain gentlemen'. Finally, the local newspaper took up the cause, and when we asked ourselves who could have supplied the information on which the relevant article was based, all the clues pointed to Samuel.

Captain of the Fire Brigade. Samuel finally organised his volunteer fire brigade and was made its Captain. It abundantly justified its existence by putting out its first fire on 16 October 1884, four days before it was officially created!

Just over a month later, the brigade succeeded in extinguishing another fire in a tavern next door to a brewery. There was a full and congratulatory report in the local newspaper, together with an apparently unsolicited letter of gratitude from one of the owners of the brewery, Mr W. S. Pope. This praised 'the prompt way in which the call was responded to by Mr Honeycombe' to whom and his staff great credit was due, he said, for saving the surrounding property. It seems very likely that Mr Pope, who had good reason to be grateful to the fire brigade, was asked to write a letter to this effect. Was it Samuel's idea also to include a sentence on the 'great and immediate necessity of a properly organised Northfleet Fire Brigade'?

But however carefully he schemed, Samuel did not get everything his own way. He had been pressing for a

39

40

39. Gordon at Thameside Fire Station, December 1975. This now covers Northfleet.

40. The Northfleet Fire Brigade, 1888. Samuel Honeycombe is the gentleman in the top hat.

properly equipped uniformed fire brigade, but the Local Board finally decided to supply only 'helmets, hatchets and belts' to the first six firemen who arrived as the result of a call. So of the twelve firemen, six were given no equipment at all, and nobody was supplied with a uniform! In view of the fine record of the fire brigade, the attitude of the Board seems to have been parsimonious.

Resignation. On the 14 April 1888, Samuel attended his last and most tragic fire. The newspaper reported that two children had been burnt to death. Just over two weeks later, on 2 May, he tendered his resignation as Captain on the grounds of age – he would be sixty the following October. The coincidence is suspicious.

It may well be that the death of the two young children had upset Samuel. Although the children seem to have died before the brigade arrived, he may have felt that the physical and emotional stress was too much for a man of his age, and that a younger man should be in charge.

Although Samuel had resigned as Captain of the fire brigade, he continued as Surveyor to the Local Board. In 1894, a Local Government Act set up Urban District Councils to replace Local Boards of Health, and gave them a far wider range of duties. Although sixty-six, Samuel Honeycombe was confirmed as Surveyor to the new Council, and the minutes show his part in a drainage scheme for which he was given a fee of twenty guineas. Samuel served until 1905, when he resigned at the age of seventy-seven. The Council showed their appreciation by making him 'Consulting Surveyor', a position he held until his death six years later.

Samuel's family. Samuel George Davey Honeycombe started life as the son of a Devonport sawyer. He died a highly respected retired local government officer. Henceforth, his descendants not only led a different way of life from their working-class ancestors and relatives, but had very different aspirations.

William: builder and undertaker. From the directories, it would seem that Samuel's eldest son, William, took over his father's building and undertaking business at 36 The Hill in 1881. On 5 February 1885, while working in Northfleet Churchyard on the tomb of the late Vicar, the Rev. Frederick Southgate, a slab collapsed, killing Thomas Gray, a thirteen-year-old boy who was helping him [41]. Although William was uninjured, according to a newspaper report the whole incident so unnerved him that his health was broken and he died on 18 February 1887, just over two years after the

In Loving Memory of

Thomas Edward George Gray,

AGED 13 YEARS AND 3 MONTHS,

Who was killed February 5th, 1885, by the falling of a flag-stone while preparing the Vault to receive the remains of the late Rev. F. Southgate in Northfleet Churchyard.

41

accident. He was twenty-nine. The local paper also carried reports of the accident and the inquest. Apparently the boy removed a chisel that was wedging a large slab covering the entrance to the vault, which then fell on him and crushed him to death. Most likely it was William who had used the chisel for this purpose and he blamed himself for Thomas's death [42].

William's funeral was attended by members of cricket and rowing clubs and of the Ancient Order of

FATAL ACCIDENT AT A GRAVE.—A serious and fatal accident occurred at the Northfleet churchyard, while the workmen were engaged in preparing the vault for the reception of the remains of the late Vicar It appears that the large slab covering at the entrance to the vault consists of two parts, one of which was removed while the other was fixed back to an iron pallisading by means of a chisel. Mr. Honeycombe, jun., Mr. Steadman, and several workmen were in the vault, and a lad named Gray, about 14, son of the blacksmith on the Hill, had just taken a bar of iron into the vault for use by the men. While returning up the steps one of the bricklayers asked for his chisel, and the lad seeing it, but not knowing that it held the stone back, removed it, and no sooner had he done so than the massive slab fell, literally crushing the boy's head, and killing him instantaneously. The men in the vault became aware of the occurrence by being suddenly thrown into darkness, and it was with the utmost difficulty that they raised the stone, and extricated the body, which was removed to the belfry until after the funeral of the late Vicar. Dr. Tippie was immediately called, but his services were of no avail. The sad event created the greatest consternation among the assembled people, and the utmost sympathy was expressed for the bereaved parents.

THE LATE VICAR OF NORTHFLEET. — It is with deep regret that we have to record the death of the Rev. Frederick Southgate, vicar of Northfleet, which took place, after a long and painful illness, at the

Buffaloes, which gave a lead to where further information about his activities might be found.

Henry: hotel proprietor. The second son, Henry, Gordon's grandfather, learned the catering trade at Simpson's in Piccadilly, became the landlord of a public house at Hampton Wick, near Kingston-upon-Thames and was catering manager on the first of the dining cars on the London and North-Eastern Railway from Kings Cross to Waverley Station, Edinburgh. Later, as we have seen, he became a hotel proprietor in Edinburgh, Torquay and Bridge of Allan.

Margaret: post mistress. According to the newspaper report on Emma's hundredth birthday, Samuel set up his daughters, Margaret and Emma, in a sub-post office at Northfleet in 1878. However, the directories show them as being at the Post Office only from 1886, and this was at 36 The Hill, the same address as William Honeycombe's building and undertaking business the previous year. So when William was no longer able to work, Samuel would appear to have had the premises converted into a sub-post office run by his two elder

been abstracted only for Honeycombes and not for other surnames appearing on the family tree. The importance of knowing about relations and neighbours is also illustrated by the marriage of one of Margaret's daughters to a James Mitchell. It was a James Mitchell, a member of the Local Board, who proposed that Samuel's plans for new fire hydrants should be accepted. In the 1871 Census we find the Mitchells living next door. James Mitchell junior was Samuel's assistant in later years, succeeded him as Surveyor, witnessed his will and finally married his grand-daughter. Relations between the two families were obviously close for many years.

daughters. That does not necessarily mean the news-paper account was wrong. Margaret and Emma may have been set up in business in 1878 and moved their sub-post office in 1885 when their brother's premises became available. However, if that were the case, it is odd that the Post Office does not appear in the directories from 1879 to 1884.

In 1890 Margaret married a Richard Fox. This photograph [43] shows the shop of a James Fox, numbered 34 and 35. It was known that the Honey-combes were at 36 The Hill. Could the Fox's have been next door? When the directories were re-examined, it was discovered that 'James Fox. Grocer and Draper', was indeed at 34 and 35 The Hill from 1879 onwards.

The 'Misses Honeycombe' appear at the Post Office, 36 The Hill until the 1889 directory. In the 1890 and 1891 directories it is 'Miss Honeycombe' and from 1892 onwards, numbers 36, 37 and 38 are described as 'R. Fox, Postal and Telegraph Office'. We know that Margaret Honeycombe married Richard in 1890, pre-sumably too late to affect the 1891 directory entry. What is interesting, however, is that from 1892 'James Fox, Grocer and Draper', was at 34 and 35, and his son at 36, 37 and 38. The Foxes seem to have almost taken over the street!

The genealogist preoccupied with the male line may well miss important clues, and in building up the family history we need to be aware not only of relations on the female side, but neighbours as well. In this case, a search had to be re-done because directory entries had

MISS EMMA SPANS MAIL COACH DAYS AND TELSTAR

NEXT Wednesday Miss Emma Honeycombe, of Dartford, for five years a resident of Bournemouth, will be 100 years old.

When she was born Abraham Lincoln was President of the United States. She saw the first mail coach on its journey from Dover to London.

In 1878 her father started his two daughters in a business with a sub-post office at Northfleet. Ten years later the postmaster of Gravesend asked Miss Honey-combe to assist at the Head Office for a few days. She stayed there for 34 years.

She was the first woman to serve at Gravesend Head Office counter and during her service saw the introduction of telegraph money orders, parcel post, radio telegrams, air mail and old age pensions.

Miss Honeycombe retired in 1922. She came to Bournemouth about six years ago and lived at 94, Richmond Wood-road until last year when because of her age she had to return to Kent to be near relatives. She now lives at Carlton House, St. James-lane, Horn's Cross, Dartford.

She is a member of Bourne-mouth and District Association of Post Office and other Civil Service Veterans.

 44

Emma: Post Office assistant. According to the news-paper account, Emma worked in the Northfleet sub-post office until 1888, when the post master asked her to assist at the Head Office in Gravesend for a few days. She stayed there for thirty-four years. We now know this was inaccurate, for Emma worked for many years in the sub-post office by Gravesend Pier, and was only later transferred to the Head Office. However, the newspaper is no doubt correct in saying that she was the first *woman* to serve at a counter in that office, and she certainly saw the introduction of money orders, parcel post, radio telegrams, air mail and old age pensions [45]. She retired in 1922, aged sixty. As we have seen, she died in 1963 at the age of one hundred [44, 46].

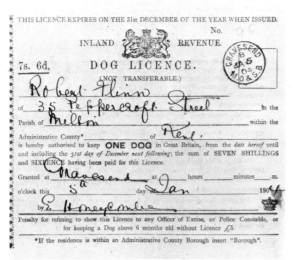

45 *A licence issued by Emma at Gravesend Post Office.*　　**46** *Emma's hundredth birthday party, 1962.*

Eleanor: headmistress. The youngest daughter, Eleanor, was appointed headmistress of the girls' department of Lawn Board School, Northfleet, when it opened on 10 June 1885, with twenty-four scholars. She was twenty years old and was a 'certified teacher of the second class'.

The school log book gives a vivid picture of school life during her headship. Many entries are devoted to the teaching of hymns and songs and to school inspections [47]. The report on Eleanor's first inspection, on 27 May 1886, says the school 'gives promise of satisfactory general efficiency'. It continues:

The elementary subjects are generally satisfactory and in the third and fourth Standards, Writing is good and Arithmetic pretty good, though no girl has solved the problem in the Third or the Reduction sum in the Fourth. Needlework is pretty good, and up to the third Standard, English and Grammar are satisfactory, but the fourth Standard fail in the latter subject.

The log book reveals some rather sad little stories. In 1889, Eleanor wrote:

Mrs Povey visited me a fortnight ago, with reference to her daughter, Alice Povey, who is attending this school. She told me that since the child had the measles last

Spring her reason has been affected. Previous to the visit of the mother I had noticed the child had been very peculiar in her ways. She has now been playing truant. This week six times.

The following year, Eleanor was at loggerheads with the Local Board of Education over the time spent on collecting the statutory penny a week from each child.

I was directed by the Board on Feb 27th to take all school pence, also to initial each child's card. . . . I have been obliged to leave my class, not only first class to lose their lessons, but also obliged to stop lessons in other classes. On Friday Morning it took me 1 hr 10 mins to count money, make up registers, and send to Bank. Friday Afternoon has been entirely lost, making up registers and cards. This makes a total of 6 hrs 53 mins loss to my class work.

The Board were adamant that 'The resolution passed by the Board at the last Meeting must be strictly adhered to.' However, the problem solved itself, for Board school education became free by an Act of 1891.

At this time, the grant to a school depended upon results as evidenced by the children's performance on inspection. In 1891 the Inspector said the general

29

July 13th. *Wednesday Afternoon. All children sent home there being only 41 present, & several very wet, on account of a severe storm.*

E. Honeycombe
Edwin Carpenter

July 15th. *Found Every thing very Satisfactory*

July 15th. *The Stock transferred to Miss Odell. Mr Baynes checked same.*

E. Honeycombe.

The Lawn Board School log book, 1892. Eleanor resigns.

Eleanor and Frederick, 1892.

working of the school was so praiseworthy that he was recommending the higher grant though he hoped to find 'distinct improvement next year in the matter of general Intelligence' and gave the full grant for singing only 'with much hesitation'.

Eleanor resigned on 15 July 1892 to get married [48]. By that time there were 225 pupils, a second assistant and two pupil teachers.

The main difference between the school log book and the minutes of the Local Board of Health which were our main source for Samuel's career is that although Eleanor obviously had to be circumspect about what she wrote, the log book was – to a certain extent – a personal document, reflecting her own point of view.

Social mobility. So in the years immediately preceding Samuel's resignation from the Fire Brigade in 1888, the Honeycombes shared between them the jobs of Surveyor and Inspector of Nuisances, Captain of the Fire Brigade, post-mistress and school-mistress. There can have been few people in Northfleet who did not know and respect them. We must, however, beware of inflating their status. The Surveyor to the Local Board was a kind of half way house between the old amateur official elected by the parish and the modern highly qualified professional. Although Samuel's chil-

dren held middle-class jobs, neither post-mistress nor school-mistress were posts of any great status.

Nevertheless, in rising from skilled worker to a minor professional post, it would appear that in true Victorian tradition, Samuel had by sheer ability and industry raised himself – and consequently his family – from the ranks of the working-class. Yet how much was really due to Samuel himself, and how much to chance? Had Samuel not seduced poor Elizabeth Frayne in 1849, he might well have thought twice about leaving the security of a pensionable job in Devonport Dockyard. Similarly, had Northfleet Dockyard not failed after the Crimean War, he might have ended his working life as a humble carpenter there. As it was, he was forced by circumstances out of secure employment and into the building trade, just at a time when the population was expanding fast, with a consequent demand for new houses. Finally, he was in the right place at the right time when the Local Board was seeking a Surveyor and Inspector of Nuisances.

Whilst Samuel undoubtedly turned each situation to good advantage, it was lucky that such opportunities came his way. As we shall see in the next chapter, his Devonport relatives were less fortunate. That some branches of a family rose, whilst others did not, was often due as much to chance as to any other factor.

5 A Dockyard Sawyer

So far, we have used standard genealogical procedures to trace Gordon's ancestry back to his great-grandfather, Samuel George Davey Honeycombe (B15), the son of William Honeycombe (B1), a 'converter' or sawyer in Devonport Dockyard.

Samuel's obituary stated that he was born in Devonport in 1828. This was confirmed as his place of birth by the 1861 and 1871 Census Returns, and so Devonport was obviously the first place to search. Gordon soon discovered however, that there was no parish of Devonport. The town which had grown up around the dockyard was called Plymouth Dock until 1824 and was in the once rural parish of Stoke Damerel.

As well as Plymouth Dock, another new town, Stonehouse, had grown up in the shadow of Plymouth.

So by 1811, there were three adjacent towns: Plymouth, Stonehouse and Plymouth Dock, later called Devonport [49].

Parish registers. For genealogical information before 1837, we turn to the parish registers of baptisms, marriages and burials. First started in 1538, most were kept in parish churches until recent years. However, since the Second World War, increasing numbers have been deposited in County or Borough Record Offices.

Many registers have been transcribed and indexed, and in the library of Devon and Cornwall Record Society at Exeter, Gordon found a copy of the marriages for Stoke Damerel, 1595–1814. There he discovered that William Honeycombe, 'millwright' married

Table B. The Devonport Honeycombes.

For ease of reference, individuals have been numbered consecutively from left to right and these numbers are used in the text. Cross references are included to Table A, page 13.

B1 (A1) William Honeycombe b. Liskeard 1786 Millwright in 1811 Sawyer, Devonport Dockyard, 1814–1855 Pawnbroker, St Helier, Jersey, 1861 d. 17 Aug 1867	=	B2 Dorothy Davey m. Stoke Damerel, Devon 12 Aug 1811 d. 2nd Oct 1849 (cholera)

B3 Mary Ann Davey Honeycombe bapt Stoke Damerel 27 Oct 1811 m. Liskeard, Cornwall, 18 Aug 1836 B4 John Hancock Shoemaker of Liskeard	B5 (A2) Margaretta Davey Honeycombe bapt Stoke Damerel 4 April 1813 d. Northfleet, Kent, 1875	B6 Elizabeth Davey Honeycombe bapt Stoke Damerel 10 July 1814 d. Liskeard, Cornwall, 1878	B7 William Henry Davey Honeycombe bapt Stoke Damerel 31 March 1816 d. 27 Dec 1884 bur Stoke Damerel = B8 Thirza Found drowned 9 Aug 1885	B9 Ann Maria Davey Honeycombe bapt St Andrew's, Plymouth 3 Aug 1817 bur Liskeard 3 July 1892	B10 Elizabeth Sarah Davey Honeycom... bapt Stoke Damer... 5 Nov 1820 bur Stoke Damere... 31 Jan 1824

49 *The Plymouth area in 1860 showing the three adjacent towns of Devonport, Stonehouse and Plymouth and the Torpoint and Cremyll ferries across to Cornwall.*

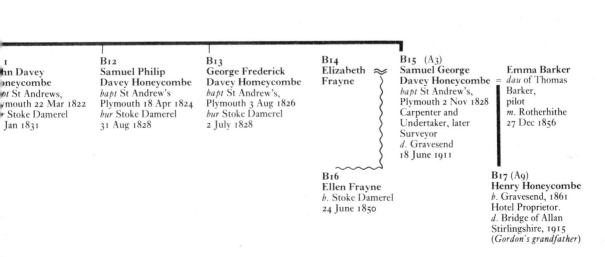

B11	B12	B13	B14	B15 (A3)	
[Jo]hn Davey [Ho]neycombe	**Samuel Philip Davey Honeycombe**	**George Frederick Davey Homeycombe**	**Elizabeth Frayne** ≈	**Samuel George Davey Honeycombe** =	**Emma Barker**
[*ba*]*t* St Andrews, [Ply]mouth 22 Mar 1822	*bapt* St Andrew's Plymouth 18 Apr 1824	*bapt* St Andrew's, Plymouth 3 Aug 1826		*bapt* St Andrew's, Plymouth 2 Nov 1828	*dau* of Thomas Barker,
[bu]r Stoke Damerel [ ] Jan 1831	*bur* Stoke Damerel 31 Aug 1828	*bur* Stoke Damerel 2 July 1828		Carpenter and Undertaker, later Surveyor *d*. Gravesend 18 June 1911	pilot *m*. Rotherhithe 27 Dec 1856

			B16		B17 (A9)
			Ellen Frayne *b*. Stoke Damerel 24 June 1850		**Henry Honeycombe** *b*. Gravesend, 1861 Hotel Proprietor. *d*. Bridge of Allan Stirlingshire, 1915 (*Gordon's grandfather*)

Mary Bradey, of this Parish, Spinster _____ were
Married in this Church by *Banns* _____
this *Twelfth* Day of *August* in the Year One Thousand *Eight* Hundred
and *Eleven* _____ By me *Williams Officiating Minister*

This Marriage was solemnized between Us { *The Mark X of William Willmott*
{ *The Mark X of Mary Bradey*

In the Presence of { *J Longman*
{ *Wm Roberts*

〰〰〰〰〰〰〰〰〰〰〰〰〰〰〰〰〰〰〰〰

N° *160* { *William Honeycombe* of th*is* Parish *Millwright &*
Dorothy Davey, of this Parish, Spinster _____ were
Married in this Church by *Banns* _____
this *Twelfth* Day of *August* in the Year One Thousand *Eight* Hundred
and *Eleven* _____ By me *Williams Officiating Minister*

This Marriage was solemnized between Us { *William Honeycombe*
{ *Dorothy Davey*

In the Presence of { *Wm Roberts*
{ *Mary Alger*

50 *The Stoke Damerel marriage register, 1811. Note William and Dorothy's signatures and the fact that William Roberts also witnessed a previous marriage on the same day. Mary Alger lived next door to the church.*

Dorothy Davey on 12 August 1811. Later, he checked with the original register [50]. It is most important to do this, as there may be transcription errors, or the omission of vital information, such as names of witnesses.[16] Gordon knew that Samuel George Davey Honeycombe's father was William. He had now found a William whose wife's maiden name was Davey. It seemed pretty certain that they were Samuel's parents, but had yet to be proved.

Baptism registers. From the obituary and census

16. In this case the names of the witnesses were not too helpful. Both William Roberts and Mary Alger witnessed many marriages.

returns, Gordon knew that Samuel George Davey Honeycombe (B15) was born in 1828. However, a search of the baptism register of Stoke Damerel did not yield the expected entry, although he did find the baptisms for five children of William and Dorothy between 1811 and 1822, the first – Mary Ann Davey Honeycombe (B3) – only two months after the parents' marriage. We must remember that before 1837 we are always dealing with *baptisms*, not births. The delay between birth and baptism was frequently months, and might be years. So Mary Ann could even have been born before the marriage.

BAPTISMS solemnized in the PARISH OF SAINT ANDREW, in PLYMOUTH, in the County of DEVON, in the Year 1828.

When Baptized.	Child's Christian Name.	Parents' Name. Christian.	Surname.	Abode.	Quality, Trade, or Profession.	By whom the Ceremony was performed.
1828. Nov.r 2 No.1666	Henry Benj.n Son of	Thomas Joanna		Plym.o	Fisherman	Jn Williams Off. Min.
2 No.1667	John Henry Wakeham Son of	Rowden Sarah		Plym.o	Boot Maker	Jn Williams
2 No.1668	Samuel Will.m George Davey Son of	Honey= =combe Dorothy		Devonport	Sawyer	Jn Williams
	Samuel Samuel					

51 *Baptism of Gordon's great-grandfather at St Andrew's, Plymouth, 1828.*

Gordon then decided to search the registers of the two parishes of nearby Plymouth and found the baptism of Samuel George Davey Honeycombe (B15) in 1828 in the register of St Andrew's.[17] [51] He was indeed the son of William and Dorothy, the last of five children baptised there since 1817. This clinched the relationship. Gordon could now add another name to the family tree – that of his great-great grandmother, Dorothy Davey (B2). Was she a relative of John

17. There seems no obvious reason why most of the later baptisms were at Plymouth, rather than at Stoke Damerel, since it is apparent that the family lived in Devonport throughout.

Symons Honeycombe's grandmother, Joanna Davey? Were both related to Sir Humphrey Davy? Certainly William and Dorothy went to extraordinary lengths to perpetuate the name, giving every one of their children Davey as a Christian name. But the Stoke Damerel registers gave no other hint of the answers to such questions, which would clearly have to await further research. However, they did give a great deal more information about the Devonport Honeycombes.

Child mortality. One of the first things Gordon noticed was that two of Samuel George Davey Honey-combe's elder brothers – George Frederick Davey (B13)

BURIALS solemnized in the Parish of STOKE-DAMEREL, in the County of DEVON, in the Year of our Lord God 182 0

Name.	Abode.	When Buried.	Age.	By whom the Ceremony was performed.
Samuel Philip Davey Honeycombe No. 426	Devonport Marlboro' St	31	4 years 5 Months	J. Jacob Officiating Minister
George Fredk Davey Honeycombe	Marlboro. St.	2	1. 10	J. Harrison Offg Minister

Burials of two elder brothers of Samual George Davey Honeycombe, 1828. The next child was given both their names.

PLACE	HOUSES		NAMES of each Person who abode therein the preceding Night.	AGE and SEX		PROFESSION, TRADE, EMPLOYMENT, or of INDEPENDENT MEANS.	Where Born	
	Uninhabited or Building	Inhabited		Males	Females		Whether Born in same County	Whether Born in Scotland, Ireland
Morice Street No 6		1	Joshua Pearse	30		Port Boy	Yes	
			Ann D		25		Yes	
			Mary D		8		D	
			Phillipa D		5		D	
			Elizabeth D		2		Di	
			Jane D		× Mo		D	
			William Honeycombe	55		Lawyer	No	
			Dorothy D		50		No	
	1		William D	25		Lawyer	Yes	

1841 Census for Devonport. Note that the ages over 16 are in five-year groups and exact birthplaces are not given.

and Samuel Philip Davey (B12) [52] had died in infancy in 1828, just before Samuel (B15) was born, no doubt the reason why the names Samuel and George were both used again for the next child. Two other children died young – Elizabeth (B10), aged three, buried in 1824, and John (B11), aged eight in 1831. So out of a family of ten children, only six survived to maturity. Child mortality was high in all towns and Devonport was no exception. It was probably just as insanitary as the new industrial towns of the north.

Occupations. In 1811, the marriage register described William (B1) as 'millwright' – a highly skilled craftsman who built and serviced mills. Since the father's occupation is very rarely given in pre-1813 baptismal registers, Gordon did not know whether he was still in this trade when their first child was baptised two months later. However, at subsequent births in 1813 and 1814, William's occupation was given as 'labourer'. It was clear that within two years his status had dropped considerably, though, of course, Gordon could not be sure that he was actually in employment as a millwright in 1811 – he would doubtless put this down as his trade even if he had been out of work for years. The baptismal register showed that by 1816 William was a sawyer, i.e. a semi-skilled worker, and this remained his description in all subsequent entries.

Gordon had no evidence of where William worked as a labourer in 1813 and 1814. However since he knew he was later a sawyer in the dockyard, it seemed a very reasonable assumption that he was recruited to it as a labourer and later promoted to a more skilled trade. After all, the dockyard would have provided nearly all the employment in the area.

Residences. The fact that William and Dorothy had ten children over eighteen years was a great advantage, as the 'abode' given for the baptisms and burials almost provided a directory of their different addresses. In the baptisms, whether at Stoke Damerel or St Andrew's, Plymouth, William's abode was given simply as Plymouth Dock – or Devonport after it changed its name in 1824. In the Stoke Damerel burial registers, however, the 'abode' was more precisely described – John St, (1824), Marlborough St (1828) and Market St (1831). As William's family increased so he moved, presumably to larger accommodation – or maybe he fell behind with the rent.

Census returns. None of these addresses, however, proved helpful in locating the family in a census, and in the end the whole of the 1841 Census for Devonport had to be searched. The family was discovered living in Morice Street [54].

Unlike the next three censuses, ages of those over sixteen were given to the nearest five years below, e.g. William Honeycombe could be fifty-nine. Nor were exact birth places given – only 'whether or not born in the same county'.

Gordon was surprised to find that only one of William's six surviving children was still at home. Neither in civil registration nor in Stoke Damerel parish registers had he discovered marriages for any of the four daughters. He would therefore have expected the search of the remainder of Devonport to have revealed other Honeycombe entries. In particular, where was twelve-year-old Samuel George Davey Honeycombe?

Finding out about an occupation. So far, the primary sources had left Gordon with only a bare outline of the lives of William and his family. However, wider reading set the biography in its context. He discovered much about Devonport dockyard and its workers in a booklet by George Dicker called *A Short History of Devonport Royal Dockyard.*

The Napoleonic Wars. In 1811, the year in which we first hear of William in Devonport, Britain was still at war with Napoleon. Although British sea power had been dominant since Trafalgar, the French Navy still remained a threat, while deteriorating relationships with the United States ended in war the following year. In Devonport, there was a sudden surge in shipbuilding about 1809. In the previous eight years only three ships had been built – yet one was completed each year between 1810 and 1812, and no less than three in 1813. Maybe there was a recruiting drive in 1811. It seems very likely that William was carrying or sawing timbers for most, if not all of these five vessels – the *Union* (1811), *Narcissus* (1812), *Creole* (1813), *Jupiter* (1813) and *Rennie* (1813).

Although William doubtless owed his recruitment to the war with France, he probably gave it little thought at the time. In 1812, however, he undoubtedly saw the French prisoners who were daily brought out

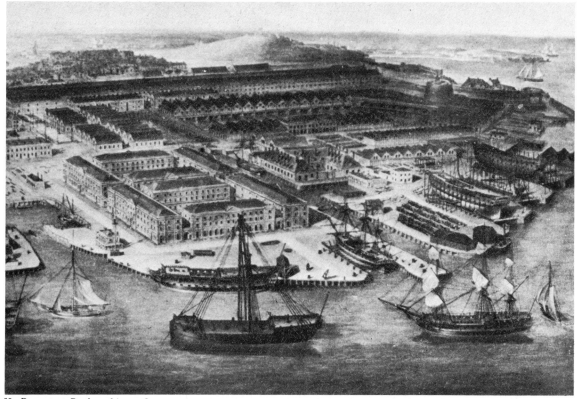

55 *Devonport Dockyard in 1798.*

of prison, chained, to work in the dockyard. He would also have seen the *Bellerophon,* which in 1815 anchored for a while in Plymouth Sound, bearing the captive Napoleon to his final exile in St Helena.

Plymouth Dock. The dockyard in which William spent most of his working life was begun in 1690. A second dry dock was built in 1727, a third in 1762, and a fourth, the huge New North Dock, in 1789. With the influx of workers to man these new docks, the town of Plymouth Dock grew rapidly. By 1801, when the first census was held, the population was already approaching that of Plymouth, and in another twenty years had 25,000 inhabitants to Plymouth's 21,500. The vast majority of these people were drawn from the villages of West Devon and East Cornwall, particularly the latter, which at this time largely lacked the mining

which absorbed the surplus population further west.

Sawyers. To find out more about the work of a dockyard sawyer, Dicker's booklet on Devonport Dockyard was supplemented with information on sawyers in Jocelyn Bailey's well-illustrated *The Village Wheelwright and Carpenter* in the Shire Album series.

In a village community the carpenter would choose and buy standing trees and they would be felled and brought to his yard to await the arrival of the sawyer. In the dockyard, wood was used in such quantity that the shipwrights could not themselves have gone far afield to choose trees for felling. The yard most probably employed special buyers to visit estates and select suitable trees. When the tree trunks arrived at the yard (almost certainly by water like the transportation of timber on Canadian rivers today) a skilled and ex-

56 *Fore Street, Devonport, in 1831 showing the entrance to the dockyard in the distance.*

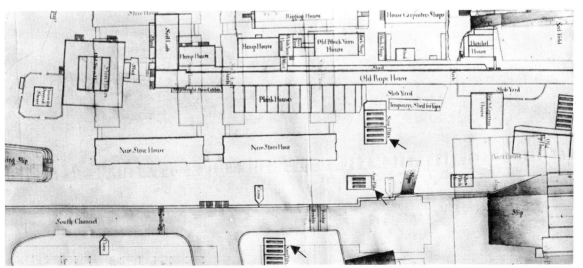

57 *Part of a plan of Devonport dockyard showing Saw pits (arrowed). Note their proximity to the water.*

58 *Sawyers at work. This photograph was taken in the 1920s but the method had not changed for centuries.*

hausting job awaited the sawyers. First, they had to manoeuvre a tree-trunk into position over the sawpit, through the adept use of levers. Then, when sawing began, the 'top sawyer' – the senior man – stood on the tree trunk, holding his end of the saw. The 'bottom sawyer' in the pit underneath, would usually wear a brimmed hat to keep the sawdust out of his eyes [58].

Much of the sawyers' time was spent not in actual sawing but in manoeuvring the timbers and setting and sharpening their saws. When the two sawyers had made several cuts along to the first supporting roller, the bottom sawyer would remove the bottom handle and the top sawyer would lift out the saw. Then the roller was moved, the saw re-inserted and the cuts continued. To prevent the plank ends vibrating as the cuts progressed, rope was wound round the ends and

wedges put in to steady them. Unlike modern steel saws, the iron saws blunted very quickly and needed frequent sharpening. Eventually, the sawyers in the dockyard were displaced by steam-driven saws, but this was long after William's retirement. It seems incredible that so long after the invention of the steam engine, the dockyard remained unmechanised.

Hours of work. Hours of work were long – in winter from 6.00 am to 6.00 pm with one hour for dinner; in summer, from sunrise to sunset, with half an hour for breakfast and one and a half hours for dinner. While William was working in the dockyard, various adjustments were made to the working week. At the time he retired in 1855, the hours were fixed at ten per day in summer and eight in winter. The eight hour day all the year round was not granted until 1894.

59 *An eighteenth-century sawyer.*

60 *An early nineteenth-century shipwright.*

Wages. Though above the labourers, the sawyer was at the bottom of all the crafts in the dockyard. During most of the eighteenth century, plumbers received 2s 4d per day; shipwrights and caulkers 2s 1d; joiners 1s 6d; sail-makers 1s 10d; riggers and sawyers only 1s 1d. These rates of pay had an extraordinary length of life, being first instituted in 1650 and remaining unchanged until 1788. But even in 1811, William's wages would not have been much more.

The method of paying wages in those days is almost unbelievable. Wages were paid quarterly and a quarter's pay was kept in hand, so that new workers had to wait six months for their first pay-packet. The pay was brought to the port by sea from London – a vital precaution because of the activities of highwaymen on the roads. When the time for the arrival of the frigate drew near, an anxious watch was kept on the approaches to the port, and at the first sighting of the vessel, the town and the yard went mad. Bells were pealed, and people danced in the streets as the good news spread.

Because pay-days came only every three months, local traders and tavern-keepers inevitably had to allow considerable credit, and as soon as the dockyard workers received their quarter's pay, they were almost immediately relieved of most of it to settle outstanding accounts. William arrived at the dockyard at the right time – in 1814, quarterly payments were abandoned and weekly payments instituted.

Apart from the basic rates, there was 'task and job'. This was a form of piecework, 'task' referring to work on new construction, and 'job' to repairs. The system

61 *The saw-mills in Devonport dockyard today. Note the uncut tree trunk in the foreground.*

gave rise to continual arguments which at times erupted into riots. 'Task and job' was abolished in 1833.

In 1847, a new method of payment, called 'Day work and check measurement' was introduced. Under this system, if a man's work reached the work norm, he received full pay, and nothing more if he exceeded the norm. However, if he did *less*, a deduction was made from his wages. The new system was extremely unpopular, and in 1854, there was a return to 'task and job' which lasted until after William retired in 1855.

Perks. In the eighteenth century it was the custom in the shipbuilding trade inside and outside the Yard to permit workmen to carry home quantities of waste wood known as 'chips'. The term became purely nominal, and the 'chips' became longer and the

bundles larger each day. Eventually, the maximum length of the 'chips' was limited to three feet and this led to doors, furniture and fittings in the houses of the workers assuming dimensions of this order. George Dicker believes that in the guise of 'chips' enough wood was removed from Plymouth Yard in a month to build a sloop of war. This was bad enough, but first-class timber was being ruthlessly cut up to provide the 'chips' and in the centre of many of the bundles were often secreted other items such as copper bolts. In desperation the privilege was stopped in 1803 and a monetary allowance was made in lieu. Labourers received an additional 3d a day, sawyers 4d and ship-wrights 6d. So William would have received an extra 4d above his basic wage.

62 *Hooping the mast on a Victorian timber warship.*

The Great Fire of 1840. Local histories are useful not only for providing the social context of an ancestor's life, but in finding out interesting local events through which he lived and with which he may even have been directly concerned. Thus on 27 September 1840, William must have been involved in trying to fight the greatest fire ever seen in the dockyard. A policeman on his rounds saw flames issuing from the *Talavera*, a ship under repair in the forward section of the Union Double Dock, and immediately raised the alarm. Meanwhile, the flames spread rapidly to other ships and the dockside buildings, aided by the volume of timber strewn about the yard. As fire engines rushed to the scene, hundreds of townspeople turned out to help, and in the harbour, numerous small boats tried to pull

ships clear. By daybreak, the fire was under control, but it was not finally put out until six o'clock that evening. Besides the near total destruction of three ships, there had been enormous damage to the dock buildings.

No doubt William's eleven-year-old son, Samuel George Davey Honeycombe, witnessed this terrible fire. Maybe he even helped to put it out. Could the memory still have been vivid when he founded a fire brigade all those years later in Kent?

King Cholera. An event which impinged even more closely upon the lives of William Honeycombe and his family was the cholera epidemic of 1849. Cholera was the scourge of the nineteenth century as bubonic

No.	When and where died	Name and surname	Sex	Age	Occupation	Cause of death	Signature, description, and residence of informant	When registered	Signature of registrar
211	Second October 1849 5 Fore Street Devonport	Dorothy Honeycombe	Female	62 years	Wife of William Honeycombe Sawyer Hill Dock yard	Choleaic Asphyxia Certified	Samuel Honeycombe present at the death 5 Fore Street Devonport	Second October 1849	Peter Pascoe Registrar

63 *Dorothy's death certificate revealing the cause of death. Note that 'choleraic asphyxia' is mis-spelt.*

No. of House	Name of Street, Place, or Road, and Name or No. of House	Name and Surname of each Person who abode in the house, on the Night of the 30th March, 1851	Relation to Head of Family	Condition	Age of Males	Age of Females	Rank, Profession, or Occupation	Where Born
		Ann Cudlip	Daur			1	Do Daughter	Stoke
		Hannah Do	Son		15		Scholar	Devon Do
91	10 Waterloo Street	William Williams	Head	Mar	77		Superannuated Labourer D. Yard	Plymstock
		Anne Do	Wife	Mar		71	Do Wife	Buckland
		Mary Chown	Niece			14	Smithy Daughter	Do
92		Wm Westlake Sampson	Head	Mar	68		Retired S.H. of Shipwrights	Devon Freemington
		Elizabeth Do	Wife	Mar		70	Do Wife	Tawton
93	11 Waterloo Street	William Honeycombe	Head	Widr	64		Sawyer	Cornwall Liskeard
		William Honeycombe	Son	Mar	35		Do	Devon Devonport
		Thirsa Do	Daughter in law	Mar		27	Do Wife	Do
		Ann Do	Grand daughter			9	Scholar	Jersey St Hellier
94		Roger Chappell	Head	Widr	64		Superannuated Shipwright	Devon, Appledore
		Susan Griffin	Daur			30	Housekeeper	Do
		Henry Griffin	Grand Son		14		Scholar	Devon, Devonport
Total of Houses 1 3 U B					Total of Persons... 9	12		

64 *1851 Census for Waterloo Street, Devonport. Almost every house contained two or more households.*

plague had been in earlier centuries. The first great cholera epidemic in Britain had begun in India in 1817 and reached Britain in 1831–2, causing deaths in towns and cities all over Britain. 53,293 people died in the epidemic which ravaged Britain in 1849. When it was discovered that both these epidemics caused much loss of life in Devonport, the pedigree was examined to see if any member of the family died in either year. The Honeycombes seem to have remained unscathed in 1832, but it was noted that William's wife, Dorothy, died in 1849. Could she have been a cholera victim? An application was made for her death certificate [63] and sure enough, she died of 'choleraic asphyxia'.[18]

18. This is the second, usually fatal stage of the disease. The first stage is a mild and painless diarrhoea which lasts two or three days and is often not regarded as anything serious. In the second stage,

The Plymouth weekly paper, the *Plymouth, Devonport and Stonehouse Herald*, chronicled the history of the epidemic. The first deaths were recorded on 4 July 1849, the last on 8 November. There were 921 deaths in Devonport in the quarter ending 30 September 1849, 717 of these from cholera. Poor Dorothy, dying on 2 October, must have been one of the last people in Devonport to die of the disease.

the diarrhoea becomes very violent, accompanied by continual vomiting, a severe pain at the pit of the stomach and intense thirst. The symptoms then advance rapidly – agonising cramps of the legs, feet and abdominal muscles, the surface of the body becomes cold and blue or purple, the skin dry and wrinkled, the features pinched and the eyes deeply sunken. Death often comes in as little as one day from asphyxia by vomit.

19. In a study of the Stoke Damerel Parish registers for 1849, it was discovered that the number of burials, which between January and July ranged between eighty-two and ninety-three a month, shot up to 488 in August and 280 in September. By October, they were

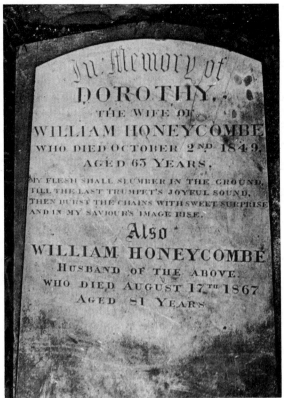

65 *Dorothy and William's tombstone – now, sadly, a step in a pathway in Stoke Damerel churchyard.*

66 *11 Waterloo Street, Devonport, where the Honeycombes, together with several other familes, were living in 1851.*

To end on a happier note, it must not be thought that the disease was invariably fatal. The *Herald* for 29 September gives the figures for the disease up to 28 September for Plymouth; there were 1,239 cases of cholera, and 1,823 of choleraic diarrhoea but only 663 were fatal.[19] It may be reasonable to suppose that William, his son and daughter-in-law also contracted the disease, but survived.

This rather melancholy episode in the Honeycombe family history illustrates two points. Firstly, the researcher needs to keep constantly in mind the relationship between the genealogical evidence and down to seventy-four, and by November, an incredibly low forty-eight, lower than any month the year before. The annual total burials for 1849 was 1,434, as compared with 958 for 1848 and 698 for 1850. Like the low figure for November 1849, the much lower figure for 1850 was probably due to the fact that most of the weak had already been weeded out, leaving a resilient population.

the social and economic history of the area. Secondly, genealogists have traditionally undervalued the English Death Certificate, for the genealogical information it gives is very limited. Yet, as in Dorothy's case, it can help to put the family in its full historical context.

In Chapter 3 we decided that the most likely explanation for Samuel's leaving Devonport was the evasion of his paternal responsibilities. Dorothy's death certificate supplies two more possible reasons. When she died of cholera he may have decided to leave Devonport to avoid contracting the disease. More probably, once his mother had died, he may have decided that there was nothing to hold him in Devonport. Perhaps he did not get on with his father.

The 1851 Census. In 1841 the Honeycombes had been living in Morice Street. Dorothy's death certificate

No.	Name	Age	Late Employment, and in what Yard, &c.	Power of Attorney, &c.		Dates of	
				Date	Gen¹ or Spec¹	Authority	Commencement
5	*Honeycombe W^m*	58	*Job Sawyer*			*Devonport*	*1853* *15 Mar 20 Mar*

67 *William the Sawyer's pension record which revealed (facing page) the Jersey connection.*

The undermentioned Houses are situate within the Boundaries of the ... 15 [Page 23]

| | Parish of *St Helier* | | Island or Isle of *Jersey* | | Town of *St Helier* | | Village of | |

No. of Schedule	Road, Street, &c., and No. or Name of House	HOUSES In-habited Unin-habited (U.), or Building (B)	Name and Surname of each Person	Relation to Head of Family	Condition	Age of Male Female	Rank, Profession, or Occupation	Where Born	Whether Blind, or Deaf-and-Dumb
116	*Hill Street* "Old Bank"	1	*Lerrier Godfray*	*Head*	*Mar.*	*38*	*Banker*	*Jersey St Helier*	
			Harriet Do	*Wife*	*Mar*	*27*	*Fundholder*	*Do Do*	
			Anna F. Saunders	*Visitor*	*Un.*	*26*	*Do*	*Switzerland, British subject*	
			Martha Stanner	*Servt*	*Un.*	*34*	*House servant*	*England*	
			Henry Purkis	*Servt*	*Un.*	*27*	*Do*	*England*	
117		1	*William Honeycombe*	*Head*	*Mar*	*72*	*Pawn Broker*	*England*	
			Margaritta Do	*Wife*	*Mar*	*46*		*England*	
			Annie Do	*Grand-dau*	*Un.*	*19*		*Jersey St Helier*	
	Wine stores (House)								

68 *1861 Census for Jersey providing more information about William.*

showed that by 1849, they had moved to Fore Street However, no Honeycombes were found there in the 1851 Census and again it was necessary to search the whole of Devonport. William was located living with his son and daughter-in-law, at 11 Waterloo St [64].

This entry contained the vital piece of evidence for taking the genealogy back further, for Gordon now knew that William was born at Liskeard, Cornwall. This was not altogether suprising, for tradition had said the family came from Cornwall. What was exciting, however, was that Liskeard is the very next parish to St Cleer, where John Symons Honeycombe was born in 1833, and where, he said, the Honeycombes owned the Manor House.

Another very interesting thing about this entry which also suggested a link with John Symons Honeycombe, was that William's granddaughter was born in *Jersey*. This was the first mention of Jersey in connection with Gordon's own relatives and was the

first step towards linking him not only with John Symons Honeycombe (who said he was born shortly after his parents returned from Jersey), but with Roy Honeycombe and his grandfather, the nineteenth-century town crier.

Finally, this entry illustrates that in Family History, you can never take anything for granted unless proven. A natural assumption would be that Ann was the daughter of William and Thirza. In fact subsequent research in parish registers and later census returns showed that she was the younger William's niece, not his daughter.

The 1861 Census. In the 1861 Census, the younger William (B7) and his wife Thirza (B8), now described as 'tailoress', were still at 11 Waterloo Street. However, William senior had gone. So too had the grand-daughter, Ann. Once again, the Census was searched for the whole of Devonport and Plymouth without

			1855			1856			1857		
Rate per Annum	Commencing	Ending	Sum paid	When paid	Where paid	Sum paid	When paid	Where paid	Sum paid	When paid	Where paid

(Stamped Receipts required for payments of £10 and upwards.) **Artificers, Laborers, &c.** *(per Act 2nd Wm. IV., Cap. 40., Sect 29.)*

20"	1st Jan. 31st March		13 4	17 Ma	Devonport	5	1 Jun	Jersey	5	1 Jun	Cust. Jersey
	1st April 30th June		5 . .	5 Sep	Cust. Jersey	5	10 Sep		5	16 Sep	
	1st July 30th Sept.		5	12 Dec		5	3 Dec		5	9 Dec	
	1st Oct. 31st Dec.		5	12 Mar		5	18 Mar		5	10 Mar	

REGISTRATION DISTRICT Stoke Damerel

1867.   DEATH in the Sub-district of Morice in the County of Devon

No.	When and where died	Name and surname	Sex	Age	Occupation	Cause of death	Signature, description, and residence of informant	When registered	Signature of registrar
464	Seventeenth August 1867 2 Tenement to 7 Queen Street	William Honeycombe	Male	nearly 81¾ years	Sawyer Superannuated from H.M.S Dockyard	Age and General Decline Certified	M. D. Honeycombe Present at the death 2d Tenement 87 Queen Street Devonport	Twentieth August 1867	W. G. Spry Registrar

69 *William's death certificate – why did he return to Devonport?*

success. One would naturally assume that William had died and Ann had married. However, neither assumption was confirmed by the civil registration indexes for William did not die until 1867 and Ann did not marry until 1864. Where were they in 1861?

Pension records. Although the records of Devonport Dockyard were destroyed during the Second World War, the three-volumed *Guide to the Contents of the Public Record Office* was checked to see if there were any pension or other records in London that might be helpful. It was discovered that by this time all dockyard workers had pensions and that there were records at the Public Record Office at Kew [67].[20] Pensions were very unusual at this time. Could this be one of the reasons why William sought work in the dockyard? When the pension records were examined, it was found that William retired on 16 March 1855 on an annual pension of £20, which was to commence on the 26th of that month. By this time he had become a top sawyer – the man at the upper end of the saw who didn't get the sawdust in his eyes! Then came a surprise. The records showed that William's pension was to be paid through the Customs in Jersey. Coming on top of the mention of Jersey in 1851 as the place of birth of his grand-daughter, this made a search of the Jersey census returns imperative.

William the Pawnbroker. In the 1861 Census for St Helier, Jersey, William was living with his daughter,

20. The unique Dockyard Superannuation Scheme began in 1764, when large reductions in numbers had to be made following the peace with France in 1763. Pensions were at first confined to shipwrights and caulkers, but in September, 1771, the privilege of superannuation was extended to all grades. Some of the earlier records include a physical description of the employees, but alas, such description books are not extant for the time when William was a sawyer.

REGISTRATION DISTRICT	St. Germans							

1885. DEATH in the Sub-district of Antony in the Counties of Devon and Cornwall

No.	When and where died	Name and surname	Sex	Age	Occupation	Cause of death	Signature, description, and residence of informant	When registered	Signature of registrar
192	Ninth August 1885 Empacombe Beach Parish of Maker R.S.D.	Thirza Honeycombe	Female	64 years	Widow of William Honeycombe a Pensioner	Found dead Probably accidentally drowned	Certificate received from Albert C.L. Glubb Coroner for Cornwall Inquest held 10th August 1885	Twelfth August 1885	Richard Wilcocks Hancock Registrar

70 *The document which led to the discovery of an interesting if melancholy episode in the Honeycombe family history.*

Margaretta (B5) – described by an enumerator's error as his wife – and his nineteen-year-old grand-daughter, Annie. Another surprise – his occupation was given as 'pawnbroker'! So after his retirement from the dockyard, William had started a third career – first millwright, then sawyer, and finally pawnbroker. He was nothing if not adaptable [68].

William had his pension paid in Jersey only until the first half of 1861. After that, it was paid to him at Devonport until his death, on 17 August 1867, at the age of 'nearly 81¼ years'. His address then was given on the certificate as '2nd tenement to 7 Queen Street' [69].

Thirza. William's elder son, William Henry (B7), was also a sawyer in the Dockyard. Perhaps father and son worked as a pair, the father as Top Sawyer, young William in the pit. He retired in 1869 on an annual pension of £21 18s 2d and died on 27 December 1884. His widow, Thirza, outlived him by less than a year. Her death certificate records that she was 'found dead' on Empacombe Beach, parish of Maker, Cornwall [70]. At an inquest on 18 August 1885, the Coroner recorded a verdict of 'probably accidentally drowned'. Once again, a death certificate provided an invaluable lead and a search was made of the local newspaper, the *Western Daily Mercury* to see if it yielded any further information. The edition of 10 August reported:

FOUND DROWNED. – *Yesterday morning the body of an old lady was found floating in the water near Cremyll. There was nothing that would convey any idea as to who the deceased was and the police are endeavouring to ascertain particulars. The deceased was dressed in black, and is about 65 years old. She wore a small black bonnet, with white frill inside. Her complexion is brown. The county coroner will hold an inquest at Mount Edgeumbe Farm (where the body now lies) this morning at 10 o'clock.*

The next day there was a full account of the inquest.

MR. A. C. L. GLUBB, *of Liskeard, held an inquest yesterday at Mount Edgecumbe Farm, in the parish of Maker, on the body of Thirza Honeycombe, aged 64 years, the widow of a dockyard pensioner. Deceased was found on Sunday morning, as announced in yesterday's* Mercury, *on Empacombe Beach, mid-way between Millbrook and Cremyll. Mr. George Wilson was appointed foreman of the jury and it appeared from the evidence that deceased had been in receipt of 1s 6d. per week, parish pay, but maintained herself chiefly by following her occupation which was that of a tailoress. – Philip Honeycombe, residing at 2, St. James-place, Morice Town, nephew of the deceased, said she had to go to Maker to get a marriage certificate in order to be entitled to draw the balance of her late husband's pension. On Sunday, the 2nd inst, she left her home and did not return that night. On the following day, Monday (Bank Holiday), witness went over to Mount Edgecumbe to see the Volunteer sham-fight and inspection, and met his aunt on the beach at Cremyll. She then told him she had not been home for the night, and had lost her way. She had been out all night and could not get across to Devonport because she had no money. She went to Maker again on Saturday last. – Anna Higman, servant in the employ of Mr. E. L. Harvey, residing at Empacombe Beach, deposed to seeing the deceased on Saturday last, and gave her some water and sandwiches. Deceased said she had been to Millbrook. – Mary Ann Collings and Elizabeth Dawe, neighbours, who lived in the same house as deceased, said she left the house between eight and nine on Saturday morning. She was not of a melancholy disposition, and they saw nothing unusual about her when she left. – The Coroner in summing up, remarked on the solitariness of the district in which the event occurred, and said it was unlikely they could get any further evidence, although what they had had was not conclusive. – A verdict of "Found dead, having been probably drowned," was returned.*

The crucial statement in this report is that Thirza had told her nephew Philip that she had to go to Maker to get a marriage certificate in order to draw the balance of her late husband's pension. We are in the fortunate position of knowing more than the Coroner. Before this report was discovered, Gordon's comprehensive search of the civil registration indexes abstracting all Honeycombes had failed to reveal a marriage of William Henry and Thirza. There are a number of possibilities: (i) the marriage was registered, but mis-indexed; (ii) it took place before 1837; (iii) it took place after 1837 but was not registered for some reason, or (iv) William and Thirza never went through a marriage ceremony.

The first two possibilities were very thoroughly researched, and can now be regarded as in the highest degree unlikely.[21]

The third possibility – that the marriage took place but was not registered, is the one favoured by Gordon. Thirza clearly expected to find evidence of her marriage at Maker because she made two visits. Moreover, since the first visit was on a Sunday, it is a reasonable assumption that she was going to a church or chapel. In the 1840s the Vicar of Maker, the Rev Darell Stephens was very aged. It seems possible that he either forgot to register the marriage or never submitted his copy-register to the Registrar-General. Alternatively, the marriage may have taken place after his death in 1848, in the interregnum between him and his successor. Perhaps the service was taken by a locum and the registers were locked up in the safe.[22]

The last possibility is that William and Thirza were never married. The poor woman needed a marriage certificate to draw the balance of the pension owing to her deceased husband. This in itself is not sufficient to provide a motive for suicide, for she was earning her living as a tailoress, and getting some parish relief. Had she told her relatives she was married at Maker, and could not face being found out, 'living in sin' all those years? Or was she wandering on the beach in a disturbed state of mind and cut off by the tide? We must agree with the Coroner that we are unlikely to get any further evidence and what we have is not conclusive. However, one thing is clear. Thirza died a pauper at a time when her brother-in-law, Samuel George Davey Honeycombe, and his family enjoyed respectable middle-class status in Northfleet.

21. With regard to the first, Gordon's work was re-checked and all Honeycombe marriages examined from 1837 to 1851 (when she appears in the census as William's wife). Moreover, a search was made under every conceivable spelling variant – Honicombe, Hun(n)icombe, etc., as well as Stoneycombe, as indexing 'H' under 'St' is very common – they look much alike in copperplate. The results were all negative. Could the marriage have been before Civil Registration started in September 1837? The younger William has no wife listed in 1841 so it does not seem very likely. Moreover, it could only have been just before – for Thirza's age was given as sixty-four, in both the death certificate and the newspaper report. So she was born in about 1821 and could only have been sixteen in 1837. A copy of Maker marriages at the Society of Genealogists was searched from 1830 to 1837 and failed to reveal any entry. The original register was then checked and again the result was negative. Marriages from January 1836 to June 1837 were also searched for Stoke Damerel, East Stonehouse and the Plymouth parishes of St Andrews, Charles and St Budeaux. Again, all negative. It is therefore highly unlikely that the marriage took place before 1837.

22. Another possibility is that William and Thirza were married in a Nonconformist chapel. At this time, such marriages were legal only if the registrar was present. Did someone fail to notify him? Was he notified but failed to turn up? Did he come but forget to bring the register?

6 Across the Tamar

We have now followed Gordon's ancestors from Scotland to Kent, and from Kent to Devonport. The 1851 Census had at last provided the firm evidence which took the family across the Tamar. From that Census we knew that William the Sawyer was born in Liskeard about 1786, a date confirmed with precision by his death certificate in 1867 – 'aged 81¼ years.'

The next step was obviously a search of the Liskeard parish registers deposited in the Cornwall County Record Office. There Gordon found the baptism on 24 December 1786, of 'William, son of William and Mary Honeycombe' (c8). If his death certificate was correct in describing him as 81¼ on the 17th August, 1867, he must have been about seven months old when he was baptised – it looks as if the baptism was deliberately postponed to coincide with Christmas.

Gordon also found the baptisms of a number of brothers and sisters, and the marriage in 1836 of William the Sawyer's eldest daughter, Mary Ann Davey Honeycombe (c19) to John Hancock (c20), shoemaker of Liskeard. One of the missing children accounted for!

A search of the Liskeard 1841 Census Return revealed not only the people Gordon expected to be there, but also his great-grandfather, Samuel George Davey Honeycombe (c23), aged twelve, whom he had failed to find in Devonport. He was not, however, with his married sister, as one might expect, but lodging in Barn Street with an uncle, John Davey (fifty), a ropemaker, his wife Mary (forty) and their seven children [71]. Samuel's entry was marked off from the others by a single line, showing he was in the same house, though not a member of the Davey household. No occupation was given for him. Samuel may have been on a short visit to his Liskeard relatives. Alternatively, he may have been lodging with his uncle while

Table C. The Liskeard Honeycombes.

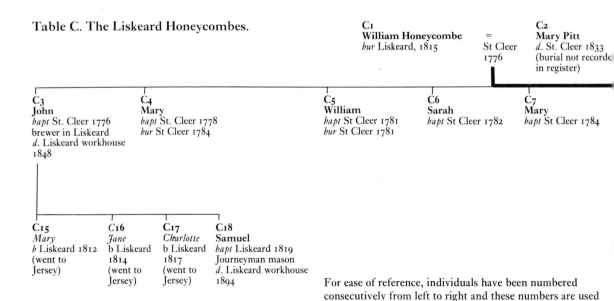

C1 William Honeycombe bur Liskeard, 1815	= St Cleer 1776	C2 Mary Pitt d. St. Cleer 1833 (burial not recorded in register)

C3 John bapt St. Cleer 1776 brewer in Liskeard d. Liskeard workhouse 1848	C4 Mary bapt St. Cleer 1778 bur St Cleer 1784	C5 William bapt St Cleer 1781 bur St Cleer 1781	C6 Sarah bapt St Cleer 1782	C7 Mary bapt St Cleer 1784

C15 Mary b Liskeard 1812 (went to Jersey)	C16 Jane b Liskeard 1814 (went to Jersey)	C17 Charlotte b Liskeard 1817 (went to Jersey)	C18 Samuel bapt Liskeard 1819 Journeyman mason d. Liskeard workhouse 1894

For ease of reference, individuals have been numbered consecutively from left to right and these numbers are used in the text. Cross references are included to Table A, page 13 and Table B, page 46.

going to school in Liskeard – in 1841 there was both a grammar school with scholarship places and a boys' school run by the British and Foreign Schools Society.

Reasons for a move. It would seem therefore, that as late as 1841 a close connection was maintained with relatives in Liskeard. But what took the Honeycombes from Liskeard to Devonport in the first place? Before we can answer this question, we need to try and find out *when* the move took place. There are three possible theories.

Theory No. 1: *William (C8) was a millwright in the Liskeard area, went to Devonport in 1811 where he married Dorothy Davey and took work as a labourer in the dockyard.*

In favour of this theory is the fact that the dockyard was recruiting at this time, that Dorothy is known to have come from Liskeard, and that William appears to have kept up a connection with the place.

On the other hand, both parties were described in the marriage entry as being of Devonport.

Theory No. 2: *William came to Devonport as an adult some time before 1811, and was a millwright in Devonport for some years before becoming a labourer in the dockyard.*

That both parties were described as being of Devonport is consistent with this theory. However, it seems unlikely there would be any great demand for millwrights in Devonport.

Theory No. 3: *That William was taken to Devonport as a child by his parents some time between 1796 and 1802 and grew up there.*

In support of this theory is the fact that on 22 July 1812 William's brother, Philip (C13), son of William and Mary, was baptised in Stoke Damerel church as an

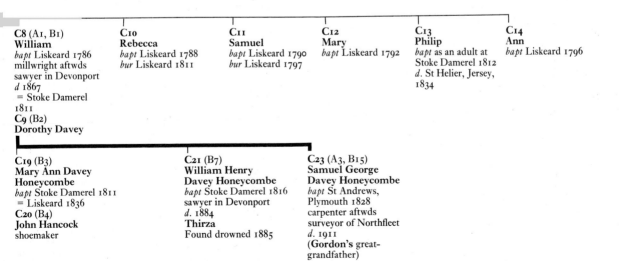

C8 (A1, B1)	C10	C11	C12	C13	C14
William	**Rebecca**	**Samuel**	**Mary**	**Philip**	**Ann**
bapt Liskeard 1786	*bapt* Liskeard 1788	*bapt* Liskeard 1790	*bapt* Liskeard 1792	*bapt* as an adult at	*bapt* Liskeard 1796
millwright aftwds	*bur* Liskeard 1811	*bur* Liskeard 1797		Stoke Damerel 1812	
sawyer in Devonport				*d.* St Helier, Jersey,	
d 1867				1834	
= Stoke Damerel					
1811					
C9 (B2)					
Dorothy Davey					

C19 (B3)	C21 (B7)	C23 (A3, B15)
Mary Ann Davey	**William Henry**	**Samuel George**
Honeycombe	**Davey Honeycombe**	**Davey Honeycombe**
bapt Stoke Damerel 1811	*bapt* Stoke Damerel 1816	*bapt* St Andrews,
= Liskeard 1836	sawyer in Devonport	Plymouth 1828
C20 (B4)	*d.* 1884	carpenter aftwds
John Hancock	**Thirza**	surveyor of Northfleet
shoemaker	Found drowned 1885	*d.* 1911
		(Gordon's great-
		grandfather)

City or Borough of *Liskeard*

Parish or Township of _____   Enumeration

PLACE	HOUSES		NAMES of each Person who abode therein the preceding Night	AGE and SEX		PROFESSION, TRADE, EMPLOYMENT, or of INDEPENDENT MEANS	Whether Born in same County
	Uninhabited or Building	Inhabited		Males	Females		
Barn Street		1	Henry Angove	66		Woolstapler	Y
			Mary do		66		Y
			John Sowden	26		Ag Lab	Y
			Elizabeth do		26		Y
			William do	2			Y
			Ann do		2 Mnth		Y
			Elizabeth Cook		45		
			Thomas do	24			
			William do	12			
do		1	John Davey	50		Ropemaker	Y
			Mary do		40		Y
			Maryann do		20		Y
			Thomas do	15		Mason	Y
			Maria do		13		Y
			William do	11			Y
			Rebecca do		8		Y
			Elizabeth do		6		Y
			Charles do	3			Y
			Samuel Honeycombe	12			
do		1	Joseph Fletcher	47		Labourer	
			Mary do		48		
			John do	16		Labourer	
			Elizabeth do		12		Y
			Susan do		8		Y
do		1	Johanna Wells		50		
TOTAL in Page 16	4			12	13		
Dd							

71

1841 Census for Liskeard. Note the single line between the Daveys and Samuel which suggests that he was living not as part of the family, but in a separate apartment.

the elder William (C1), had been there since 1802, for in that year the marriage at Stoke Damerel – the parish church of Devonport – of an Elizabeth Honeycombe was witnessed by a William Honeycombe. Elizabeth seems to have been born in Devonport in 1781, the daughter of a John Honicombe, a baker, and if the William who witnessed the marriage was our man, it would imply close relationship with these Devonport Honeycombes. It would also seem to be likely that he was living in Devonport.

Against this theory is the fact that the elder William (C1) was, as we shall show later in this chapter, buried in Liskeard on 30 October 1815.

The balance of probability is in favour of the first theory – that William, an adult millwright, left Liskeard for Devonport in about 1811, to marry Dorothy Davey. She was twenty-four at the time and must have had some occupation. It seems possible that she was working in Devonport.

Nevertheless, the third theory cannot be lightly dismissed, for it is possible either that William senior returned to Liskeard when he retired, or that his body was taken back for burial.

Researching an occupation. Despite the lack of conclusive evidence, let us provisionally assume that the first theory is correct, and consider what factors might have made a country millwright move to Devonport. To do this we need to ask certain questions about the nature of the job. Was it a static one like that of tailor or shoemaker, where the craftsman spent most of his working life in one place? Or was it an itinerant one, like that of a mason, in which the craftsman tended to go wherever there was work? How far might such a craftsman have to travel? Was the work all the year round or seasonal? Did it provide a small but steady income, or alternating periods of reasonably high income and complete unemployment?

The millwright. The millwright is a good example of the itinerant job. Unlike the dockyard sawyer it was neither static nor produced a steady income. As a skilled craftsman the millwright could hope to earn good money as long as he could obtain regular work. But he might have to travel some distance to find it, and if unlucky, or if he gained a reputation for not being

adult. Also, when his sister Ann (C14), was married in St Helier, Jersey, in 1826, she was described as 'of Devonport'.

These entries could mean nothing more than that Philip and Ann followed their brother to Devonport after 1811. However, it is possible that their father,

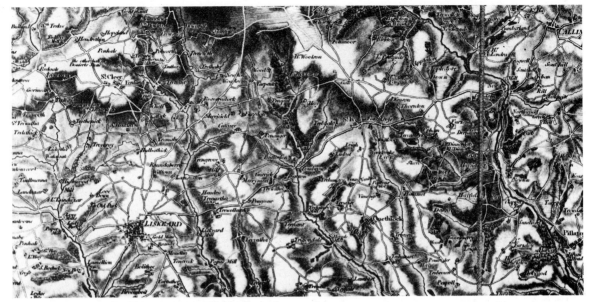

72 *The Liskeard area from the first edition of the Ordnance Survey, 1812.*

very skilful, he could have some very lean times.

To find out more about the millwright, we consulted R. A. Buchanan's *Industrial Archaeology in Britain.* Buchanan sees him as one of the ancestors of the modern engineer. The millwright, he says, developed from the tradition of the village blacksmith, wheelwright and carpenter:

Such men could shoe horses, make cart wheels, or turn pieces of wood on simple lathes and assemble the parts into furniture which could be graceful or utilitarian. They were the vital craftsmen of the early industrial community, but the new demands and resources of this community stimulated the emergence of the millwright as a sort of itinerant specialist in the construction of machines, industrial buildings, or improved roads and canals. The millwright was thus the representative of a significant transitional stage from the traditional crafts to the modern engineer.[23]

Useful though this description is, when researching an occupation it is important if at all possible to read not just general books on the subject but local histories as well, for with most occupations there were wide regional variations in both the scope of the job and the conditions of work. A. C. Todd and Peter Laws' *Industrial Archaeology of Cornwall* states that the Cornish millwright was responsible for maintaining not only the water-wheels which still powered most mills, but also furnaces and forges and the pumps of many of the tin, copper and china-clay mines. However, at this time, there was relatively little mining in East Cornwall, and the mainstay of William's business would probably be the maintenance of corn mills in the Liskeard area, especially Liskeard's town mills at Bodgara. According to John Allen's *History of Liskeard* (1856), these declined at the beginning of the nineteenth century. Until then, all the inhabitants of the town were compelled to grind their corn there. But after they succeeded in freeing themselves from this obligation, the mills lost a large part of their custom.[24]

In itself, the rundown of Bodgara mills would not have been enough to make William abandon his trade for unskilled work in Devonport dockyard. It may be,

23. R.A. Buchanan *Industrial archaeology in Britain* Penguin Books 1972. p. 103.

24. J. Allen *History of Liskeard and its vicinity* 1856. p. 357

however, that there was a general decline in the mills in the locality for reasons which have yet to be explored, and that William was forced by insufficient work to seek employment elsewhere. As we have seen, this was a period when the dockyard was recruiting. Perhaps William preferred the security and pension of unskilled work in the dockyard to the job satisfaction but uncertainties of the millwright's trade.

There is one irony in the story of William the millwright. William was perhaps born in Liskeard a generation too early. In the 1850s, the mines in St Cleer parish, just to the north of the town had 'one of the largest concentrations of waterwheels anywhere in Cornwall',[25] and millwrights must have been at a premium. Unluckily for William, most of the twenty-five copper mines around St Cleer were not opened until he was nearing retirement in the dockyard.

Influencing factors in family history. The move to Devonport is a good example of the interplay of the five types of factor which influence the history of any family.

Firstly, there are *national, and even international events*, such as wars, slumps and government decisions – in this case, the Napoleonic Wars, the worsening relations with America and the upsurge of ship-building 1809–1811.

Secondly, there are *regional and local factors* – the local environment, its raw materials, industries and traditions – in this case, the probable decline of the mills around Liskeard and the proximity of Devonport dockyard where work was available.

Thirdly, there are *family factors*, eg, the economic status of the family, hereditary trades, the sudden death of a breadwinner – in this case the fact that the Honeycombes probably had relatives in Devonport.

Fourthly, there are *personal factors*, – whether the individual is cautious or adventurous; his personal friends – in this case, William's getting Dorothy pregnant and their subsequent marriage.

Fifthly, there are *chance factors*. Who knows what actually brought about William's decision to move? Maybe he had a chance conversation with a relative of

someone working in the dockyard. Beyond living memory, only letters, diaries and autobiographies will reveal such chance factors, and since these are rare, we must always recognize the limitations of our own knowledge.

Change of occupation. The second point exemplified by the move to Devonport is change of occupation. There is a temptation to think of an occupation as a rather permanent thing. If the first reference to an ancestor describes him as a sawyer, it is all to easy to enter 'sawyer' tidily on the family tree, making the unconscious assumption that he was a sawyer all his life. However, there has always been a certain flexibility of occupation, and this has been more marked since the Industrial Revolution. William (A1) was successively millwright, sawyer and pawnbroker, Samuel (A3) was a carpenter, builder, undertaker, surveyor, and part-time fireman, Henry (A9) was railway catering manager, restaurant manager and hotel proprietor. Gordon (A23) has been an actor, newsreader and writer. Only Gordon's father (A15) had a single occupation for most of his working life, and this was in India, away from the rat-race at home. Presumably a life of relative ease and leisure with servants and status provided little incentive to move on. Yet although on the face of it Gordon and most of his Honeycombe ancestors over the last few generations had several changes of occupation, in most cases skills learned in one job were transferable to the next.

Migration. The move to Devonport was also typical of Gordon's family in another respect. For the last two hundred years, each generation has been born in a different place – William (A1) in Liskeard (1786), Samuel George Davey (A3) in Devonport (1828), Henry (A9) in Gravesend (1861). Gordon Samuel (A15) in Edinburgh (1898), and Gordon (A23) in Karachi (1936). This speaks volumes for population mobility since the Industrial Revolution and it is not entirely coincidental that each generation moved further than the previous one.

Migration has always been the toughest nut the genealogist has to crack, and many pedigrees grind to a halt at some point in the eighteenth or early nineteenth century because the earliest known ancestor

25. A.C. Todd and P. Laws *Industrial archaeology of Cornwall* David and Charles 1972. p. 115.

NAME	SEX M MALE/F FEMALE/H HUSBAND/W WIFE, FATHER/MOTHER OR SPOUSE	TYPE	EVENT DATE	TOWN, PARISH				BATCH
HONYCOMBE, MARY								
HONYCOMBE, MARY	JOEL HONYCOMBE/	F C	18MAY1709	HATHERLEIGH	INFANT	INFANT	21JUN1974LD	C05255
HUNNYCOMBE, PEDRICKE	BENJN HONYCOMB/ELIZTH	F C	18JUN1718	WEARE GIFFARD	26AUG1974LD	12OCT1974LD	26APR1975LD	M00183
	ELIZ HALLETT	H M	21OCT1610	PLYMOUTH, SAINT ANDREW			30JAN1975SL	C05001
HUNNYCOMBE, RICHARD	STEPHEN HUNNYCOMBE/	H M	18AUG1606	PLYMOUTH, SAINT DAVID	16NOV1963SL	03FEB1964SL		
HONYCOMBE, RICHERDE	ANDREW HONNYCOMBE/	H C	07MAY1615	EXETER, SAINT DAVID	INFANT	INFANT		
HONICOMBE, SALLY	JOHN HONICOMBE/RACHEL	F C	13APR1784	STOKE DAMEREL	INFANT		02JUL1973SL	C01242
HONYCOMBE, SAMUEL	JOEL HONYCOMBE/	H C	08JUN1713	HATHERLEIGH			26APR1975LD	M00183
HUNNYCOMB, STEVEN	JANE LENDON	H M	19SEP1603	PLYMOUTH, SAINT ANDREW			20APR1975LD	
HONYCOMBE, THOMAS	MARGERY COLIVER	H M	23JUN1645	PLYMOUTH, SAINT ANDREW			04FEB1974CB	
HONEYCOMBE, WILLIAM	DOROTHY DAVEY	H M	12AUG1811	STOKE DAMEREL				
HONEYCOME, ** SEE HONEYCOMBE								
HONEYE, ** SEE HONEY								
HONYFORDE								
HONYFORDE, JANE	SIPRIAN HONYFORDE/	F C	05MAY1633	EXETER, HOLY TRINITY	05MAR1976PV	04MAY1976PV	29MAR1976PV	C05009
HUNNAFORD, REBEKAH		F C	07MAR1675	DARTINGTON	26JUN1974OG	13AUG1974OG	07DEC1974OG	C05077
WILLIAM HUNNAFORD/MARGRETT								

73 *Microfiche from the Devonshire section of the Mormon International Genealogical Index which has revolutionised searches.*

suddenly appears in a place and extensive research fails to establish whence he came.

In Gordon's case, he had now traced his pedigree back to the baptism of William the Sawyer (c8) in Liskeard in 1786. As we have seen, he was the son of another William (c1) and his wife Mary (c2). However, Liskeard registers yielded no marriage of a William and Mary, and there were no earlier Honeycombe entries which seemed relevant. The elder William and his wife Mary had clearly come to Liskeard from elsewhere. How could their marriage be located and William's ancestry traced further back?

Until recently, there was no answer except a systematic search of neighbouring parishes or an effort to find more evidence in other records. Solving a problem like this was extremely difficult, often taking years of fruitless searching.

International Genealogical Index. The situation has been revolutionised through the activities of the Church of Jesus Christ of Latter-Day Saints, popularly known as the Mormons. They lay enormous stress on genealogy, encouraging their members to trace their ancestors in order to baptise them posthumously, since they do not recognise the validity of baptisms by other denominations. The Mormons have microfilmed all kinds of genealogical source material, but have concentrated upon parish registers.

From the point of view of the British researcher, however, the main value of their work lies not so much in the microfilms themselves, as in the enormous index to their parish register collection. Called the International Genealogical Index (or IGI), it has over thirty million entries in the British section on many hundreds of microfiches. Copies of this invaluable Index are in Mormon branch libraries (see page 165) and at the Society of Genealogists (see page 161). Many Record Offices and Societies are obtaining the microfiches for their own county. Although there are some marriages in the IGI, the vast majority of the entries are of baptisms. So an inspection of the relevant microfiches for Cornwall did not reveal the *marriage* of a William Honeycombe and a Mary. However, under the nearby parish of St Cleer, we found many Honeycombe entries including baptisms of older children of William and Mary – John (c3) in 1776, Mary (c4) in 1778, William (c5) in 1781, Sarah (c6) in 1782 and another Mary (c7) in 1784.

A search of the St Cleer registers provided the marriage of William Honeycombe and Mary Pitt on 7 July 1776. There were also two relevant burials – those of a William (c5) in 1781 and a Mary (c4) in 1784, so two of the children died young. These entries show how wary one must be of using the IGI. The IGI is a finding aid, not a source. Looking at the entry for that William, there is no way of knowing from the IGI that he died in infancy. Many an incautious user of the IGI has seized upon a seemingly appropriate entry and carried on from there, blissfully unaware that the luckless 'ancestor' died as an infant.

If we look in the *Devonshire* section of the IGI, we find there the marriage of William Honeycombe and Dorothy Davey in Stoke Damerel in 1811. Had Gordon being doing his investigations today, once his work on Civil Registration was complete, he could have gone straight to the IGI and found this marriage, though not Samuel's baptism, since the Stoke Damerel baptisms are in the IGI only up to 1801. Nowhere near all baptisms are in the IGI, but it has enough to make it one's first port of call after civil registration and census returns.

Pinpointing a move. We were able to pinpoint Samuel's moves to Rotherhithe, Gravesend and Poplar through the complementary use of civil registration certificates, census returns and directories. None of these is available for the period before 1837 when parish registers of baptisms, marriages and burials are often the only source for migration. As we saw in the case of the move to Devonport, these do not always establish the date of a move with certainty. If it took place before marriage, as in the case of William the sawyer and Dorothy, or after the family was complete (as would be the case if the elder William did go to Devonport), the first recorded entry in a parish register may be many years after the move. However, when a family moved while children were coming regularly off the production line, parish registers will date it with a fair degree of precision. In the case of the elder William (c1), we know he was in St Cleer on 25 December 1784 for the baptism of Mary (c7), but he was in Liskeard when William (c8) was baptised on 24 December 1786.

Unfortunately, we do not know the older William's occupation. However, as we shall see later, his father and brother were masons and his son Philip probably was. So too was a grandson (c18). On the other hand, his son William (c8) was a millwright and later a sawyer, and a brother, Philip, was a carpenter. So though it seems very likely that William was either a mason or a carpenter, we cannot be sure which. The move to Liskeard may well have been in connection with building works in the town. However, we must remember firstly that a move to an adjacent parish may only have been from one side of the boundary to the other, and secondly, that the ecclesiastical parish of Liskeard included a large rural area. William need not have become a townsman.

A question of identity. Gordon now knew that the elder William Honeycombe (c1) married at St Cleer in 1776, had children baptised there between 1776 and 1784, and further children (starting with Gordon's ancestor, William) baptised at Liskeard between 1786 and 1796.

There was only one William baptised at St Cleer who could have been old enough to marry in 1776 – a William, son of John and Mary Honicombe, baptised on 12 March 1750. This in itself would not be sufficient to justify assuming the connection, for the William married in 1776 could have been born in another parish, or born in St Cleer and unregistered. However, Gordon found a William Honeycombe, buried at Liskeard on 30 October 1815, aged sixty-five, which seemed to be irrefutable proof. But was it? In genealogy it is very easy to look for evidence which fits one's preconceptions and find it. Were there no other Honeycombe entries in the Liskeard register, the presumption would be very strong that Gordon had found the baptism, marriage and burial of his ancestor.

There must be many pedigrees where a series of such entries is cited as 'proof'. However, the genealogist has a duty not just to cite the entry which fits his assumption, but to demonstrate why other entries for people of the same name have been discarded as irrelevant.

There were, in fact, two other Williams having children baptised at Liskeard between 1789 and 1805, one married to a Catherine and the other to an Elizabeth. On the face of it, either of these could be the William who died in 1815, aged sixty-five, and hence the William born in 1750 in St Cleer, especially as there were no baptisms of a William in Liskeard.

In a situation like this there are two things we are seeking to do. We want to find positive evidence in favour of one hypothesis and negative evidence to destroy alternative hypotheses.

Positive evidence: Mary. A Mary Honeycombe received poor relief in St Cleer from 1816 until her death in 1833. This made it highly probable that the William who died in 1815 was Gordon's ancestor, who was married to a Mary, his widow being forced to 'go on the parish' after his death. No burial has been found in Liskeard or elsewhere of any other Mary who could conceivably be Gordon's ancestress, Mary Honeycombe née Pitt.

Negative evidence: (i) *William and Catherine.* The

Table D. Relationship between Gordon and John Symons Honeycombe.

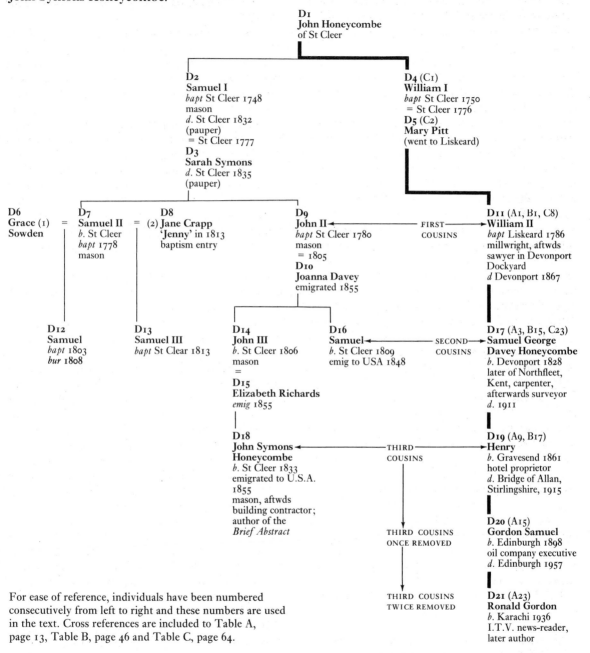

D1
John Honeycombe
of St Cleer

D2
Samuel I
bapt St Cleer 1748
mason
d. St Cleer 1832
(pauper)
= St Cleer 1777
D3
Sarah Symons
d. St Cleer 1835
(pauper)

D4 (C1)
William I
bapt St Cleer 1750
= St Cleer 1776
D5 (C2)
Mary Pitt
(went to Liskeard)

D6
Grace (1)
Sowden
=

D7
Samuel II
b. St Cleer
bapt 1778
mason
= (2)

D8
Jane Crapp
'Jenny' in 1813
baptism entry

D9
John II ◄——————— FIRST
bapt St Cleer 1780   COUSINS
mason
= 1805
D10
Joanna Davey
emigrated 1855

D11 (A1, B1, C8)
►**William II**
bapt Liskeard 1786
millwright, aftwds
sawyer in Devonport
Dockyard
d Devonport 1867

D12
Samuel
bapt 1803
bur 1808

D13
Samuel III
bapt St Clear 1813

D14
John III
b. St Cleer 1806
mason
=
D15
Elizabeth Richards
emig 1855

D16
Samuel ◄————— SECOND
b. St Cleer 1809   COUSINS
emig to USA 1848

D17 (A3, B15, C23)
►**Samuel George**
Davey Honeycombe
b. Devonport 1828
later of Northfleet,
Kent, carpenter,
afterwards surveyor
d. 1911

D18
John Symons
Honeycombe ◄——————— THIRD
b. St Cleer 1833   COUSINS
emigrated to U.S.A.
1855
mason, aftwds
building contractor;
author of the
Brief Abstract

D19 (A9, B17)
►**Henry**
b. Gravesend 1861
hotel proprietor
d. Bridge of Allan,
Stirlingshire, 1915

THIRD COUSINS
ONCE REMOVED

D20 (A15)
Gordon Samuel
b. Edinburgh 1898
oil company executive
d. Edinburgh 1957

THIRD COUSINS
TWICE REMOVED

D21 (A23)
Ronald Gordon
b. Karachi 1936
I.T.V. news-reader,
later author

For ease of reference, individuals have been numbered
consecutively from left to right and these numbers are used
in the text. Cross references are included to Table A,
page 13, Table B, page 46 and Table C, page 64.

74 *Baptism of John Symons Honeycombe at St Cleer in 1833. Note the spelling of the surname and the apparent error of his mother's name.*

75 *Extract from St Cleer Vestry Minutes, 1829.*

IGI helped us to identify one of the Williams as the William Honeycombe buried in the nearby parish of Broadoak in 1833. There we also found the burial of his wife Catherine, and the marriages of the children baptised at Liskeard. (ii) *William and Elizabeth.* The William who married Elizabeth proved much more difficult to discount, but poor relief records eventually firmly identified him as a William aged sixty-four, buried in Liskeard in 1828.

So neither of the two other Williams living in Liskeard could have been the one who died in 1815 aged 65 who was almost certainly the one baptised in St Cleer in 1750.

Absolute proof is very difficult to obtain in genealogy. However, the circumstantial evidence is sufficient for us to be confident of the accuracy of Gordon's assumption that his ancestor, the William who married Mary Pitt in 1776 was the one baptised in St Cleer in 1750.

John Symons Honeycombe. We have now traced Gordon's family firmly back to St Cleer. This was the parish where John Symons Honeycombe's *Brief Abstract* said he was born in 1833. From the St Cleer parish register, Gordon was able to confirm that the *genealogical* information in the *Brief Abstract* was substantially correct and at last he was able to establish his own connection with John Symons Honeycombe (D18). He was a third cousin of Gordon's grandfather (D19), or Gordon's third cousin, twice removed.

But John Symons Honeycombe did not confine himself to genealogical details. The *Brief Abstract* tells how in the latter part of the eighteenth century, 'the Honeycombes and Symonds secured properties in the parish of St Cleer, Cornwall, a few miles west of Honeycombe Hall, and members of both families took up their abode there, my great-grandparents, [i.e. Samuel Honeycombe (D2) and Sarah Symons (D3)] being among them; and there were born my grandfather, John Honeycombe (D9), in 1780 and later, his brother Samuel (D7).' Sarah Symons was, said John Symons Honeycombe, a prima donna and friend of Mrs Inchbald, a famous actress, dramatist and novelist in the reign of George III. 'Whenever we get a glimpse of our people off their manor,' he said, 'we find them as soldiers in the army. One, an officer under Abercrombie, was killed in Alexandria, in Egypt, in 1801.' He brings the story down to his immediate forebears: 'My great-grandfather (D2) died in December, 1832, within a month of my birth in 1833, and his wife, Sarah Symons (D3), survived him about four years', and later, 'During the Crimean War, 1854–5, we resolved to seek America, and my grandparents

Table showing columns: Paupers' Names, Rate pr Week, No of Weeks, Amount of Pay, Clothing, Fuel, Casual Relief, House Rent, Total.

Paupers' Names	Rate pr Week	No of Weeks	Amount of Pay	Clothing	Fuel	Casual Relief	House Rent	Total
			£ s d	£ s d	£ s d	£ s d	£ s d	£ s d
Gedye Eliz.	2/	53	5-6-	" 10-3½	—	" 2-6	—	5-18-9½
Gilbert Rich.d Jun.r	—		—	1-1-4	—	" 2-6	—	1-3-10
Gill Mary	2/3	53	5-19-3	" 8-10½	" 2-6			6-10-7½
Gundry Will.m Sen.r	2/6	53	6-12-6	1-1-1		{1-19-9 / Lodgings &c}	9-13-4
Gundry Will.m Jun.r	—		—			" 11-6		" 11-6
Honeycombe Sam. & Wife	5/	53	13-5-	—	" 5-	" 5-6	1-11-6	15-7-
Harris Jane's Child	{14/6 / 1/6}	{31 / 22}	4-4-8	" 1-6	—		—	4-6-2
Harris Tho.s & Family	6/	6	1-16-	" 12-	—		2-10-	1-18-

76 St Cleer Overseers' Accounts showing payments to John Symons Honeycombe's great-grandparents.

(D9, D10) made up their minds to accompany us too. So grandfather (D9) sold his interest in the old Manor House at St Cleer, as well as his remaining interests in the celebrated Honeycombe Hall estate.'

Although the parish register evidence confirmed most of the genealogical details in the *Brief Abstract*, Gordon was somewhat disappointed to find that they gave no support to John Symons Honeycombe's description of the status of the family. Occupations are not given in the parish register before 1813, but in that year, Samuel (D13), son of Samuel (D7) and Jenny (D8) was baptised. His father was a mason, living at Church Town, St Cleer. On 27 January 1833, there was John Symons' own baptism – he was the son of John (D14) and Elizabeth (D15) of Trelosk, St Cleer, though curiously Elizabeth is given as *Ann*. His father was also described as 'mason' [74]. Whatever could have happened that such close relatives of the Lords of the Manor were only humble craftsmen?

Poor law records. Parish registers were not the only records maintained by the parish. Like other parishes, St Cleer was run by the 'vestry', a body consisting of the more substantial parishioners. By an Act of 1598, each parish was responsible for its own poor and annually the vestry elected Overseers of the Poor – in rural areas usually farmers – who were responsible for giving relief to those unable to maintain themselves or their families. The money was raised through a poor rate levied on owners and occupiers of lands and buildings. Both the vestry and the overseers kept detailed records and one would certainly expect local landowners like the Honeycombes to appear in them. And so they did – but not quite in the way Gordon expected.

The St Cleer Vestry Minutes included tables of payments to paupers, in which John Symons' great-grandfather, Samuel Honeycombe (D2) and his wife, appeared from 28 November, 1828, receiving relief of 5s a week [76]. It was apparent that Samuel and Sarah had not been able to save anything for their old age. Nor were their sons able to maintain them.

At the vestry annual meeting, on 25 March, 1829, it was reported that Samuel Honeycombe applied for a half year's rent [75]. It was decided he should 'have his full pay and pay his own rent' – i.e., his weekly payments were deemed to be sufficient to pay his rent. However, Samuel clearly could not manage, for in the overseers' accounts for 1829–30, in addition to fifty-two weeks at 5s, 15s 9d was paid for Samuel Honeycombe's half year's house rent, due on 25 March 1829 and £1 11s 6d for 'this year's rent'. One can imagine Samuel pleading in vain for his rent to be paid and,

The Weekly Pay of the Poor, as settled by

East Side

	Sep.	Oct.		Nov.		Dec.	1833 Jan.		Feb.		Mar.	
1832	20	12.	26.	9	23.	7.	21.	4	10.	1.	15.	1	15.
	pr week												
Borrow Jane	2/3	2/3	2/3	2/3	2/3	2/3	2/3	2/3	2/3	2/3	2/3	2/3	2/3
Bawden Maria	1/0	1/0	1/0	1/0	1/0	1/0	1/0	1/0	1/0	1/0	1/0	1/0	1/0
Cook Will —	2/9	2/9	2/9	2/9	2/9	2/9	2/9	2/9	2/9	2/9	2/9	3/3	3/3
Gilbert Richd	1/6	1/6	1/6	1/6	1/6	1/6	1/6	1/6	1/6	1/6	1/6	1/6	1/6
Govett John & Wife	4/.	4/.	4/.	4/.	4/.	4/.	4/.	4/.	4/.	4/.	4/.	4/.	4/.
George Elizth	2/6	2/6	2/6	2/6	2/6	2/6	2/6	2/6	2/6	2/6	2/6	2/6	2/6
Honeycombe Saml & wife	5/, 6/.	6/.	6/.	6/.	6/.	6/.	3/3	3/3	3/3	3/3	3/3	3/3	3/3
Hooper Sarah Child	1/6	1/6	1/6	1/6	1/6	1/6	1/6	1/6	1/6	1/6	1/6	1/6	1/6
Harris Jane's Child	1/6	1/6	1/6	1/6	1/6	1/6	1/6	1/6	1/6	3/.	3/.	3/.	3/.

77 *Payments to paupers, St Cleer Vestry Minutes. The death of Samuel Honeycombe led to reduction in relief.*

when he was on the verge of eviction, eventually getting it.

The following year, Samuel and his wife, Sarah, received fifty-three weeks' relief at 5s, two seams of wood at 5s and eleven weeks at 6d per week 'for their attendance' (i.e. a home help). Clearly, the old couple could no longer look after themselves. The 1832–3 accounts also had an entry 'for removing his household goods at different times – 16s 0d'. This was not a parish confiscation, but doubtless referred to several parish-assisted moves to cheaper accommodation. The sum seemed a large one – more than three times as much as the couple's weekly relief [**78**].

The weekly payments continued until 7 December 1832, when there is a note 'he died' and the payment changes from 5s 0d to 3s 3d per week [**77**]. The last payment for Sarah was 11 March 1835 when there was another note 'died'. Sarah was perhaps fortunate that she died in 1835, for this was the last year when the Old Poor Law was implemented in St Cleer. As has been mentioned previously, an act of 1834 grouped parishes into 'unions' and had Sarah lived longer, she would doubtless have had to go into Liskeard Union Workhouse.

One thing was plain, the owner of the Manor House at St Cleer and his wife, the prima donna 'a daughter of the house of Symonds', died in abject poverty. The conclusion was inescapable. Their great-grandson, John Symons Honeycombe (D18) who, in true American tradition had risen from penniless immigrant to wealthy industrialist and railroad contractor, deliberately set out to conceal his humble origins by embellishing a basically accurate genealogy with romantic but spurious pretensions to gentility.

	£	s	d
Paid Samuel Honeycombe & Wife 37 Weeks at 5/	9	5	.
P.d her 15 Weeks at 2/6	1	17	6
P.d 37 Weeks at 1/ and 15 Weeks at 9.d for attendance	2	8	3
P.d for a p.r of Shoes, Scuits & Nails	..	9	.
P.d for 1 Seam of Wood	..	2	6
P.d for removing his Houshold goods at different times	..	16	.
	14	18	3

Paid Sarah Hooper's Child 52 Weeks at 1/6	3	18	..
P.d for a pair of Shoes, Scuits & Nails	..	3	9
P.d for p.r Shoes. Scuits &c for S. Hooper	..	6	6
	4	8	3

Paid Grace Hender (?) her two Children 10 Weeks at 3/ p.r Week	1	10	..
P.d 10 Weeks House Rent at 6.d	..	5	..
P.d her relief	..	1	..
P.d her & two Children their Passage	18	..	..

78 *St Cleer Overseers' Accounts, 1832, showing the wide range of relief given by the parish.*

7 The Jersey Connection

When Gordon began his quest, he was looking for answers to three main questions. Firstly, how was he related to John Symons Honeycombe? Secondly, how much of the *Brief Abstract* was true? Thirdly, how was he related to Roy Honeycombe? His researches at St Cleer had largely answered the first two questions, though he still had to find out whether there was any connection between his family and Honeycombe Hall. It seemed clear that an answer to the third question would be found only in Jersey. In fact, Jersey seemed to hold the key to a whole group of unanswered problems, for time and again it cropped up unexpectedly in Gordon's investigations. The 1851 Census return for Waterloo Street, Devonport, gave St Helier as the birthplace of William the Sawyer's granddaughter, Ann. Then the Dockyard pension records showed William's pension as being paid in Jersey. Finally, William, his daughter, Margaretta, and granddaughter, Ann, were found in the 1861 Census for St Helier.

There was also, of course, the reference to Jersey in the *Brief Abstract*. John Symons Honeycombe (E33) tells how his father, John Honeycombe (E23), 'early in life 1825 went to the island of Jersey and there married on the 15th day of July, 1826, Elizabeth Richards (E24), a native of St Neot, Cornwall, born in December, 1804.' They had ten children: 'The first three died in infancy on the island of Jersey; I the fourth child was born at St Cleer, Cornwall, England, on January 9th 1833.' What took John Symons Honeycombe's father (E23), to Jersey in 1825, and why did he return shortly before January 1833? How was he connected with the Jersey Honeycombes whom Gordon had now discovered?

Parish registers. To try to answer these questions, Gordon went to Jersey and searched the parish registers of St Helier. He turned to 15 July 1826, and there, sure enough, was the marriage of John Honeycombe of St Cleer (E23) to Elizabeth Richards of St Neot (E24). Somewhat to his surprise, however, only a week earlier, on 7 July, there was another Honey-

combe marriage. Ann Honeycombe 'of Devonport' was married to Sgt John Montgomery of the 76th Regiment. Ann could only be the Ann born in Liskeard in 1796 (E15), the daughter of William (E5) and Mary (E4) and sister of William the Sawyer (E12).[26]

Clandestine marriages. Since the earliest Honeycombe entries in the St Helier register were two marriages a week apart, one theory was that they might be *runaway* marriages against the wishes of the parents. Maybe Elizabeth Richards' (E24) parents felt she was marrying beneath her, or Ann's (E15) brother did not approve of her marrying a soldier. This theory was not improbable since, in 1753, the English 'Hardwicke' Marriage Act had made marriage with a minor illegal without the consent of parents. The Act did not, however, apply to the Channel Islands, which, with

> Mr URBAN, *Gravesend, Jan. 24.*
> THere has lately eloped from this place a young nymph of 15, with a considerable fortune in her pocket, in company with a little dapper swain of her own chusing. After an ineffectual pursuit by her careful guardian, news is at length arrived from the island of *Guernsey*, that they have been married there.
> Upon enquiry it appears, that at *Southampton* there are vessels always ready for carrying on the trade of smuggling weddings, which, for the price of five guineas transports contraband goods into the land of matrimony; and this trade, it seems, has been car-

79

26. Not only was she described as 'of Devonport' (where we know her brother was living at the time) but Gordon found the burials of her sister, Sarah (E11) who died in 1840, aged fifty-eight, and of another brother, Philip (E14) who died in 1834, aged forty-two years ten months.

no such legal constraint, acted as a kind of Gretna Green for southern England. The *Gentleman's Magazine*, in 1760, reported that sailing vessels were always kept ready at Southampton, which, for a fee of five guineas, would carry runaway couples to the Channel Islands.[27] [79]

However, Elizabeth Richards (E24) was twenty-one in December 1825, and so of age when she married. Ann (E15) was twenty-nine and subsequent research showed that her groom, Sergeant John Montgomery (E16), was stationed on the island in 1826. So this theory had to be abandoned.

As we pointed out in the last chapter, personal factors are nearly always present and the decisions of the individual have always been crucial. Rarely, however, do they provide a full and sufficient explanation divorced from national and local factors.

National and local factors. The first Honeycombe baptism in the St Helier registers was in 1828. It was of a daughter of John Symons's great-uncle, Samuel II (E6) and later there were numerous entries for his descendants, which enabled Gordon to draw up a fairly substantial family tree of the Jersey Honeycombes.

The common denominator with all except one of the early male Honeycombes in Jersey was that they were masons. The exception was Ann's brother, Philip (E14) whose occupation we did not know, but a newspaper reference to his death in 1834 stated that he was 'killed by a fall of earth where he was working', which suggested that he was also a mason. Could the Honeycombes have been recruited for building work in Jersey?

Fort Regent. Background reading showed that during the period 1815–52 the island saw the construction of many public works, especially for defence. In the hope of finding information on the recruitment of masons, a search was made in the *Engineers Papers in the Channel Islands 1787–1856*, among the War Office files in the Public Record Office.[28] It was discovered that by far

the greatest of these projects was the construction of Fort Regent, St Helier, begun in 1806, when invasion threatened. For some years local labour was used, but from 1810 onwards, masons were brought over from Plymouth and elsewhere on the mainland. By the spring of 1812, there were over 280 masons at work, made up of 123 London masons at 5s 3d a day; forty-seven Plymouth masons at 4s 3d a day; thirty-five Jersey masons at 4s 0d a day; and fifty-two military masons at 1s 8d a day. These wages appear to have been high by the standards of the day, and must have proved attractive to the Plymouth masons.

After the completion of Fort Regent in 1817, government employment of masons fell off, though in 1824 tenders were invited from local contractors to repair fortifications. There were, however, a number of other local projects – in 1818 the New Quay was built and the Royal Square repaved and the Old South Pier was built between 1820 and 1822. That Cornish masons enjoyed a high reputation on the island is shown by an advertisement for workers in the *Chronique de Jersey* in 1832, which said 'Cornishmen will be preferred'.

Seasonal migration. One explanation of the 1825 migration is that John III (E23), Samuel II (E6) and Philip (E14) were recruited for the stonemasons' work for which tenders were invited in 1824, their arrival in 1825 being the beginning of a permanent settlement. However, there is no reason to suppose that this was their first period of employment there. The Channel Islands Engineers papers in the Public Record Office make it clear that for the building of Fort Regent most of the masons were sent home at the onset of winter and were re-engaged in the spring. Some of the Honeycombe males may have been coming over regularly on a seasonal basis for some years – possibly as early as 1810. The seasonal pattern of work may have become so regular that in the end they decided to bring their families and settle down. To test this theory, we examined the baptism dates of the Honeycombe children from 1810 onwards, back home in Cornwall, to see if they were winter conceptions, but the evidence was inconclusive.

In 1828, as we have seen, Samuel II (E6) had a daughter baptised. Samuel might have emigrated in 1825 with his family. However, the long gap in the

27. *Gentleman's Magazine* 1760. pp. 30–31.
28. P.R.O. W.O. 55: Engineers Papers, Channel Islands, 1787–1856. Papers looked at: W.O. 55/809 (1811–18); 810 (1819–1877); 811 (1828–30). These consist largely of correspondence between the Commanding Officer of the Royal Engineers on Jersey and the Ordnance Office, London.

Table E. The Jersey Honeycombes.

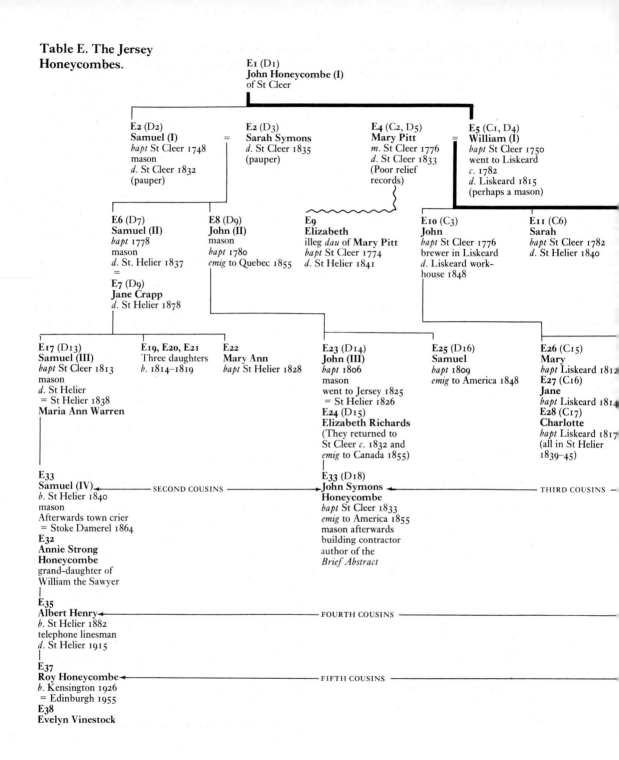

E1 (D1)
John Honeycombe (I)
of St Cleer

E2 (D2)
Samuel (I)
bapt St Cleer 1748
mason
d. St Cleer 1832
(pauper)

=

E2 (D3)
Sarah Symons
d. St Cleer 1835
(pauper)

E4 (C2, D5)
Mary Pitt
m. St Cleer 1776
d. St Cleer 1833
(Poor relief records)

=

E5 (C1, D4)
William (I)
bapt St Cleer 1750
went to Liskeard
c. 1782
d. Liskeard 1815
(perhaps a mason)

E6 (D7)
Samuel (II)
bapt 1778
mason
d. St. Helier 1837
=
E7 (D9)
Jane Crapp
d. St Helier 1878

E8 (D9)
John (II)
mason
bapt 1780
emig to Quebec 1855

E9
Elizabeth
illeg *dau* of Mary Pitt
bapt St Cleer 1774
d. St Helier 1841

E10 (C3)
John
bapt St Cleer 1776
brewer in Liskeard
d. Liskeard work-house 1848

E11 (C6)
Sarah
bapt St Cleer 1782
d. St Helier 1840

E17 (D13)
Samuel (III)
bapt St Cleer 1813
mason
d. St Helier
= St Helier 1838
Maria Ann Warren

E19, E20, E21
Three daughters
b. 1814–1819

E22
Mary Ann
bapt St Helier 1828

E23 (D14)
John (III)
bapt 1806
mason
went to Jersey 1825
= St Helier 1826
E24 (D15)
Elizabeth Richards
(They returned to
St Cleer *c.* 1832 and
emig to Canada 1855)

E25 (D16)
Samuel
bapt 1809
emig to America 1848

E26 (C15)
Mary
bapt Liskeard 1812
E27 (C16)
Jane
bapt Liskeard 1814
E28 (C17)
Charlotte
bapt Liskeard 1817
(all in St Helier
1839–45)

E33
Samuel (IV)
b. St Helier 1840
mason
Afterwards town crier
= Stoke Damerel 1864
E32
Annie Strong
Honeycombe
grand-daughter of
William the Sawyer

——— SECOND COUSINS ———

E33 (D18)
John Symons
Honeycombe
bapt St Cleer 1833
emig to America 1855
mason afterwards
building contractor
author of the
Brief Abstract

——— THIRD COUSINS ———

E35
Albert Henry
b. St Helier 1882
telephone linesman
d. St Helier 1915

——— FOURTH COUSINS ———

E37
Roy Honeycombe
b. Kensington 1926
= Edinburgh 1955
E38
Evelyn Vinestock

——— FIFTH COUSINS ———

For ease of reference, individuals have been numbered consecutively from left to right and these numbers are used in the text. Cross references are included to Table A, page 13, Table B, page 46, Table C, page 64 and Table D, page 71.

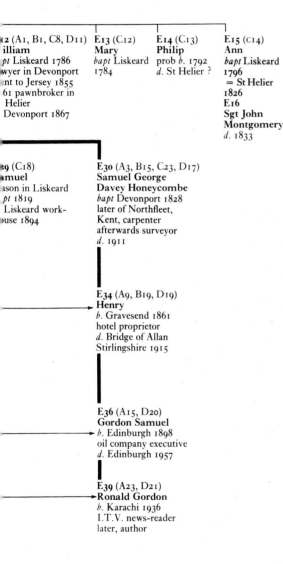

2 (A1, B1, C8, D11)	E13 (C12)	E14 (C13)	E15 (C14)
illiam	Mary	Philip	Ann
pt Liskeard 1786	bapt Liskeard	prob b. 1792	bapt Liskeard
wyer in Devonport	1784	d. St Helier ?	1796
nt to Jersey 1855			= St Helier
61 pawnbroker in			1826
Helier			E16
Devonport 1867			Sgt John
			Montgomery
			d. 1833

29 (C18)
amuel
ason in Liskeard
pt 1819
Liskeard work-
ouse 1894

E30 (A3, B15, C23, D17)
Samuel George Davey Honeycombe
bapt Devonport 1828
later of Northfleet, Kent, carpenter
afterwards surveyor
d. 1911

E34 (A9, B19, D19)
Henry
b. Gravesend 1861
hotel proprietor
d. Bridge of Allan
Stirlingshire 1915

E36 (A15, D20)
Gordon Samuel
b. Edinburgh 1898
oil company executive
d. Edinburgh 1957

E39 (A23, D21)
Ronald Gordon
b. Karachi 1936
I.T.V. news-reader
later, author

baptisms of his children (1819–28) suggests that he may have been living there on his own before 1825 and was joined around July 1827 by his wife and family.

Going to relatives. So the Honeycombes may have all come to the island in 1825. Alternatively, they may have gone in ones and twos as relatives already over there told them of job opportunities. Be that as it may, the important thing is that once one member of a family was already settled in an area, others were very likely to follow. Indeed, we know that other members of the family came over in the 1830s.[29] To understand what happened in the past we have only to look at the pattern of immigration to Britain since the Second World War.

Another point to remember is that even if the date of the Honeycombes' first connection with Jersey could be established (e.g., by the lucky discovery of masons' pay-books) it would not follow that this was the first *family* connection with the island, for, like immigrants to Britain today, families were just as likely to join relatives on the female side as on the male. Had Gordon abstracted Jersey parish register entries for the surnames of families into which the Honeycombes had married back home in Cornwall, or entries for any surnames which showed links with parishes where there were Honeycombes, such entries might have thrown further light on why the first of the Honeycombes went to Jersey.

'Push' factors. In the case of William the Sawyer's move to Devonport, we looked not only at factors of 'pull' but those of 'push', e.g., whether there was difficulty in finding employment at home.

It may be that the Honeycombes were not so much pulled to Jersey, as pushed from Cornwall by the slump of the early 1820s. Frank Booker notes that this particularly hit the building trade. For example the carriage of granite on the Tavistock Canal which ran from Tavistock to Morwhelham on the Tamar River completely ceased.

Temporary migration. The return of John Symons Honeycombe's parents (E23, E24) to St Cleer about 1832 highlights the fact that not all emigration was permanent. Although in this case the fact that Samuel I

29. Mary, Jane and Charlotte (E26–29), daughters of John (E10), brewer in Liskeard.

Table F. Ann and Annie.

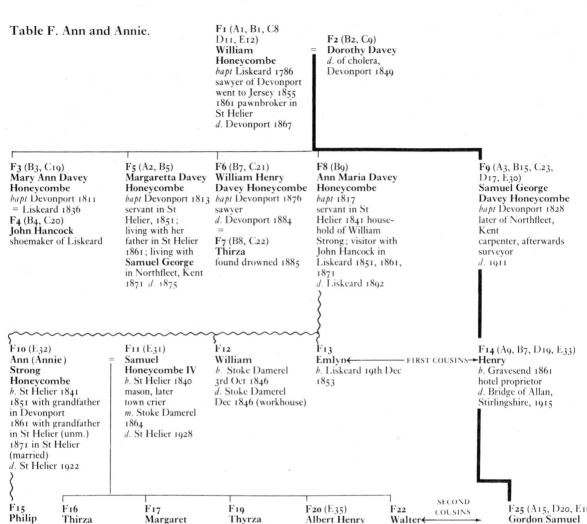

F1 (A1, B1, C8 D11, E12)
William Honeycombe
bapt Liskeard 1786
sawyer of Devonport
went to Jersey 1855
1861 pawnbroker in
St Helier
d. Devonport 1867

=

F2 (B2, C9)
Dorothy Davey
d. of cholera,
Devonport 1849

F3 (B3, C19)
Mary Ann Davey Honeycombe
bapt Devonport 1811
= Liskeard 1836
F4 (B4, C20)
John Hancock
shoemaker of Liskeard

F5 (A2, B5)
Margaretta Davey Honeycombe
bapt Devonport 1813
servant in St
Helier, 1851;
living with her
father in St Helier
1861; living with
Samuel George
in Northfleet, Kent
1871 *d.* 1875

F6 (B7, C21)
William Henry Davey Honeycombe
bapt Devonport 1876
sawyer
d. Devonport 1884
=
F7 (B8, C22)
Thirza
found drowned 1885

F8 (B9)
Ann Maria Davey Honeycombe
bapt 1817
servant in St
Helier 1841 house-
hold of William
Strong; visitor with
John Hancock in
Liskeard 1851, 1861,
1871
d. Liskeard 1892

F9 (A3, B15, C23, D17, E30)
Samuel George Davey Honeycombe
bapt Devonport 1828
later of Northfleet,
Kent
carpenter, afterwards
surveyor
d. 1911

F10 (E32)
Ann (Annie) Strong Honeycombe
b. St Helier 1841
1851 with grandfather
in Devonport
1861 with grandfather
in St Helier (unm.)
1871 in St Helier
(married)
d. St Helier 1922

=

F11 (E31)
Samuel Honeycombe IV
b. St Helier 1840
mason, later
town crier
m. Stoke Damerel
1864
d. St Helier 1928

F12
William
b. Stoke Damerel
3rd Oct 1846
d. Stoke Damerel
Dec 1846 (workhouse)

F13
Emlyn ← FIRST COUSINS →
b. Liskeard 19th Dec
1853

F14 (A9, B7, D19, E33)
Henry
b. Gravesend 1861
hotel proprietor
d. Bridge of Allan,
Stirlingshire, 1915

F15
Philip
b. 1862
Plymouth

F16
Thirza
b. Devonport 1864
d. St Helier 1865

F17
Margaret
b. Devonport 1864
F18
Thomas le Breton
emig to Salt Lake City,
Utah, USA

F19
Thyrza
b. St Helier 1866

F20 (E35)
Albert Henry
b. St Helier 1882
telephone linesman
d. St Helier 1915
=
F21
Alice Maud Delamare
|
F26 (E37)
Roy ← THIRD COUSINS →
b. Kensington 1926
= Edinburgh 1955
F27
Evelyn Vinestock

F22
Walter ← SECOND COUSINS →
b. St Helier 1887
d. St Helier 1959
= (1) **F23**
Alice le Mercier
=
(2) **F24**
Mary Blanpied

F25 (A15, D20, E16)
Gordon Samuel
b. Edinburgh 1898
oil company executi[ve]
d. Edinburgh 1957

F28 (A23, D21, E39)
Ronald Gordon
b. Karachi 1936
ITV newsreader, lat[er]
author

For ease of reference, individuals have been numbered
consecutively from left to right and these numbers are used
in the text. Cross references are included to Table A,
page 13, Table B, page 46, Table C, page 64, Table D,
page 71 and Table E, page 78.

Baptêmes Célébrés dans la Paroisse de St. Hélier, en l'île de Jersey.

Baptisms Solemnized in the Parish of St. Helier, in the Island of Jersey.

DATE DU BAPTÊME. WHEN BAPTIZED.	JOUR DE LA NAISSANCE. WHEN BORN.	NOM DE BAPTÊME DE L'ENFANT. CHILD'S CHRISTIAN NAME.	NOMS DES PÈRE ET MÈRE. PARENTS' NAMES.		ÉTAT, PROFESSION, ET NOM DU PÈRE. FATHER'S NAME, TRADE OR PROFESSION.	SIGNATURE DU MINISTRE OFFICIANT. OFFICIATING MINISTER'S SIGNATURE.
			DE BAPTÊME. CHRISTIAN.	DE FAMILLE. SURNAME.		
1842 January 16th	General Hospital December 25th 1841	Ann Strong Illegitimate daughter of John L. Marie & Marguerite L. Marie	Ann	Honeycombe Sponsors		Jas Gallichan Offg Minister

80. *Baptism of Annie Strong Honeycombe at St Helier, 1842. Unlike English registers, dates of both baptism and birth are given.*

(E2) was dying was most probably the crucial factor, this was a time when the situation in the Cornish building trade was improving. Booker says that the 1830s ushered in better times, and by 1835, the Tavistock Canal was carrying 15,500 tons, much of it granite for building.[30] In fact, the same personal, family, local and national factors operate in the case of a return as with the original migration.

Samuel III and Mary Ann. Of the four branches of the Honeycombes who eventually settled in Jersey, three left Jersey or died out in the male line. So all the Honeycombes living in Jersey today are the descendants of Samuel II (E6) and his wife, Jane (E7). Samuel died in 1837. Jane lived on until 1878, dying at the age of ninety. Their eldest son, Samuel III (E17) married Maria Ann Warren (E18). In the 1861 Census, Samuel and Maria Honeycombe are found living at 77 Great Union Rd, St Helier. He was described as a mason, his wife as a grocer. Samuel III died in 1865, and in the same year, his wife appears in a Jersey directory[31]

30. F. Booker *Industrial archaeology of the Tamar Valley* David and Charles, 1967 p. 117.

31. *Jersey Express Almanac: a directory of professional, mercantile and trading classes.*

as a 'grocer and tea dealer'. Alas, Maria later went bankrupt and died in 1874.

Ann and Annie. Samuel and Maria Ann's eldest son, Samuel IV (E31) was married in Devonport in 1864. His bride was also a Honeycombe – Annie Strong Honeycombe (E32). The marriage certificate did not give her father's name. Since there was no Annie Strong Honeycombe in the St Catherine's House birth indexes she was clearly identical with the Ann Strong, illegitimate daughter of Ann Honeycombe, baptised at St Helier on 29 December 1841 [80]. But who was this Ann? Gordon thought she was probably a daughter of Samuel II (E6) and Jane Honeycombe (E7). There was a convenient gap between 1819, when Samuel II had two daughters (E20, E21) baptised at St Neot, Cornwall, and 1828 when, as we have seen, another daughter was baptised in St Helier (E22). This would mean that it was a marriage of first cousins. At the time that Gordon favoured this solution, it was not known that William the Sawyer went to Jersey. This discovery, coupled with the fact that Annie's marriage to Samuel was in Devonport, made it quite possible that the elder Ann was, in fact, William's daughter, Ann Maria Davey Honeycombe (F8).

No.	(1) When married	(2) Name and surname	(3) Age
64	6 August 1864	Samuel Honeycombe	24
		Annie Strong Honeycombe	23

200	Seventeenth July 1864 3h.51m. p.m. 15 Fort Street	Thirza Elizabeth	Girl	Samuel Honeycombe

1841 Census entry for Ann. The single line separating Ann from three other residents suggests that she was living with the Strongs. She is also shown as being born outside Jersey.

Entries showing the birth of a child before the marriage.

The clinching piece of evidence was the 1861 census return for St Helier, which showed William the Sawyer (now William the Pawnbroker!) living with his 46 year old daughter, Margaretta, (F5) and his 19 year old grand-daughter Annie Honeycombe. She could only be Annie Strong Honeycombe.

So Annie (F10) was the illegitimate child of William's daughter, Ann Maria Davey Honeycombe (F8).

The 1841 Census. Unexpectedly, the one missing piece of the jigsaw, the identity of Annie's father, was provided by the 1841 Census for St Helier. This listed an Ann Honeycombe, a servant in the household of a thirty-year-old coachman, William Strong, his wife and three children. Ann's age was given as 20 (i.e. 20–24), William's as 30 (i.e. 30–34). There can be little doubt that *he* was the father of Ann's daughter [81].

Curiously, this same entry solved another problem – why Annie should marry such a distant relative (Samuel and Annie were not first cousins, as was at first thought but *third* cousins). In fact, William Strong lived in Great Union Rd, next-door but one to Samuel's father, Samuel Honeycombe III (E19). So the probability is that Samuel IV and Annie (who were almost exactly the same age) grew up together as children. Again, as with Margaret Honeycombe, the Surveyor's daughter, and Richard Fox, this emphasises that it is important when studying census returns and directories to look at the *total* context of where people were living, and not just to pull out a series of isolated entries for a single surname.

Mother of three! We can now reconstruct Ann Maria Davey Honeycombe's life in fair detail. The daughter of William the Sawyer (F1) and Dorothy (F2), she was born in 1817 and baptised at St Andrew's Plymouth. In 1841 she was in St Helier and had an illegitimate child, Ann Mary, known as Annie (F10). By 1846, she was back in Devonport but she would appear to have left her infant daughter in Jersey. True in 1851 Annie, then aged ten, was in Devonport, living with her grandfather, but her being given the name 'Strong' does suggest that an amazingly tolerant Mrs Strong brought her up with her own children, and the fact that the Strongs were next door but one to the Honeycombes, and that Annie later married Samuel (F11) would seem to indicate she spent a number of years there. So the balance of probability is that Annie went to Devonport only in, or very shortly before, 1851. This is a reminder that evidence of where people were *in* census years cannot be taken as any indication of where they were *between* census years.

On 3 October 1846, the Stoke Damerel baptismal registers showed that Ann Maria had a *second* illegitimate child, William (F12) baptised. At this stage she would seem to have been disowned by her parents or was too ashamed to tell them, – for poor William died two months later in the workhouse.

In the 1851 Census, we found Ann in Liskeard as a 'visitor' in the house of her brother-in-law, John Hancock (F4). John was a 'cordwainer' or shoemaker. Since his wife was not there, and there were three

Parish [or Township] of	City or Municipal Borough of	Municipal Ward of	Parliamentary Borough of	Town of	Hamlet or Tything, &c., of	Ecclesiastical District of			

The undermentioned Houses are situate within the Boundaries of the   [Page 5]

No. of Schedule	Road, Street, &c., and No. or Name of House	HOUSES (In-habited / Un-in-habited (U.), or Building (B.))	Name and Surname of each Person	Relation to Head of Family	Condition	Age of (Males / Females)	Rank, Profession, or Occupation	Where Born	Whether Blind, or Deaf-and-Dumb
24 a	do		John Hancock	head	widr	47	Master shoemaker	do	Liskeard
			Louisa Hancock	dau	un	20	dress maker	do	do
			Elizabeth Hancock	dau	un	18	Dress Maker	do	do
			Joseph Hancock	son	un	16	Carpenter (app)	do	do
			Mary Hancock	dau	un	40	Dress Maker	do	do
			Mary Barker	aunt	wid	75	Formerly a nurse	do	Helston
			Ann Honeycombe	visitor	un	40	No occupation	Devon	Devonport
			Emily Honeycombe	niece	un	7	Scholar	Cornwall	Liskeard
			Elizabeth Bastin	boarder	un	37	No occupation	do	do
			David Bastin	son	-	8	scholar	do	do

84   *1861 Census, Liskeard, showing the unusual composition of the Hancock household. Emlyn Honeycombe appears as 'Emily'.*

young children, it looked as if Ann Maria's eldest sister, Mary Ann Davey Honeycombe (F3) had died and Ann was looking after the children. Although her relationship to John, as head of the household was given as 'visitor', her occupation was given as 'house-servant'. As we have seen, her daughter Annie was not with her, but was living at 11 Waterloo St, Stoke, Plymouth, with her grandfather the sawyer, and her uncle and aunt, William (F5) and Thirza (F7).

Emlyn. In 1853 Ann had a third illegitimate child, a daughter, Emlyn (F13), born in John Hancock's house in West St, Liskeard. We had no evidence as to the father, but suspected that it might not be just the Hancock *children* Ann Maria was looking after. Emlyn appeared with Ann in the Hancock household's return in 1861 (when she is described as 'Emily' – an under-standable error on the part of the enumerator). Again, Annie was not living with her mother. This time she was living with her grandfather in St Helier.

In 1871, Ann Maria was still with John Hancock, in West Street. She was then described as 'servant'. Emlyn, though seventeen, was described as a scholar, an unusual age for a working class girl to be continuing her education. Perhaps she was a pupil-teacher. The interesting thing is that the St Catherine's indexes provided us with no evidence either of Emlyn's marriage or her death. She might have adopted the name of Hancock and been married under that name. A search at St Catherine's House for the marriage of Emlyn Hancock would confirm or refute this. Alterna-

tively, she may have emigrated.

Her mother, Ann Maria Davey Honeycombe (F8), was buried in Liskeard on 3 July 1892.

Annie. Let us now take a look at the life of Ann Maria's daughter, Annie (F10). It is said that history never repeats itself but Annie came close to following in her mother's footsteps – except that she did marry eventually.

As we have seen, in April 1861 Annie, now aged nineteen, was living with her grandfather, William, in St Helier. We know that William was back in Devonport by the end of the year, for his pension for the second half of 1861 was paid in Devonport. On the 19th April, 1862, Annie gave birth to an illegitimate son, Philip Theodore (F15), at 2 Jubilee St, Plymouth. In other words, the return to Devonport coincided almost exactly with Philip's conception. Was Philip conceived in Jersey, William taking his grand-daughter back to have her baby in Plymouth? Or was Annie's arrival in a naval town the cause of her downfall?

In 1864, the Stoke Damerel registers and Civil Registration certificates record Annie's marriage to Samuel Honeycombe IV (F11) and the birth of twin daughters, Thirza (F16) doubtless named after her aunt, (who was later so tragically drowned) and Margaret (F17). The marriage certificate and one of the twins' birth certificates reproduced here, serve as a warning that it is not always enough when looking in Civil Registration marriage indexes to start with the date of birth of the eldest child and work backwards

⁸⁵ *A chance photograph of Samuel Honeycombe the Town Crier taken at St Helier at the annual festival of flowers. Samuel, clutching his newspapers, is on the far left.*

until the marriage is found. The marriage took place on 6 August, but the twins were born on 17 July. Samuel and Annie were back in St Helier by March 1865 when Thirza died [82, 83].

Annie Strong Honeycombe's husband, Samuel IV (F11) was, like his ancestors, a mason and was so described when his first two children were born or baptised in 1864 and 1865. However, in the 1871 Census, he was down as *labourer*. But in July of that year, at a daughter's birth he was a mason again, as he was in 1872. In 1874, he was a *merchant* living in Great Union Rd, the same road where he had spent his childhood. He was *mason* again in 1876 and 1878, but thereafter was *newsagent* (1881) and *town crier* (1882 and 1887). In 1972, when Gordon Honeycombe was a television news-reader, he was sent a cutting from a Jersey newspaper, which left Samuel's job in no doubt whatsoever. Writing from Chicago, a ninety-two-year-old ex-Jerseyman recalled that in his boyhood days in

Jersey, part of the news came from town criers Landrick and Honeycombe. Nearly a hundred years before Gordon, Samuel Honeycombe had also been a news-reader! [85]

Here again, we have yet another example of a person who changed his occupation. According to family tradition, in Samuel's case the reason was that he worked for a while on the building of the Victoria and Albert Museum in London. While travelling back to Jersey from Plymouth he had an accident in which he injured his right arm. On his return to Jersey, the injury worsened and in the end he was forced to give up being a mason.

Samuel died in 1928, aged eighty-eight [86].

Roy Honeycombe. The later Jersey Honeycombes are all descended from Samuel and Annie, who had fourteen children, or from Samuel's brother, Richard. Roy Honeycombe (E27, F26) whose marriage an-

86 *Samuel and Annie.*

(F11) was born and died in St Helier – but his marriage and the births of his first two children were in Devonport, and so appear at St Catherine's House though the birth of his youngest son, Walter (F22), does not. Both Walter's marriages are there – one at St Pancras, London (F23) the other in Essex (F24). Even Roy Honeycombe (F26) was born in Kensington. His birth accordingly appears in St Catherine's House indexes, though his marriage does not, being in Scotland!

Migration and assimilation. In this chapter, we have seen longer distance migration patterns at work. In all probability, (though firm proof has so far been lacking) the Honeycombes first came to Jersey as seasonal migrant workers, returning home each winter. Then they became immigrants. At first, they were probably not accepted very readily by the host population. The nineteenth century saw a great immigration of English people in Jersey. By 1840 there were 15,000 English residents, mainly living in new streets which grew up on the outskirts of St Helier. These people tended to live as an English colony, with their own churches or chapels, their own newspapers and their own social life. They rarely mixed with Jerseymen. So Samuel III (E17) though only a child when he was brought to the island, married a girl with an English name; his son, Samuel IV (E31 F10) as we have seen, married his third cousin, Annie Strong Honeycombe (E32 F10); Samuel IV's brother, Richard, married an Ann Ellis; his sister, Maria Ann, a John Doran. This exclusiveness seems to have lasted only for two generations, for both Samuel's and Richard's children married people with Jersey names, such as Thomas le Breton (F18), Alice Maud Delamare (F2) Alice le Mercier (F23) and Mary Blanpied (F24). There could not be a more complete indication of assimilation.

nouncement first aroused Gordon's interest in the family history, is the town crier's grandson. However, although only very distantly related to Gordon (E39, F28) in the male line, there is, strangely enough, a closer relationship in the female line. For, as we have seen, his grandmother, Annie Strong Honeycombe (F10) was, like Gordon's grandfather Henry (F14), a grandchild of William the Sawyer of Devonport (F1). So Gordon (F28) and Roy (F26) are fifth cousins on one side (Table E) and third cousins on the other (Table F).

Other registration systems. The story of the Jersey Honeycombes serves as a reminder that one must not forget the separate registration systems of Scotland, Ireland, the Channel Islands and India.[32] The later Jersey Honeycombes flit in and out of the St Catherine's House indexes in a way which would baffle a genealogist unaware of the Jersey connection. The town crier

32. Civil Registration began in England in 1837 and in Scotland in 1855; in Ireland it was 1864; in Jersey it has never been started! So there are still only parish registers (see p. 153). However, as with Scottish parish registers, there is the great advantage that a wife's maiden name is usually given in the burials, though not, alas, in the baptisms.

8 Establishing the Pedigree

Of the three 'stages' in building up a family history – the genealogical, the biographical and the historical – the first is obviously basic. Without a genealogy, there can be no family history; with a wrong genealogy, the family history is at best distorted and at worst you may be writing the history of a totally different family.

Gordon's pedigree was proved from civil registration back to Samuel George Davey Honeycombe (E30). From census returns, he knew that Samuel was born in Devonport and he located his baptism at St Andrew's Plymouth, in 1828. The marriage of Samuel's parents, William Honeycombe (E12) and Dorothy Davey (E13), was found at Stoke Damerel in 1811. Census returns showed that William was born in Liskeard in 1786 and his baptism was duly found there. The marriage of *his* parents, William Honeycombe (E5) and Mary Pitt (E4), was located at St Cleer in 1776, and after some problems of identification, it was established that this William was the son of John (E1) and Mary Honicombe and was baptised at St Cleer on 12 March 1750 [**126**].

There are two interesting points about this entry. Firstly, the most common spelling was now Honicombe. Until the nineteenth century, the spelling of surnames was very flexible. Since most people were illiterate, the parish clerks wrote the names as they thought fit. Sometimes the spelling varies in a single entry.

Secondly, the date – 12 March 1750 – is very misleading for the beginner, for up to 1752, the year began not on 1 January but on the 25 March, – Lady Day. The calendar was reformed in 1751, and the year started with January in 1752. So 1751 was nearly three months short! Today, to avoid confusion, we usually put both the old style and the new style dates. So William Honeycombe was baptised on 12 March 1750/1. The register called it 1750. We would call it 1751.

The St Cleer registers. The William Honicombe baptised in 1750 (G11) was the third surviving son of John and Mary Honicombe (G5–6). The eldest child (G9), was baptised in 1737, and the marriage of John Honicombe (G5) to Mary Ough (G6) was found in

1736. Working back from the marriage, Gordon found a John baptised in St Cleer in 1706/7. No other John was baptised between 1683 and 1737, and no John was buried there between 1706/7 and 1736. Gordon therefore assumed that he had found the right person. However, with such a common Christian name, one cannot be sure that our John Honicombe might not be missing from the baptism register because he was not baptised, was baptised but unregistered, or – most likely of all – had come into the parish from elsewhere. Moreover, according to the *Brief Abstract* he was born in 1708 and was the son not of a John Honi-

Table G. St Cleer Honicombes.

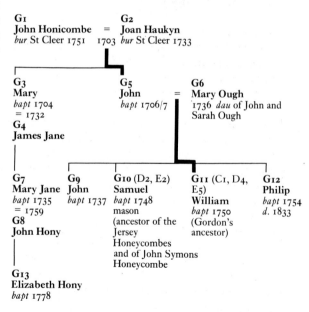

G1
John Honicombe = G2 Joan Haukyn
bur St Cleer 1751   1703   *bur* St Cleer 1733

G3
Mary
bapt 1704
= 1732
G4
James Jane

G5
John
bapt 1706/7   = G6 Mary Ough
1736 *dau* of John and Sarah Ough

G7
Mary Jane
bapt 1735
= 1759
G8
John Hony

G9
John
bapt 1737

G10 (D2, E2)
Samuel
bapt 1748
mason
(ancestor of the Jersey Honeycombes and of John Symons Honeycombe

G11 (C1, D4, E5)
William
bapt 1750
(Gordon's ancestor)

G12
Philip
bapt 1754
d. 1833

G13
Elizabeth Hony
bapt 1778

For ease of reference, individuals have been numbered consecutively from left to right and these numbers are used in the text. Cross references are included to Table C, page 64, Table D, page 71 and Table E, page 78.

combe, but of a Philip and was the first to come to St Cleer from Calstock. Leaving aside the nonsense about manor houses, could this enshrine a genuine oral tradition? On the face of it, it seems quite likely. The youngest son (born in 1754) was called Philip (G12) and could well have been named after his grandfather. The name Philip was found among the Calstock Honeycombes. Whatever tales John Symons Honeycombe had invented about the family history, his genealogy, no doubt obtained from his grandfather (with whom he emigrated), had been fully substantiated from parish registers up to this point. Philip, in fact, was the earliest Honeycombe in John Symons' consecutive pedigree, making it very likely that this was the limit of his knowledge from oral evidence.

So here we have alternative hypotheses – the preferred one, that John was baptised at St Cleer in 1706/7, and the alternative one, that he was the son of a Philip Honeycombe from Calstock. It was necessary to look for further evidence.

Registers of other parishes. A search of the registers of neighbouring parishes, including Calstock, showed that there was no baptism which could be that of John married in 1736 nor was there any burial which could be that of John baptised in 1706/7.

Wills. Potentially the most useful source for complementing the parish register is *wills*. Until 1858, wills were proved by the church courts. In general it was normal for a will to be proved in the court of the archdeaconry in which the testator died. Most of these wills have, however, ended up in the County Record Offices. (See page 144.)

Gordon searched the index in the Cornwall County Record Office and obtained photocopies of all Honeycombe wills. There were eighteen of them, almost all with an inventory attached. Most were for Honeycombes living in Calstock and Callington; a few were for other places. None was for St Cleer. Wills were also searched for Ough, Haukyn and the married surnames of daughters but no relevant ones were found.

Other parish records. Unfortunately, the St Cleer overseers' accounts, which as we have seen are very

informative, started only in 1770. There were churchwardens' accounts, however, from 1720 and these included a number of references to 'John Honicombe':

1742	Pd John Honicombe for 2½ bushels of lime and carriage of the same	0- 3-6
1744	Pd John Honicombe for pointing the windows	0- 5-0
1747	Pd John Honicombe as by his Bill	0- 1-0
1752	Pd John Honicombe for Building the Wall over the Church door	0- 1-6
1759	Pd John Honicombe for taking off some of the Helling[33] to repair the Timber of the Church and laying the same again	0-18-0
	Pd John Honicombe and his Partners as by his Bill	1- 0-6
1760	Pd John Honicombe and his partners as by their Bill	0-16-3
1761	Pd John Honicombe for Nails 2d and for pointing the windows 16d	0- 1-6

These entries seem to refer to Gordon's ancestor, the John Honicombe who married Mary Ough (G6) in 1736. They show that John was, like his son Samuel (G10) and his Jersey descendants, a mason. They also show that he did reasonably well, for by 1759 he had taken on partners. The churchwardens' accounts reveal that most members of the Ough family were also masons, supporting the assumption that the John in the accounts was the one who married Mary Ough. Perhaps John's partners were relatives of his wife.

There are also a number of entries for 'John Honicombe' between 1726 and 1729 [87].

1726	John Honnicomb for carying boards for plancking under the Tower leads	0- 4-0
1726	To John Honicombe for three bush lls lime and carryage	0- 4-4
1726	To John Honnicomb for fetching the Church ladder	0- 1-0
1728	Pd John Honicombe for one days work	0- 1-0
1729	Pd John Hunicombe as by his Bill	0-15-6

These could also refer to the John (G5) who married Mary Ough, but are more likely to refer to the John Honicombe (G1) who married Joan Haukyn in 1703. We know that this John was still alive in 1733, for when Joan died she is described as 'wife' not 'widow' of John Honicombe. That the early entries refer to him is also suggested by the gap between 1729 and 1742 when there are no Honicombe entries, and by the fact that

33. *Helling* was tiling and a *hellier* a tiler. One of the later Honeycombes was described as 'mason and hellier'.

87 *St Cleer Churchwardens' Accounts, 1726, itemising sums spent on the upkeep of the church and other parish expenses.*

the John who married in 1738 would be fairly young in 1726 – only nineteen if he was baptised in 1706/7. The 15s 6d paid in 1729 must have been for more than just minor repairs and the responsibility for such work on an important building like the church would probably not be given to one so young.

That the elder John (G1) was also a mason is indicated by the second entry for 1726 which is almost identical to the entry for 1742 which we know refers to a mason.

We now have three pieces of evidence to support Gordon's assumption that the John married in 1738 was the one baptised in 1706. (i) No other Johns are

baptised either at St Cleer or in neighbouring parishes. (ii) There is no burial in St Cleer or neighbouring parishes which could suggest that the John baptised in 1706 may have died before 1738. (iii) The churchwardens' accounts point to two John Honicombes, both masons, and living in the same parish.

Although cumulatively strong, none of these is conclusive. The clinching piece of evidence comes from an entry for the marriage of John Hony to a Mary Jane in 1759. This marriage was witnessed by a John Honicombe. We can establish from the parish register that Mary Jane (G7) was the daughter of James Jane (G4) and Mary Honeycombe (G3), who married in 1704, the elder sister of the John Honey-combe (G5) baptised 1706/7.[34] Thus John was the uncle of the bride. So the John baptised in 1706/7 had not died young or gone to another parish but was still alive and in St Cleer in 1759. It seems certain he was the John who appears in the churchwardens' accounts for that year. It is worth noting, incidentally, that Gordon missed this vital piece of evidence, since he used only a printed copy of the marriage register, which did not include witnesses.

Transport in St Cleer. Having established Gordon's pedigree back to the John Honicombe (G1) married in 1703, what do we know about him? The answer is very little. We know he married in 1703, and was alive in 1733 when his wife died. He had children baptised in 1704 and 1706 and was almost certainly the John Honicombe buried in 1751. Apart from those entries, our knowledge is entirely confined to the five entries in the churchwardens' accounts which almost certainly refer to him rather than to his son. However, these can tell us more than one would think at first sight. Let us take another look at the three Honeycombe entries for 1726 (page 87 above).

As we have seen, the middle entry establishes that John was a mason. On the face of it, though, fetching and carrying looks like a labourer's job. However, it seems clear that John was not paid for physically carrying the boards and ladder but for providing *transport*. John was almost certainly a mason who, transporting stone all the time for his job, had a suitable vehicle. But what kind of vehicle did he provide? This is difficult.

In 1856, John Allen, in his *History of Liskeard*, wrote that since the roads were 'too bad and steep to be convenient for carriages the general mode of travelling was on horseback, or on foot, goods being conveyed on pack horses, with short or long crooks, or merely slung over the back of the animal'. However, sledges or slides appear also to have been used. According to Allen, 'the first dray having wheels was said to have been introduced into the district about the year 1750, by Salmon

Bowden of St Cleer. The first wagon built in Liskeard was about 1790 for Matthew Johns, of Baytree Hill. Both these were considered curiosities and great advances. The wagon was made of such large timber and found so heavy, that it was seldom used. Even the axle was of wood covered with sheet iron.'[35]

It seems incredible that in 1726, a mason in St Cleer would not transport stones in a cart. Was the church ladder brought by pack-horse? By sledge? We need more evidence than Allen's second-hand report over a century later before we come to any firm conclusion.

But what was John transporting the planks and ladder for?

The Budge affair. The entries for John Honicombe furnish an excellent example of the need to take entries in context, rather than pillaging the records for isolated entries for a surname and ignoring all others. We find that these entries are part of a group of entries for 1726:

Spent when the Parish[ns] mett to weigh the Leads of the Tower	0- 4-0
for fetching and returning the weights	0- 2-0
spent on the Plummers	0- 0-6
Spent when the Parishioners mett to weigh the new Leads of the Tower	0- 1-0
Spent when the Parishioners made up the account with the Plumber	0- 3-4
To the Plumber as by his Bill	19- 0-0
John Honnicomb for carrying boards for plancking under the Tower Leads	0- 4-0

It seems clear from the context that John was transporting boards for scaffolding to be erected to take the lead off the tower to be weighed. The references to the plumbers remind us of the original meaning of the word, workers in lead. But why was the lead being weighed?

To understand what was happening, we need to study the previous year's accounts. A memorandum for 2 February 1725/6 records a meeting held at the house of one Peter Knight 'for the Inspecting the procedures of Charles Budge, one of the Church-wardens for ye year last past relating to his Running ye Leads of ye Church'. The eight leading parishioners who signed the memorandum adjudged these proceed-

34. It could not be a re-marriage of her mother, Mary Jane née Honeycombe (G3) for the couple had many children, the youngest (G11) born in 1778 when the first Mary was seventy-four! This was a case where it was necessary to follow through several generations to establish identity.

35. J. Allen *History of Liskeard and its vicinity* 1856. pp. 337-8.

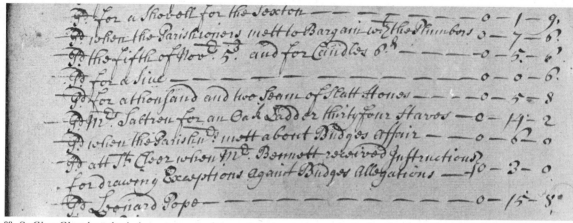

88 *St Cleer Churchwardens' Accounts, 1725. Apparently uninteresting entries lead to the unravelling of a fascinating story.*

ings to be 'all-together unnecessary, Illegall and a great Imposition on ye Parish' and decided to defend the Parish against Budge's allegations which were adjudged 'very fraudulent and unjust'.

What were Budge's allegations? To try and find out we searched the Act Books of the Archdeacon of Bodmin's Court, now deposited in the Cornwall County Record Office at Truro.

On 31 May 1725, there is an entry for Charles Budge 'of the Church of St Cleer' against John Langdon.

The business of rendering account of the leads of the church of St Cleer promoted by Charles Budge, late Churchwarden of St Cleer aforesaid for the last year charged against John Langdon of the other part, formerly churchwarden.[36]

Charles Budge and his fellow churchwarden, John Langdon, should have submitted their accounts for audit soon after 25 March 1724/5. Budge refused to agree to them and so Langdon submitted them alone and they were approved by five leading parishioners. On 31 May, therefore Budge charged his fellow churchwarden in the Archdeacon's Court. It would seem that he claimed that Langdon had misrepresented the amount of lead used in re-leading the church roof and by implication presumably accused him of

36. Cornwall Record Office, Archdeaconry Act Book, No. 28.

pocketing the difference in cost.

On the 17th January, 1725/6 Budge produced his own accounts at the Court and summoned the current churchwardens, Bray and Mullis 'to take his separate account'. The meeting on 2 February recorded in the churchwardens' accounts was the immediate result.

Here we have exactly the same kind of problem as when we studied the minutes and newspaper accounts relating to the founding of the Northfleet Fire Brigade. Only minute attention to detail, together with 'reading between the lines' will reconstruct the full story.

The meeting of 2 February was ostensibly a general meeting of parishioners, notice of which had been given in the church by the churchwardens. However, the memorandum was signed by only eight people – Carew, Langdon, Borrow, Truscott, Bealley, Trubody, Coppelston and Knight. Of these, Langdon was the fellow churchwarden of 1724 whom Budge was accusing. Carew, Borrow, Truscott, Bealley and Knight were the five auditors of Langdon's accounts. So only Trubody and Coppelston were disinterested parties.

It was apparently decided to refute Budge's allegations by taking up all the lead from the roof and weighing it. So for the year 1725, the following entries appear in the accounts:

Pd when the Parishioners mett to bargain with the Plumbers	0- 7- 6
Pd when the Parishioners mett about Budges affair	0- 6- 0

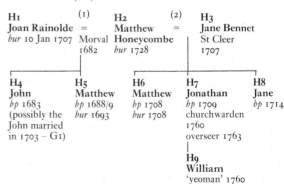

The Accompt of Richard Sowden and Jonathan Honicombe Churchwardens of the said Parish for the year 1760 Rendered to the Parishioners the 24th day of March 1761 as followeth

Receipts
Received of the Preceeding Churchwardens — — 1 11 1
Received, five Rates at 4£ 15s 0d p Rate — — 23 15 0

Total 25 6 1

Disbursments
Pd for Bread and Wine for the Holy Communion — — 2 0 0

39 *St Cleer Churchwardens' Accounts, 1760, showing Jonathan Honicombe as Churchwarden.*

Pd att St Cleer when Mr Bennett received Instructions for drawing Exceptions against Budges Allegations	0- 3- 0
Pd expenses att the Court about Budges affair	0-12-10
Spent when the Parishioners Mett and took up and weighed the leads runn by Charles Budge	0- 6- 0

The weighing of the leads would seem to have been started shortly before the year ended on 24 March and continued into the next year, for there are also the entries for 1726 that we have already noted.

On 20 May 1726, the affair came once again before the Archdeacon's Court. Bennett, a notary public, reported that Peter Truscott had examined Budge's allegations and found them baseless. The case against Langdon and the 1725 churchwardens would appear to have been dismissed.

Was Langden guilty? Or did the weighing of the lead really show that Budge's charges were without foundation? Peter Truscott was scarcely unbiased, being one of the five auditors of the 1724 accounts. Was it a case of corruption in local government with a Watergate-type cover-up? Should one feel sorry for Budge? Had his conscience refused to let him participate in a fraud by his colleagues, perhaps with the connivance of other leading parishioners? Or was he just a lonely and embittered old man – he was about sixty-five years old and his children had long since died. We shall probably never know. But one thing is certain. Gordon's ancestor got some work out of the affair.

Other events in parish records. The Budge Affair shows how parish records may yield not only entries specifically relevant to a family history but ones which help to build up a general picture of life in the parish in the period your ancestors lived there. We learn, too, of celebrations in which they must have participated. For example, in 1759, the accounts record expenditure on celebrations for the capture of Quebec and in 1761 there are entries recording the purchase of a tar barrel and a hogshead of cider to celebrate the coronation of George III.

A weak link. In linking up the Honeycombe entries in the St Cleer parish registers, Gordon identified the John Honicombe married in 1703 (G1) with the John baptised at St Cleer in 1683 (H4), the son of Matthew Honicombe (H2).

H1 (1) H2 (2) H3
Joan Rainolde = Matthew = Jane Bennet
bur 10 Jan 1707 Morval Honeycombe St Cleer
1682 *bur* 1728 1707

H4 H5 H6 H7 H8
John Matthew Matthew Jonathan Jane
bp 1683 *bp* 1688/9 *bp* 1708 *bp* 1709 *bp* 1714
(possibly the *bur* 1693 *bur* 1708 churchwarden
John married 1760
in 1703 – G1) overseer 1763

H9
William
'yeoman' 1760

The main objection to this identification is that Jonathan (H7) the younger brother of the John baptised in 1683 (H4) was almost certainly a farmer. He became a churchwarden in 1760 and overseer in 1763. His son, William (H9), was described as 'yeoman' on his marriage allegation in 1760. Jonathan married in 1726 at the unusually young age of seventeen. Since his father died in 1728, probably aged about sixty-eight, it seems likely that he married on taking over the farm when his father was no longer able to run it. If the elder Matthew (H2), was a farmer, was it likely that his eldest son was a mason? Why did the eldest son not inherit?

There are objections to identifying the John married in 1703 (G1) with the one baptised in 1683 (H4) but they are not insuperable ones. The farm may have been inherited through the second marriage. Alternatively, it may have been too small to support the eldest son who was apprenticed to a mason. By the time Matthew (H2) died or was too old to farm, John (G1) was well established in the trade, as the church-wardens' accounts bear witness.

If that was the case, the decision – perhaps fairly arbitrary – to apprentice John to a mason rather than some other craftsman exerted a profound influence on the family history, for seven consecutive generations were masons, the last being Samuel George Honey-combe, son of the St Helier town crier and uncle of Roy Honeycombe. He died in 1952.

Although Gordon's identification is possible, there is a complete lack of corroboration – either positive evidence supporting it or negative evidence which might help to discount other possibilities. The surviving parish registers of St Cleer start only in 1678. However, some *Bishop's Transcripts* do survive for an earlier period. This is the name usually given to the copies of the parish register sent annually to a vicar's ecclesiastical superior – usually, but not always, the Bishop. They were started in 1598 to provide a security duplicate in cases of forgery, loss or damage. (See page 132.)

Since there was a gap in the bishop's transcripts between 1673 and 1678, we cannot be sure that there was not another John baptised then. Since the St Cleer registers do not differentiate between adults and children, the John Honicombe baptised in 1683 could easily be the one buried in 1690.

Neighbouring parishes. The registers of neighbouring parishes revealed other possibilities. The John baptised in St Cleer in 1683 might have been the John married at St Germans in 1709 and buried there in 1751. Equally, Gordon's ancestor, the John married in St Cleer in 1703, could have been the John baptised at Menheniot in 1668. It is a great mistake to treat a parish as an isolated unit. As we have seen in previous chapters, many craftsmen and labourers did move from parish to parish seeking work. If the John married in 1703 was a mason, he probably moved around more than most of the other craftsmen, for a mason tends to be a mobile occupation, like a millwright, rather than a static one like a sawyer.

Gordon's pedigree, therefore, cannot at present be substantiated beyond the marriage of 1703.

Further back. In striving to push his genealogy further back, Gordon collected a considerable number of Honeycombe entries from seventeenth-century Cornish parish registers. At Calstock, there were several different Honeycombe families when the parish registers started in the mid-seventeenth century. There was also a substantial branch at Callington, of which it was established that the Honicombes of Menheniot, the next parish to St Cleer, were an offshoot. It therefore seemed virtually certain that the St Cleer Honeycombes were descended from those of Calstock or from those of Callington. Many sources such as bishop's transcripts, wills, protestation returns and tax returns were used to try and find the link.

Bishop's transcripts. The surviving St Cleer bishop's transcripts before the start of the parish register in 1678 were not very helpful, revealing only a 'William, base son of Margaret Honicombe' baptised in 1635. However, that the Honeycombes were in St Cleer through most of the seventeenth century is suggested by the burial in Liskeard on 8 January 1653/4 of Elizabeth, wife of Anthonye Honnicombe of St Cleere and the burial at St Cleer itself of an Anthony Honicombe in 1697.

Wills. Gordon had searched for Honeycombe wills and had drawn a complete blank as far as St Cleer was concerned. A search for all surnames of related families proved equally unproductive. It was then

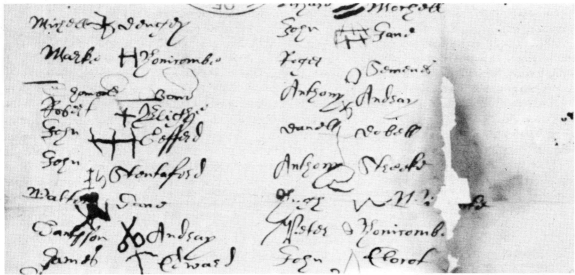

90 *Protestation return for Calstock, 1641. Note the personal marks, including that of a tailor. There are two marks made by Honicombes, by Mark and Peter.*

decided to study *every* seventeenth-century will for St Cleer and neighbouring parishes in case any of them mentioned Honeycombe relatives. For St Cleer, this produced an inventory of 1696 attested by Matthew, and wills and inventories in 1677, 1679 and 1680 witnessed by an Anthony Honeycombe. In 1670, a John Honeycombe junior was left one sheep.

The Protestation returns. In 1641, the Long Parliament, finding that 'by the designs of priests and Jesuits' there were 'plots and conspiracies to subvert the fundamental laws of the kingdom and to introduce Arbitrarie and Tyrannical government' made a declaration of abhorrence of such designs and took an oath to oppose them. All males over eighteen years of age were invited to sign, and virtually all did. The original returns, county by county, and parish by parish, are in the House of Lords Record Office. In the case of Cornwall, we were doubly fortunate. Firstly, the Cornish returns are the most complete in England. They contain 30,000 names and only four parishes are missing, though unfortunately these include Truro and St Austell, where we know from parish records there were Honeycombes. Secondly, Cornwall is one of the counties for which the returns have been printed. They list five Honeycombes in Calstock, [90]

two in Callington and a few others scattered among various parishes. The most obviously relevant entries, however, are those for St Cleer, where there are three Honicombes – an Anthony senior, an Anthony junior and a John.

Hearth tax. For 1662 and 1664 there are hearth tax returns at the Public Record Office.[36a] All householders were taxed according to the number of hearths they had. Although there is a very full list for St Cleer, with ninety-one names on it, there are *no* Honeycombes. It is possible that the Honeycombes were too poor to be listed and were lodgers in some other household. However, this does not seem like the John junior or the Anthony who witnessed wills in 1670, 1677, 1679 and 1680. Moreover, the St Cleer list is very comprehensive. There are ninety-one names on the main list, eight on an 'arrears received' list and another seventeen on a list of 'Hearthes not mentioned in the former returns', so it is far more likely that they simply were not there. What is very puzzling, however, is that they

36a. For some counties, there are also returns in the county record office, and for many others at least some of the returns have been published. An indispensable finding aid for both published and unpublished returns is Jeremy Gibson's *The Hearth Tax, Other Later Stuart Tax* lists and the Association Oath Rolls (*See p.177*) do not appear either for the neighbouring parishes of Menheniot or Liskeard. But there was a John at Lawhitton.

It could be that the John Honeycombe at St Cleer in 1641 was the same man who was at Lawhitton in 1642. He could also be the John baptised at Menheniot in 1607, the John who had a child baptised at Menheniot in 1643 and the John Honeycombe of the parish of Lanreath, labourer whose will was made and proved in 1676/7.

Unfortunately, with a name as common as John, such identifications can be little more than conjecture. But in his will, the last John was described as 'labourer' and a series of moves like this would be consistent with hirings for one year at different places. Landless labourers have always had to move about to a certain extent. When sources for identifying moves peter out, wishful thinking tends to make the genealogist assume that the John who was in a parish in 1641 and 1670 was there in between. This may well be the case and, equally well, it may not. At the same time, we must not fall into the trap of identifying as a single individual Johns in two or three different places who are nothing to do with each other.

Other tax lists. There are a number of other tax returns at the Public Record Office. Poll taxes were levied on all over the age of sixteen in 1641, 1660, 1666 and 1677. Where the returns survive, they are very useful as they often give relationships. Alas, they exist only for some Cornish parishes, St Cleer not among them.

Conclusion. It can be seen that although the pedigree is firm back only to a marriage in 1703, we have many pieces of the jigsaw for a few generations before that, and though there are not enough yet to distinguish the whole picture, parts of it are clear, and we shall continue trying to get more.

In general terms, the main possibilities are: (i) If we accept Gordon's assumption that the John married in St Cleer in 1703 was the one baptised in 1683, the pedigree is possible for three generations further back – Matthew, Anthony junior (over 18 in 1641,

witnessed documents in 1677, 1679 and 1680, and died in 1697) and Anthony senior, (probably born about 1590, wife buried at Liskeard in 1653). (ii) There may have been a second family – John senior and John junior – resident in St Cleer from before 1641 to John junior's death in 1716. On the other hand, these Johns may equally well be a John father and son who appear on the pedigree of the Menheniot Honeycombes. In either case, it is just as likely that Gordon's ancestor, John, who married in 1703 belonged to this family as to that of the Anthonys and Matthew.

About the only place in Cornwall for which we have any reference to the surname before the sixteenth century is Calstock, and it seems a very reasonable assumption that all the Honeycombe families in the area eventually go back to the Calstock Honeycombes. Whatever speculations we make, we must, however, always bear in mind Anthony Camp's salutary words of warning:

There is very rarely anything to be called a 'gap' in a pedigree. A pedigree goes as far as the evidence will take it and then it ends. The further ancestry, when found, is practically bound to lie in the direction least expected.[37]

He goes on to stress the necessity of approaching the matter with an open mind, without attempting to force the evidence to meet any preconceptions.

In the nineteenth and twentieth centuries, the evidence is fairly extensive and usually only one hypothesis fits the facts. Even here, however, it is easy to make errors. of identification, particularly with common surnames. As the amount of evidence diminishes, so are there more and more possible pedigrees which will fit the available data. Further research may eliminate some of these, but before 1750 it is unusual to be able to establish a pedigree of a landless family with absolute certainty. Often the best you can hope for is *reasonable probability*. In the case of the Honeycombes before 1703 we do not have even that.

37. A.J. Camp *Everyone has roots: an introduction to genealogy* Star Books, 1978. p. 21.

9 Honeycombe Hall

It could be argued that as we have taken the Honeycombe family history as our example, this book should have ended with the previous chapter. Gordon's pedigree cannot be established beyond a marriage in 1703, and anything further back cannot really be said to be part of his family history.

However, assuming that you have been more fortunate than Gordon, and have established your pedigree back to the sixteenth or seventeenth century, how can you find out more about the lives of your ancestors?

Without the newspapers, which, as we have seen from the stories of Samuel and Thirza, can prove such a rich source for family history in the nineteenth century, we may have to rely upon painstakingly collecting brief references from such local records as happen to survive – one ancestor may witness a document, another appear on a list of tenants. However, what tends to be forgotten is that the basic sources can often be almost as useful for amplifying the family history as they are for constructing a genealogy.

Parish registers. On 21 June 1626, an Anthony Honicombe was buried at Tavistock and on 18 September, his brother, Edmund. We have not established their connection with the St Cleer Honeycombes, but it seems likely that the Anthonys at St Cleer, Calstock and Tavistock were closely related. Two or more family deaths in one year, though not unusual at that time, are always worth investigating. 1626 turned out to be a plague year. The 575 burials in Tavistock include thirty-five for June, forty-nine for July, 115 for August and 131 for September. The average for these months over the previous few years had been eight. With the onset of the colder weather there was a dramatic decline – eighty-six in October, twenty-nine in November and thirteen in December.

On 2 December 1626, Prudence Honeycomb, probably Edmund's widow, married a widower, Giles Collamore. A period of high mortality was usually followed by a substantial increase in the number of marriages. This was because wages tended to rise with the shortage of labour, because young people inherited the property of their deceased relatives and because, as in our example, at least one of the partners had been bereaved and had a young family which needed looking after. In the following few years there is usually a 'bulge' in the baptisms. So a plague year has quite a ripple effect on the registers.

As in the case of Dorothy's death from cholera in 1849, the date of an ancestor's death may well provide the clue to an interesting story, though without death certificates, we must rely heavily upon the circumstantial evidence of statistics unless the vicar or clerk helpfully recorded an outbreak of plague or smallpox [91]. A simple count of the numbers of baptisms, marriages and burials is always worthwhile to see what trends become apparent. In this way, the baptisms, marriages and burials of your family can be related to the demography of the local community as a whole.

St Cleer register, 1741, recording a smallpox epidemic.

Wills and inventories. If parish registers may help to highlight years of pestilence or famine, wills and inventories can provide plenty of clues about the day to day lives of the testators. Nearly all the eighteen Honeycombe wills which Gordon located for the sixteenth, seventeenth and eighteenth centuries mention not only furniture, household articles and working tools, but farm animals, showing how most people drew part of their livelihood from agriculture. Thus John Honeycombe, blacksmith of St Kew in

92 *An inventory of the goods of a seventeenth-century blacksmith. Note the corn and animals as well as the tools of his trade.*

1620 [**92**], left not only 'one pair of bellows, an anvil, and the other working tools' valued at £4, and 'fourteen scythes, other edge tools and other ironwork' valued at £5 6s 8d, clearly his stock, but also four cows, two heifers and one little yearling' valued at £13 13s 4d, 'six ewes and lambs, one ram and four little pigs' valued at £3, and 'geese and other poultry' valued at 3s 4d. So his farm animals were worth a great deal more than his blacksmith's working tools and stock.

Some of the bequests on wills really are quite extraordinary. In 1607, Joan Honeycombe of Calstock left to her son Anthony (perhaps the Anthony who died at Tavistock in 1626,) 'the fourth part of one spit, the fourth part of an iron bar, and the fourth part of one winding-sheet'. Joan mentioned four other children

in the will. These peculiar bequests were not repeated for any of them. Nor did any of these items appear in the inventory. Could it be that Anthony was being cut out of the will, not with the proverbial shilling, but with significantly useless items? This may be the only clue we have to a family quarrel. On the other hand, Anthony may have already received his share.

Church seating plan. Among the documents in Calstock parish church was a church seating plan. This was useful as it was both virtually a census of all adults in the parish and an indicator of status.

Before the Reformation there were few pews in churches. Shortly after the Reformation the gentry families began to instal private pews in the nave and

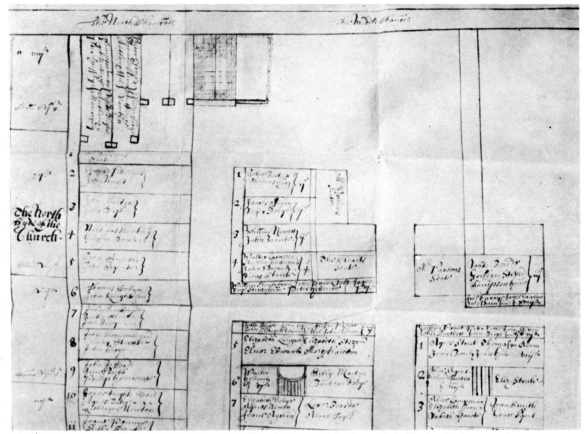

93 *Part of the Calstock Church seating plan, c. 1590. Note the absence of the altar and the Honicombes in pews 4, 8, 9.*

they were followed by the farmers and craftsmen and eventually by the labourers. By 1600, in most parishes, people had fixed places – in a time of compulsory churchgoing this made it easy to check absences.

Many seating plans of the period owed their existence to the *Instrument of Government* of December 1653. This installed Cromwell as Lord Protector and ended the religious uncertainty of the previous few years. In effect, parish churches became independent congregations, and though all Puritan sects were tolerated, such toleration was not extended to Roman Catholics or to 'prelatists', i.e. Anglicans who held fast to episcopacy and the Book of Common Prayer. Church attendance was, however, still obligatory and persistent absence a sure indication of

papistry or prelacy. So an up-to-date seating plan was essential to identify those who rejected the new settlement. But the Calstock plan is much earlier than this; the Honeycombes listed were living *c.* 1590.

In working out the seating, an order of precedence was strictly observed, and the right to seats descended with the possession of the particular farm or cottage to which they belonged. In this way the social structure of the community was formalised. Thus in 1701 the antiquarian, Richard Gough based his survey of the parishioners of Myddle, Shropshire on such a plan.[38] In Calstock, of no less than eleven Honeycombes on

38. R. Gough, *Observations concerning the seatings in Myddle and the families to which they belonged*, 1701

the plan, Stephen Honicomb would seem to have had the highest status. He was in the fourth pew from the front on the left-hand side of the nave, beside the clerk's seat – a pew for four costing 4s 0d a year [93].

Tax returns. Before the seventeenth century, records listing individuals are rather scanty. Tax returns, however, may still be useful. In most cases only the better-off were taxed, but the great subsidy of 1524–7 fell on the working population as well. Where the returns survive, they are as useful as the poll tax or hearth tax. Unfortunately, there were no returns for East Cornwall. What did survive, however, at the Public Record Office, was a return for a subsidy in 1558, which covered most hundreds in Cornwall. This revealed Honeycombes only at Calstock. However, they must have been of some standing, or they would not have appeared at all – only fourteen names were listed for that parish. Two Honeycombes appear – Stephen and Richard. They had no land and so were not freeholders. However, they had goods valued at £6 on which they paid a subsidy of 10s 0d. Only two landowners paid more. Most paid only 8s 4d. No Honeycombe entries were found for Calstock in subsidies levied in 1613, 1624, 1625 and 1626. So there was no Honeycombe of any standing in Calstock at that time. However, in each case, a William Honicombe appears under Southill and Callington.

The most exciting tax reference, however, was in the Calstock returns for the 1327 Lay Subsidy, when a John Honycome paid 12d. This is the earliest known reference to the surname.

94 *Lay subsidy 1327 showing John Honycome. His name appears halfway down the list, reflecting his social position.*

Manorial records. Far more informative than tax returns are *Manorial Records*. These are probably the most valuable class of genealogical records after parish registers and wills. Indeed, some claim that they are of even greater importance than either, for not only may a single entry provide a three generation pedigree, but some court rolls go back to the thirteenth century, and many to the fourteenth. For the bulk of the population they are almost the only source for both genealogy and family history during the medieval period.

Calstock was (and still is) a manor of the Duchy of Cornwall, the title of Duke going with that of Prince of Wales. The earlier manorial records are in the Public Record Office, the later ones in the Duchy of Cornwall Office. These records are in three series, – *Assession Rolls*, dealing with the assessment of the rents every seven years[39] and which record land transactions in some detail, *Manor Court Rolls*, dealing with admissions between assessions and with lawsuits, and the *Court Leet* records, dealing with the general maintenance of law and order.

Assession Rolls. Although there were a few Calstock assession rolls for the fourteenth century, the continuous series does not start until 1500. From them Gordon was able to build up a number of tenuously connected pedigrees of Honeycombes from 1500 to 1750 and transfers between assessions – recorded in the Manor Court rolls – added further details. In the seventeenth and eighteenth centuries, these pedigrees were, of course, amplified from parish registers and wills.

39. In 1640, the Duchy of Cornwall consisted of seventy-eight manors. These included seventeen 'ancient manors' which were originally part of the Earldom of Cornwall and were conferred on the Duchy by a charter of Edward III in 1337. These seventeen ancient manors (which included Calstock) were known as *assessional* manors from the fact that from the early fourteenth century, when the records start, there were, in addition to the freehold tenements and a decreasing number of ordinary tenancies in veilleinage (i.e., where the tenants were still villeins or serfs), a large proportion of tenements held by a system peculiar to Devon and Cornwall, according to a *convention* or agreement and a payment of an *assessed rent*. The tenants holding lands under this agreement were called *conventioners* or *conventionary tenants* and the rents were assessed periodically, generally at intervals of seven years. By the sixteenth century, the seven year period was disappearing and the lease of a life or three lives was the rule. (*Victoria history of the County of Cornwall 1924*. ed. by W. Page, vol. 1, p. 8)

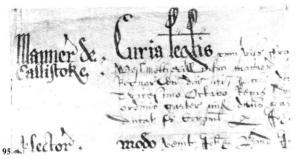

95

Manor Court Rolls. As well as land transfers, the Calstock Manor Court dealt with civil suits, frequently for trespass. For example, in 1501, Thomas Honeycombe complained that a white sheep belonging to Robert Hylland had strayed at Dyzyth on 10 August, and that a male mule of his had strayed at Calstock on 9 September. In 1516, Thomas himself was presented for striking John Coker with a billhook and drawing blood. The poor scribe, not knowing the Latin for billhook was forced to resort to '*Vi et armis videlicet uno Estrumento vocato Bylhoke*' (by force of arms, that is to say an instrument called a bill-hook).

Court Leet Rolls. The Court Leet dealt in the main with various offences against the custom of the manor. Offenders were presented by one of the manorial officials, usually the tithing man. There are several hundred entries concerning Honeycombes, which together present a vivid picture of manorial life which needs only a Hardy to recreate it.

Thus in 1470, Geoffrey Honycombe and seven others were presented for not repairing their ruined

96

houses, and in 1487, Richard and Geoffrey Honycomb and their servants were accused of killing four sheep belonging to John Taylor.

In 1541, Joan Honeycomb, Thomas Honeycomb and six others were presented for brewing and breaking the 'assize.' This referred to the 'assize of ale', an attempt to ensure the quality of ale by having assessors for each county fixing the proportions of the various ingredients. An ale-taster elected by the villagers was responsible for presenting offenders at the manorial court. The assessors came round unannounced from time to time to see that the ale tasters were doing their job.

On 27 March 1559, there was a family tragedy. Philip Honycomb who held a moiety (half) of a holding at Crosse hanged himself. This was reported to the next court on 10 April. His goods and chattels were valued by Richard Honycomb and Roger Daukin at 25s od. His widow, Margaret, inherited the moiety for the remainder of her life, did homage for it and was admitted on payment of 8d [96].

The interesting point about this entry is that the luckless Margaret not only lost her husband so tragically, but lost all her goods and chattels as well – for the property of a suicide was forfeit to the Crown. We may presume that she bought them back for 25s od, this no doubt being paid, like a fine of admission, over several years.

The overall impressions obtained from the large number of Honeycombe entries are firstly, the continuous extraction of money from tenants for one reason or another; secondly, the number of Honeycombes presented for debt, and thirdly, the way everything you could or could not do was regulated by manorial custom. For example, in 1606, John Honicombe was presented 'in that he had cultivated corn on the customary land of the king within the aforesaid manor and carried off the straw out of the manor against the custom of the manor'.

Lastly, the Court Leet also dealt with cases that one might rather have expected to find in the ecclesiastical court. Thus in 1607, Susanna Honeycombe was presented as *communis rixatrix et obcurgatrix* (a common scold and shrew) 'to the nuisance of her neighbours and to the bad example of others'.

The origins of the Honeycombes. What is the earliest evidence we have for the use of the surname in Calstock? Although the main series of assession rolls starts in 1500, we have rolls for four years in the fourteenth century: 1333, 1340, 1347 and 1356.

The first Honeycombe of whom we have any knowledge is found in the first assession roll for

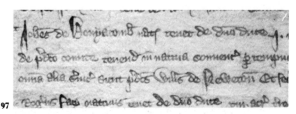

97

Calstock dated 1333, and is almost certainly identical with the John Honycome of the 1327 Lay Subsidy. In the 1333 roll we learn that: 'John de Honya combe "nativus" (ie, serf) took 1 dwelling, 32 acres of English land in Cornish furlongs which the same held at Honyacombe to be held for the aforesaid time at the Lord's will.' For this, he paid 3s 10d a year plus 22d for a further four acres to be reclaimed from the waste. He had to put in two days a year compulsory work at the hatch at Calstock Weir.

There are several interesting points about this extract. Firstly, we are back to the very beginning of the system by which the Honeycombes held their first land for centuries. This system, known as *Conventionary Tenure*, was introduced in 1333 by John of Eltham, Earl of Cornwall and with its seven year rent assessments, fines and certain customary services, marked an improvement in status from the condition of villeinage in which the villein (i.e. serf) could not move from his holding without his lord's permission and his chattels were forfeit to the lord on his death. Conventionary tenants, however, were of two kinds. There were 'free conventioners' whose heirs made a payment known as a 'heriot' on their death (this was usually the best beast but later became converted into money payments) and villein conventioners (*conventionari nativi*) who forfeited all their goods. It seems clear that John was a villein or serf, who, in 1333, when the new system was started, was granted as a villein conventioner the thirty-two acres of land which he had previously held as an ordinary villein.

Secondly, the steward took pains to point out that the holding was in Cornish furlongs, or half acres. In many English manors, the holding would be in scattered strips in the open fields. A strip was originally one acre – one furrow long (furlong) or 220 yards and twenty-two yards wide. Hence, an acre was 4,840 square yards. The open field system, however, never operated in Cornwall. In Calstock, the holdings seem

to have been enclosed and based on the Cornish unit of half an acre; 220 yards by eleven yards.

Thirdly, although there were no other compulsory services, John was obliged to put in two days' service a year maintaining the hatch at Calstock Weir.

In 1337, a manorial 'extent' or survey, listed John as holding only thirty-two acres of English land in Cornish furlongs, the four acres of waste being by then held by a Michael Burgess. He still had to put in two days work a year at the hatch, had to attend the manorial court every three weeks, and might be called upon to be reeve, tithing man or beadle. At his death, his chattels would go to the lord [97].

We can trace almost the exact date when the Honeycombes ceased to be villeins and became free, for in 1356, William Honyacombe appeared on the list of 'free conventioners' when he took possession of one dwelling, thirty-two acres of English land in Cornish half acres 'which John Honyacombe took in "villein convention" at the last assession' at a rent of 3s 10d. He paid a fine of 16s [98, 99]. It seems likely that William was the son of John.

98

99

Historical background. As with work on later periods, a series of entries like this becomes intelligible only after finding out about national and local history.

It surely cannot be coincidence that this is the very first assession roll after the Black Death which devastated England in 1348–9. Even in 1352 and 1353, the receiver of the Prince's revenues in Cornwall said that he had neither been able to let the lands nor draw the rents 'because the said tenements for the most part have remained unoccupied and the lands laid waste for want of tenants in place of those who died in the mortal pestilence lately raging in the said county'.[40]

When tenants were everywhere at a premium, the only way to keep a villein from running away was to give him his freedom. The Black Death undoubtedly speeded up the process of manumission – the grant of freedom – which was already in train. In 1355, a Commission was appointed to lease and rent all lands in Cornwall, whether held by tenants or landowners, whether for life or for a term of years, and to convert fines or tenements leased for life into fixed yearly rents.[41] It would seem very probable that William received his freedom as a result of the rationalisation that resulted from the work of this commission.

Surnames. It would be nice to be confident that despite a few 'gaps' here and there, we have here Gordon's two earliest-known ancestors. This may well be the case. However, it may not. To put these entries into perspective, we must know something about the origin of surnames.

Although surnames for a few landed families go back to the eleventh century, for the mass of the population, surnames developed in the second half of the thirteenth century, when the increase in population, and the over-use of a few very popular Christian names such as John, Richard and William made a further means of identification essential. At first neither fixed nor hereditary, they grew out of patronymics, i.e. naming after the father (John Johnson), occupational descriptions, (John the Miller), place names, (John of Honeycombe) and personal descriptions or nicknames, (John Short, John Peacock).

The one thing we can say with certainty is that the surname Honeycombe is derived from the place in the parish of Calstock, and not vice versa, as John Symons Honeycombe would have us believe in his fictitious account of the family's origins.

When the more or less consecutive series of manorial rolls for Calstock started in 1470, we are, at most, only a couple of centuries away from the origin of surnames. Indeed, since Cornwall tended to lag somewhat behind the rest of the country in the adoption of hereditary surnames it may well be only three or four generations. This was ample time for the descendants of one original Honeycombe progenitor to have spread over the various hamlets of the parish of Calstock. However, one's first reaction is to regard it as improbable. *Honeycombe* is typical of rarer surnames, which are usually derived from place names. However, if a name is rare, it is usually not a place name you will find on a small-scale map, but a hamlet or district within a parish, as Honeycombe is in Calstock. In some cases a topographical surname derives from an ancestor owning land in the place of that name, like the Moncreiffes of Easter Moncreiffe in Perthshire, or the Stonors of Stonor in Oxfordshire. More often a topographical surname was assumed when an ordinary person had left the place of that name and was used in his new place of residence as a means of distinguishing him from another person of the same Christian name.

If this is what happened in the case of the Honeycombes of Calstock, it would not be suprising that in 1500, we find families of Honeycombes in virtually all the hamlets of Calstock except Honeycombe. Unless there is evidence to link one family with another, the first presumption must be that several different individuals moved from Honeycombe to the nearby hamlets and were known perhaps, as Richard of Honeycombe, John of Honeycombe, and William of Honeycombe, but were not related to each other at all.

We have seen how the earliest manorial records of Calstock reveal Honeycombes in the fourteenth century. Alas, not only is it by no means certain that later Honeycombes are descended from them, but we cannot even be certain that their surname was hereditary. 'Of Honeycombe' may well be a description rather than a surname in the modern sense of the word. The fact remains, however, that although the Honeycombes in 1500 were living elsewhere in Calstock, the first Honeycombes of which we have any record *were* living in Honeycombe. What is the most likely explanation?

40. Quoted in *Victoria history of the County of Cornwall* 1924. vol. 1, p. 11.

41. L.E. Elliott-Binns *Medieval Cornwall* Methuen 1955. p. 172.

Honeycombe. The clue is provided by the long series of entries for Honeycombe in the assession rolls. There is always only one entry for Honeycombe – for one messuage and thirty acres of land. Even in 1846, when Honeycombe was held by Edward Williams, if one discounts land he held in the other side of the road and elsewhere, we are left with a holding of thirty acres with clearly defined boundaries on all sides save one.

Why the thirty-two acres of the fourteenth century had become thirty acres in 1500 is a matter for speculation. Perhaps the construction of one of the roads or a house and garden robbed the tenement of two acres. However, it seems highly probable that although a villein, John of Honeycombe was so called because his thirty-two acres *was* Honeycombe. He was, in a very literal sense, Honeycombe of Honeycombe. The villein status was clearly by this time little more than a technicality for he must surely be the John of Honycombe who was assessed at 12d in the subsidy roll of 1327, one of thirty-five persons paying between 6d and 4s. One would hardly expect to find a villein on the list.

In 1364, Honycombe had passed from William Honycombe to John, son of John Clerk. We have no record of William's acquiring a larger holding, and unfortunately, this roll is the last one extant before 1500. However, since in 1500 John Honycombe of Trehill paid precisely the same rent, and owed the same services as John and William paid in the fourteenth century, (3s 10d plus two days work in the demesne land) it does seem possible that the later Honeycombes do, in fact, descend from the two fourteenth century ones. However, it cannot be stressed enough that we have no proof.

And what of Honeycombe Hall which, according to John Symons Honeycombe, was built by the Honeycombes in the reign of Elizabeth? As Gordon discovered on that first, exciting trip to Calstock in 1959, there is indeed a house at Honeycombe, now the headquarters and shop for a caravan park. The most charitable observer, however, could not describe it as a Hall. Nor, of course, was there ever any manor of Honeycombe – it was always held of the manor of Calstock. The house is such a queer hotch-potch of buildings of various dates tenuously linked together, and refaced in the early nineteenth century, that it is very difficult to put a date on the oldest part. Over the door is the date 1656, but older photographs show that this was once 1856, and EW can only be Edward Williams, to whom there is a memorial stained glass window in Calstock Church: 'In memory of Edward Williams Esq., of Honicombe 1892 [100].

There was certainly a house of some kind there when the property was purchased in 1798 by John Pearson Foote, who installed George Marshall as his tenant. In 1806, it was bought by John Williams of Scorrier, a mine-owner, and it probably took on something like its present apperance in 1856 when Edward Williams presumably added the porch.

One thing is clear – the house had nothing whatever to do with the Honeycombe family, whose last known date of residence in Honeycombe was 1364. One cannot help feeling that whether or not he was the ancestor of John Symons Honeycombe (and of Gordon) John de Honyacombe, the villein who held Honeycombe in 1333, must somewhere be having a quiet chuckle.

100

Sources and Approaches

I Family History

In recent years an increasing number of people interested in their ancestors have decided that merely making family trees with names, dates, places and occupations is not satisfying enough. They do not want just to find out *who* their ancestors were; they want to know what sort of people they were and what kind of lives they lived. Many people think of history as a vast accumulation of facts from which the historian selects those he wishes to put into his book. However, history is not merely a chronicle of past events, but *an enquiry into the thoughts and actions of people in the past*. Family history has, until recently, been much neglected by academic historians. Yet the family is the most fundamental social unit. It could be argued that in studying the history of a family, the individual comes much closer to an understanding of people in the past than he does by traditional approaches to either national or local history. For studying the history of large units often involves the risk of losing human beings altogether in a haze of abstraction and generalisation. Family history, however, is the hub where national, local, family and personal factors all meet in individual experiences of slumps and booms, of migration and of war (see page 68). As has been stressed elsewhere (pages 28 and 68), the historian must also remember the importance of chance in human affairs.

Historical insights. The family historian can utilise the history of his particular family as the example through which to seek four kinds of historical insights.
Environmental insights. Firstly, he wishes to understand the physical environment in which his ancestors lived, the local industries and the patterns of communication. To what extent were their lives influenced by local factors? How did they in turn seek to modify their environment? If they lived in small rural communities, as most did before the Industrial Revolution, were they farmers, labourers or craftsmen? Was the farming arable, pastoral or mixed? What was the local system of land tenure – scattered strips in open fields, small peasant holdings or large tenant farms?

Social insights. There is, however, more to an environment than fields and hedges, bricks and mortar, crafts and factories. The family historian is also seeking *social* insights. How was the family organised and what were the predominant patterns of family life? What was the structure of the community in which an ancestor lived and worked? What was his role and status?
Ideas, beliefs and values. Thirdly, the family historian is also very much concerned with religious and political beliefs, moral values and accepted modes of conduct.
Personal insights. Fourthly, we must not forget that our ancestors were not mere products of their physical, social and ideological environment, but were individuals with their own personalities and motives. However, unless we are fortunate enough to have old letters, diaries or memoirs, we can gain a 'personal' insight only into ancestors within living memory, for biographical details gained from impersonal records may well not be the events which our ancestors would have regarded as the most significant in their lives.

Similarities and differences. In striving for various insights into the lives of our ancestors, we should ask ourselves how they were similar to us and how they were different. Like biography, family history is concerned with individuals, but it has the additional advantage of spanning several generations. It is, therefore, well placed to throw light upon which aspects of human behaviour are universal and which are most strongly influenced by time and place.

Evidence. The writing of any kind of history must be based upon evidence. The most reliable evidence is that obtained from *primary* sources (i.e. original records such as parish registers or manorial records), though even these vary in reliability. A printed pedigree or family history cannot be regarded as reliable, though it may well be soundly based. If no sources are cited, as in the case of the *Brief Abstract*, every statement is suspect.

II Oral Evidence

It is important to contact as many elderly relatives as possible as soon as possible. Unlike most other stages of the investigation, you cannot postpone it until your retirement. By all means file the information away and come back to it in twenty years time, for, barring an unlucky accident, the records will still be there – your relatives may not.

You do not only need the *memories* of your relatives, but also their *documents* – family Bibles, letters and above all, photographs, and every effort should be made to locate these before the thoughtless destruction which so often occurs on the death of an older member of the family. Many relatives are, understandably, reluctant to part with their treasures, but are usually willing to lend documents and photographs for copying.

The oral stage is never completed, as documentary evidence prompts further questions to ask relatives and helps them to be more precise about things they have heard. Oral evidence and work on records should go together.

Locating relatives. To locate relatives you will often have only the most slender clues to go on. An elderly cousin may say, 'I remember that when I was a child we used to visit relatives at Harwich, called Thompson, but I don't know how they fitted in.' Such clues should be followed up assiduously. There is nearly always a way of tracing someone if you try hard enough. Even if your relatives left the district years ago, there may still be someone who remembers where they went – a next-door neighbour, the lady in the post office, friends in the pub!

Researching a surname. Your name does not have to be as rare as Honeycombe for it to be worth collecting every instance of the name you come across. Relatives are likely to turn up in the most unlikely places, and a bank of miscellaneous material may provide possible leads when your researches have ground to a halt. British and foreign telephone directories are extraordinarily useful, and as Gordon discovered, can locate unsuspected branches of the family. Telephone directories may even be useful for more common surnames, for it is often easier to discard ninety-eight percent of the material as irrelevant than to find the relevant two percent by any other method. Telephoning people produces an instant answer, and is still relatively cheap.

Female lines. One error Gordon made was to take too little interest in the female lines. He did not care very much what children his great-aunts had, because they were not Honeycombes. However, as he discovered much later, he would have done better to contact their descendants than those of *male* Honeycombes, for a daughter of his great-aunt, Margaret Fox, had several crucial family documents, including the obituary of his great-grandfather. This should hardly have been surprising. For while men tend to be mainly concerned with their jobs, politics and sport, interest in family matters is more often a female pre-occupation.

Documents may have been handed down the female line time and again. Sometimes, with two or three changes of name on marriage, the memory may have been lost as to how the people mentioned in the documents were connected. So it is important to trace sideways and downwards before trying to get back any further.

Letters. When the first contact with a distant relative is by letter, explain exactly who you are, what you are trying to achieve, and why, as people may be suspicious of your intentions if you are unknown to them. Suggest also, that if for any reason they cannot help you, they recommend another member of the family who might. It is best in the first letter to concentrate upon the genealogical information. Enclose a copy of the relevant branch of the family tree. Include on this all the details which you know and ask them to add to or amend it. In particular, you should mention the six kinds of genealogical information itemised below.

If the first letter elicits a favourable response, it may be worth making a personal visit or telephone call, or if these are impracticable, sending a list of specific points which need clarification. At this point, you might tentatively raise the question of borrowing documents or photographs for copying. Later letters may take up biographical or more general historical points, though correspondence is the least satistifactory way of obtaining such information.

Finally, it is courteous to repay relatives' helpfulness by later sending them a more complete copy of the relevant parts of the family tree, including their relationship with you, and, if possible, biographical notes as well. These may well have a spin-off in that they may be proudly shown to other relatives who may be interested enough to contact you.

It is worth trying to persuade your relatives to write down their memoirs as Gordon did with his Aunt Dorothy. This should not, however, be regarded as a substitute for the personal interview, for elderly people often place little importance on what they regard as mundane items, and hesitate to commit family gossip to paper.

What to ask. When questioning elderly relatives, it is best to try and separate out the *genealogical*, *biographical* and *historical* information. Although they will inevitably spill over into each other, if they are kept distinct in the interviewer's mind, important points will not get overlooked. Usually, each of them will require a separate visit.

Genealogical information. In particular you should ask for:
  (i) full names and relationships;
 (ii) exact dates (or failing that, approximations) of births, marriages and deaths;
(iii) occupations (remembering that people may have had a number of different occupations during their careers);
(iv) all the places where each person resided, including full addresses of all living relatives;
 (v) any family documents or photographs which might be helpful;
(vi) any traditions about the family's origins.

Without such a check-list, many researchers return home only to find that they lack important dates, places or occupations.

The information is best recorded in the form of mini family trees, each showing exactly the information which has been obtained from a particular relative – no more and no less. When these are copied up on to your master chart, check carefully for their completeness, and make a list of any points which need clarification on the next visit.

Biographical information. It is advisable to approach this systematically, asking about each of the individuals on the family tree in turn and obtaining a brief outline of their lives. Do not go into great detail initially, or many individuals may not be covered at all. Although the information may be rather sketchy, if further talks with the relative are not possible, it will at least provide something to go on. Further details can be added at subsequent visits, until a whole series of mini-biographies has been built up.

Relatives are often very vague about dates. However, reference to events in their own lives, (How old were you? Where were you living?) or national events (Was it before the War?) will often narrow the period down very considerably.

Historical information. If time permits, pick out an interesting period in your informant's life and try to obtain information on the full environmental and social context. As with the genealogical data, it is helpful to have a check-list of questions, thus ensuring the coverage of some of the more interesting topics, such as the relationship between parents and children, or the impact of religion. These questions should not be rigidly adhered to, or they might destroy the spontaneity and individuality of what the relative has to say. But they may serve as a reminder when there is a lull in the conversation, or when something that has been said provides a natural lead-in.

In setting your immediate ancestors in their total context and in recreating the fabric of the society in which they lived, you are not limited to the memories of relatives. Although your grandfather may have died many years ago, many people who knew him may well still be alive. Many others will have grown up in the same town or village, or have worked in the same occupation.

Historians have traditionally emphasised the unique and the particular, and when you never get to know people in the past as individuals it is all too easy to see them as living a totally different way of life from our own. What the memories of living people (and for more remote periods, letters, diaries, memoirs and autobiographies) can do is to help us to see the *similarities* and to achieve a deeper empathy with the past.

The need for caution. Important though oral evidence is, beware of accepting it uncritically. Not only do elderly people often make factual mistakes through failing memory, but their accounts may be coloured by later events. Sometimes they may even conceal unsavoury facts or distort the truth to put themselves in a better light. Wherever possible, corroboration should be sought either from other relatives or from documentary sources. Where this is not possible, there must always be a slight element of doubt.

Oral evidence and personal memoirs are strongest where other kinds of historical sources are weakest, for they can say a great deal about personal feelings, motivation and family circumstances. They gain, not lose from being personal and although their account of events may be biased, the bias itself is often interesting historically, giving us an inkling of thoughts and feelings as well as actions. Moreover, through specific examples, they give us an insight into the physical and social environment and into the ideas, beliefs and values of the time.

III Recording

Making a family tree.

1. *Use large sheets of paper divided into A4 sections.* In drawing up his family trees, the genealogist is faced with a dilemma. The sheets must be large enough to contain the whole of one branch with clarity but small enough to photocopy for other members of the family.

This dilemma can be overcome with sensible planning. Whatever size paper you use, it is worth dividing it up into faintly ruled grids of A4 size 297 mm × 210 mm) so that it can be easily folded and each section photocopied. As far as possible, try and avoid writing over the grid-lines.

A handy size for a family tree is A1 (840 mm × 594 mm) which will divide into eight A4 grids. You may prefer, however, to use A3 (420 mm × 297 mm) as this can easily be photocopied in two A4 sections. Some libraries and offices have A3 photocopiers.

2. *Do not include more than one family on a chart.* It is important to make separate charts for your father's family, mother's family, grandmother's family and so on. Nevertheless, wives should be identified clearly by the inclusion of dates of birth, parentage and their father's occupations and places of residence.

3. *Include all basic information on the family tree.* Too many family trees are strewn with people in a kind of limbo, without places, occupations or even approximate dates of births, marriages and deaths. However, do not clutter your tree with too much data. Further information can be kept in a separate loose-leaf file.

4. *Whenever possible, put husband and wife side by side.*

5. *Try to keep people of the same generation level with each other.* If your paper is not big enough, continue some of the branches on new sheets rather than cram information into odd corners.

6. *Make 'deep' rather than 'broad' entries.* Deep entries stretching to about five lines down the page are preferable to broad entries which leave less room for people of the same generation.

7. *Use the standard genealogical abbreviations.*

b.	born	*dau.*	daughter
bapt.	baptised	*div.*	divorced
bur.	buried	*s.*	son
d.	died	*umn.*	unmarried
d.umn.	died unmarried	=	married
d.s.p.	died without children (Latin *decessit sine prole*)	↓	left descendants

It is especially important to distinguish between dates of birth and baptism (and also death and burial).

8. *Include reference numbers.* It is important to be able to refer to individuals on the charts. One way of doing this to to give each main chart a letter – A, B, C, and so on, and each person on the chart a number, (A1, A2, etc). This system has been used throughout this book. For ease of reference:

(i) Number every person on the chart in strict order, husbands and wives having consecutive numbers. The lowest numbers will therefore come at the top of the chart and the highest at the bottom, and any person can be located in seconds.

(ii) Include for each person the reference numbers for that person on every other chart, so that a pedigree may easily be followed from chart to chart. The references to other charts should, however, follow the main reference. Thus on Table E (page 78) Gordon has the number E39, but cross references are given to A23 and D21. This also tells us he does not appear on tables B and C.

In this book, to avoid cluttering the tables, cross references have been put in only to *preceding* tables. However, for normal use it is best to put in cross references to *all* other charts on which an individual appears. By this system, on Table E Gordon would also have the cross-reference F28. On Table A (page 13) Gordon (A23) would have the cross references D21, E39, F28, and Samuel (A3) the cross references B15, C23, D17, E30 and F9.

(iii) If people are added to the chart, it is best to use 'a' numbers so that they can still be located easily. Thus on Table A a second marriage has been discovered for Ada Lizzie Phillips (A8) after the compilation of the chart, so Henry Cooper has been given the number A8a.

Searching and recording When searching parish registers and census returns, it is useful to duplicate a number of forms with headed columns which can be completed during the search and filed without the necessity of retyping.

Dates should always be recorded in the form 27 Sept 1811 and not Sept 27 1811 (or 27.9.1811, for September has not always been the ninth month). June and July should be written in full, and January abbreviated to Jany to avoid confusion.

Keep a detailed record of all searches and enquiries made *and for which surnames.* This is just as important for oral enquiries as for searches in records. It is as important to record negative searches as positive ones.

Filing. The best way of filing source material is in a loose-leaf file subdivided by sources. A fundamental principle is one file per family. If in searching records or talking to relatives you have taken down details about several different families, they should either be copied up on separate sheets, or photocopied, striking out entries for other families. They are then filed in separate files. Nothing is more muddling than having a collection of notes with bits and pieces on half-a-dozen families. *Each* page in your file should be headed with the surname, source, source's reference number and dates searched, in case pages get misplaced. Gaps and illegible portions of records should be noted on the sheets for *each* of the families for which abstracts have been taken.

Card index. It is wise to keep a card index for each individual you encounter. Cards for individuals who appear on the family trees need give little more information than the charts on which they are to be found.

Cards for individuals not appearing on a family tree may include more information.

Of course, until an identification is proved, there may be several cards for the same person. When fresh

evidence enables a firm identification to be made, the material can either be recopied on the same card, or the cards stapled together.

Biographical data. More detailed biographical information and copies of documents can be filed. It is probably better to file them by reference numbers (A1, A2, etc) rather than alphabetically, so that the information on close relatives all comes together.

Here are some of the entries from the sheet on William the sawyer.

Recording is the area in which many family historians are least successful. Family trees often contain inadequate data and no cross references to further information. Records of searches do not always show clearly which sources have been searched and for which surnames, and abstracts on several families may be jumbled together. Systematic recording not only clarifies your own thoughts on what to do next, but is essential if your records are to be of value to a future researcher.

IV Has it been done before?

Printed pedigrees. Genealogists have sometimes spent years researching a family, only to discover a pedigree already in existence. Many pedigrees have been printed in *Burke's Peerage*, or *Burke's Landed Gentry*, in county histories, in Heralds' Visitations (made in the sixteenth and seventeenth centuries by heralds checking on whether families were bearing arms legitimately), in journals and elsewhere. There is a series of comprehensive indexes to them (see p. 186). However, two words of warning are necessary. Firstly, no existing pedigree whether printed or manuscript, should be taken on trust, but checked wherever possible. Secondly, do not assume a relationship simply because a family has the same name. Not all *Russells* are relatives of the Dukes of Bedford or *Osbornes* of the Duke of Leeds. A tradition that you are connected with a well-known family may have originated only when a relative discovered that you shared the same surname. Similarly, when a person with a distinctive surname (like *Kitchener* or *Churchill*) rises to prominence, everyone of that surname wishes to claim kinship. So it is rarely profitable, except in the case of very unusual names, to try and 'extend' one of these pedigrees in the hope of linking it with yours. Nevertheless, the value of knowing about other families of the same name is obvious, and one must not assume that one's family is so humble that relatives could never appear in these works, for many of the pedigrees in *Burke's Peerage* and *Burke's Landed Gentry* are of families which acquired wealth, land or title in the last century or so.

Manuscript pedigrees. The Society of Genealogists (see p. 158) has a substantial collection of manuscript pedigrees, as have many local libraries, museums and record offices. Pedigrees in the British Library (see p. 161) are listed in the indexes to its various manuscript collections. These are in major libraries.

The Mormons. The British collection of pedigrees pale into insignificance beside that of the Mormons. Apart from a vast collection of microfilms of records, the library at Salt Lake City holds several million family group sheets and thirty million cards on individuals. These records can be searched through the Mormon 'accredited genealogists', a list of whom can be obtained from the Genealogical Department, Church of Jesus Christ of Latter-Day Saints, 50 East South Temple St., Salt Lake City, Utah, 84101.

A family group sheet from the Mormon Genealogical Library can be very valuable, but great care must be taken in using them. This one has many inaccuracies.

Others interested in the same family. Most family history societies keep a record of the families in which members are interested and many have published lists of these. Apart from the strong possibility that the other family historian may have got further than you, the future saving of time in co-operating with research may be enormous – and this applies quite as much to common surnames where no evidence of relationship has been found as to rare surnames like Honeycombe. Also making such contacts helps to make family history a social rather than solitary hobby. In recent years two major series of annual indexes of surnames in which genealogists are interested have been produced and lists of one-name studies are in progress (pp. 186–7).

V How many families?

The assumption in the text has been that you are tracing one family. However, many genealogists are interested not just in specific families, but in tracing as many ancestors as possible: their two parents, four grandparents, eight great-grandparents, and so on. Gordon's ancestry chart is shown opposite [**104**].

The first point of interest is that Gordon is three-quarters Scottish. It is ironic that despite his Scottish Christian name he is much more interested in his rather diluted English strain than his solid block of Scottish forbears! It can be seen that only three generations back, Gordon already has an interesting social spread. The Honeycombes were on the way up, his great-grandfather Samuel, having risen from joiner to surveyor. Gordon's other great-grandfathers were a Perth master baker, who was later a potato merchant, and finally a van man; an ironmonger, who went bankrupt in 1876, was discharged in 1879, became a wine and spirit dealer, and finally a commercial traveller; and a Church of Scotland minister, the son of a farmer. Gordon's four great-grandmothers were the daughters of a Thames river pilot; a plumber of South Leith near Edinburgh; a sugar merchant in Dingwall, Cromarty; and the manager of a calico printing works in Kirkintilloch, just north of Glasgow.

This kind of ancestor collecting is not without interest, if only for the variety it gives to your researches. Also, if you trace enough ancestors, you are almost certain to find one who had some slender claim to fame. The great disadvantage, however, is that it is difficult to see families and individuals in any kind of context as you are investigating too many to know a great deal about them. The Mormons emphasise this approach to genealogy, which increases the chances of them discovering a relationship with other Mormons. Similarly, the non-Mormon genealogist is likely to discover that at least one of his ancestral lines is on file in Salt Lake City.

Tracing several families. Most family historians neither concentrate exclusively upon one family nor try to trace *all* their ancestors. Instead, they study a number of families from which they are descended. Having done an enormous amount of work on the Honeycombes, Gordon has recently taken an interest in the families of his mother, the *Frasers*, and of his grandmother, the *Spiers*. Alas, because he was not interested in these families at the time he began his investigations, he failed to contact some of his elderly relatives before they died. The golden rule in genealogy, then, is that whether you are interested in one line or many when you start your investigations, get round *all* your living relatives and take down every scrap of genealogical information you can.

RECORD OF ANCESTRY

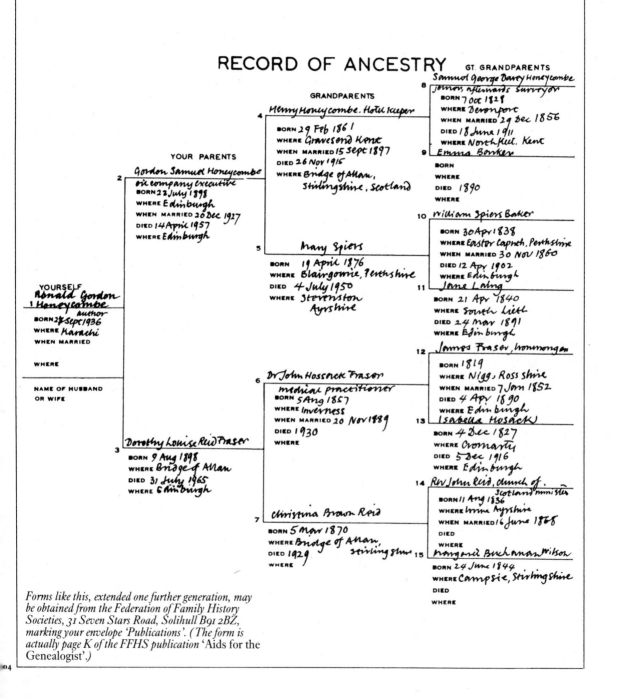

GT. GRANDPARENTS

GRANDPARENTS

YOUR PARENTS

YOURSELF

1 Ronald Gordon Honeycombe
author
BORN 27 Sept 1936
WHERE Karachi
WHEN MARRIED

WHERE

NAME OF HUSBAND OR WIFE

2 Gordon Samuel Honeycombe
oil company executive
BORN 22 July 1898
WHERE Edinburgh
WHEN MARRIED 20 Dec 1927
DIED 14 April 1957
WHERE Edinburgh

3 Dorothy Louise Reid Fraser
BORN 9 Aug 1898
WHERE Bridge of Allan
DIED 31 July 1965
WHERE Edinburgh

4 Henry Honeycombe. Hotel keeper
BORN 29 Feb 1861
WHERE Gravesend Kent
WHEN MARRIED 15 Sept 1897
DIED 26 Nov 1915
WHERE Bridge of Allan, Stirlingshire, Scotland

5 Mary Spiers
BORN 19 April 1876
WHERE Blairgowrie, Perthshire
DIED 4 July 1950
WHERE Stevenston Ayrshire

6 Dr John Hossock Fraser
medical practitioner
BORN 5 Aug 1857
WHERE Inverness
WHEN MARRIED 20 Nov 1889
DIED 1930
WHERE

7 Christina Brown Reid
BORN 5 Mar 1870
WHERE Bridge of Allan, Stirlingshire
DIED 1929
WHERE

8 Samuel George Davey Honeycombe joiner, afterwards surveyor
BORN 7 Oct 1829
WHERE Devonport
WHEN MARRIED 29 Dec 1856
DIED 18 June 1911
WHERE Northfleet. Kent

9 Emma Bonker
BORN
WHERE
DIED 1890
WHERE

10 William Spiers Baker
BORN 30 Apr 1838
WHERE Easter Capneth, Perthshire
WHEN MARRIED 30 Nov 1860
DIED 12 Apr 1902
WHERE Edinburgh

11 Jane Laing
BORN 21 Apr 1840
WHERE South Leith
DIED 24 Mar 1891
WHERE Edinburgh

12 James Fraser, Ironmonger
BORN 1819
WHERE Nigg, Ross shire
WHEN MARRIED 7 Jan 1852
DIED 4 Apr 1890
WHERE Edinburgh

13 Isabella Hosack
BORN 4 Dec 1827
WHERE Cromarty
DIED 5 Dec 1916
WHERE Edinburgh

14 Rev John Reid, church of Scotland minister
BORN 11 Aug 1836
WHERE Irvine Ayrshire
WHEN MARRIED 16 June 1868
DIED
WHERE

15 Margaret Buchanan Wilson
BORN 24 June 1844
WHERE Campsie, Stirlingshire
DIED
WHERE

Forms like this, extended one further generation, may be obtained from the Federation of Family History Societies, 31 Seven Stars Road, Solihull B91 2BZ, marking your envelope 'Publications'. (The form is actually page K of the FFHS publication 'Aids for the Genealogist'.)

VI English Civil Registration

General. From 1 July 1837 all births, marriages and deaths in England and Wales were supposed to be registered, and national *indexes* to them can be consulted free of charge, at St Catherine's House, Aldwych, London.

Applying for certificates. To obtain information from the original records, which are not open to the public, it is necessary to apply for a certificate by entering the appropriate details from the index on an application form, and paying, (at the time of writing) £5.00. Postal applications cost £10.00. So if you cannot apply in person, it is cheaper to employ an agent. It is also much quicker as postal searches are currently taking five to six weeks.

Variations in surnames. Spelling of surnames was still fairly fluid in the early years of civil registration and even in the 20th century members of the same family may appear under different spellings of the surname. Also surnames are occasionally mis-indexed ('St' for 'H' is a common error and vice versa).

Variations in Christian names. If a person had two Christian names, he might favour the second one. Thus Gordon was registered as *Ronald* Gordon and was generally known as Ronald until he was eighteen, when he chose to use Gordon instead. Sometimes the order of names might change between certificates, and some variations are quite extraordinary. Among Gordon's collection of Honeycombe certificates, there is an *Edwin Charles James* Honeycombe, born 1870, married in 1892 as *James Edwin*. His death in 1933 was registered as *James*. A *Louis Rowland* Honeycombe, born 1890, was married as *Reginald Lewis* in 1919.

Errors in certificates. Ages on certificates are notoriously unreliable, particularly on death certificates through ignorance on the part of the informant, and on marriage certificates when the groom was younger, (or very much older) than the bride.

Certificates obtained from St Catherine's House may contain mistranscriptions. In the death certificate reproduced on page 58 'H.M. Dockyard' has been transcribed as 'Hill Dockyard' and 'Choleraic Asphyxia' as 'Choleaic Asphyxia'. 'Fore St' might be correct but

it could just as easily be 'Fort St' in Devonport.

Local Copies. The original registers of births and deaths are held by local *superintendent* district registrars. Each of these looks after a *district*, which is usually divided into *sub-districts*, presided over by registrars. Ordinary registrars do not hold completed registers, but if you think family events took place in a certain area, it is often better to search their local copies, rather than visit St Catherine's House, because this is an easier way of tracing all the members of a family in the area. However, unlike St Catherine's House, there is a charge for inspecting the indexes. Although the superintendent registrar should have all but the most recent births and deaths, he will have a copy of only some of the marriages. Registers of Church of England marriages are completed in duplicate and retained in the church until they are filled up. When the church's copy of the register is full, it will probably be deposited at the County Record Office. When the duplicate book is full, it goes to the local superintendent registrar. But, of course, many small churches are still using the marriage register begun 50 years ago, and some even one begun in 1837. So you may have to wait a long time to consult this at the superintendent registrar's office! He does, however, hold registers of civil, noncomformist, Roman Catholic, Jewish (and more recently Moslem, Hindu and Sikh) marriages. The Registrar General at St Catherine's House obtains his marriage copies from quarterly returns submitted by the superintendent registrars. They in turn have obtained these from the local registrars, who have visited the churches in their sub-districts and paid 50p for a copy of every marriage which has taken place there during the previous quarter.

Birth certificates.

Delay in registration. The indexes to births, marriages and deaths are arranged by quarters – March, June, September and December. As there was often some delay between birth and registration, a September birth, for instance, might well not appear until the December quarter.

Registration districts. It is important to remember that the place given in the index is the *registration district* and not the exact place of birth. So although you may know exactly where your ancestor was born, you are unlikely to find it in the index.

Checking for people of the same name. Even with the rarest surnames, more than one person with the same Christian name may be found. When you find an entry which seems to be the right one, you should nevertheless continue the search for the whole of the period in which the entry might have occurred in case there is another possible entry. Gordon was lucky. His grandfather was the only Henry Honeycombe born between 1837 and 1875, though there was a *James Henry* in 1870. If he had found several Henry Honeycombes he could have completed a special form listing them all together with identifying criteria (e.g. the father's name – Samuel). Only the certificate which fitted the criteria would be issued. He could either have had all the entries checked to ensure that there was not more than one possibility, or have asked the checkers to stop when they came to the first register entry which fitted the criteria. The charge for this service is currently £5.00 for the first index entry submitted and £2.50 for each subsequent entry. If the desired certificate is found before all the 'possibles' have been exhausted, £2.50 is returned for each entry not examined. If the certificate is not found, the £5.00 is returned.

In the case of very common surnames it may be necessary to seek further information before applying for Civil Registration Certificates. For example, a tombstone might give a mother's Christian name.

Extended searches. You may not have an exact date of birth, or even a year – only 'Grandad died around the First World War' and 'I think he was about 60'. You would then have to start searching the birth indexes in 1854 and continue with the years either side until you found it. If the information had been so imprecise in the case of Henry Honeycombe, it would have been quite a long search (with four quarters each year) before Gordon got to 1861, and found that 'about 60' was really 54.

A direct ancestor's certificate not always the best. Where the names of an ancestor's brothers and sisters are known with certainty, it may well be better to get the birth certificate of one of them born in, or near, a Census year, *instead* of that of the direct ancestor. It will give precisely the same genealogical information and the additional bonus of an address where the family can be followed up in Census Returns.

It may also be safer to get the birth certificate of a brother or sister in preference to one for a direct ancestor if the latter has a very common Christian name (e.g. John) whereas the brother or sister has either a much rarer one (e.g. Eleanor), or else two names (e.g. William Thomas).

Lastly, although a direct ancestor might be born before the start of Civil Registration in 1837, census returns may reveal a younger sibling born after.

Checking on identification. To check that you have obtained the correct birth certificate, you must know the name of at least one of the parents. In this case, oral evidence had supplied Gordon with the name of Henry's father – it was Samuel George Davey Honeycombe. So when he obtained Henry's birth certificate (see p. 15) he could be sure that he had obtained the right one. If he had not known Henry's father's name, then he would have had to obtain it by first getting Henry's *marriage* certificate, on which his father's name is given.

Marriage certificates. To find a marriage in the index when you have only the date of birth of one of the children to go on, it is advisable to start looking in the quarter *following* the birth (as sometimes the first child was born before the marriage) and then work backwards. Since Gordon knew from Henry's birth certificate that his parents were Samuel George Davey Honeycombe and Emma Barker, and from the Family Bible that Henry's brother, William Thomas was born in October 1857, he started searching in the March quarter of 1858 and worked backwards, looking in the marriage indexes for each quarter until the marriage was found. The best way of doing this is to look for the *less common* of the two surnames. In Gordon's case, it was *Honeycombe* rather than *Barker*, but often the surname of the bride may be much less common than that of the family you are studying.

When an entry is found which could be the right one, look up the other surname – in Gordon's case, Barker – and see if there is a person of the right name (Emma) with exactly the same reference number. If so, you know you have the right marriage. From 1912 onwards, you need not look up the other party, as his or her surname is given in brackets.

Looking under Honeycombe back from 1858, Gordon reached the following entry in the December 1856 quarter of the Marriage Index: '*Honeycombe: Samuel George Davey* Rotherhithe 1d 741'. He then looked up Barker and found '*Barker: Emma* Rotherhithe 1d 741'. So he knew that he had found the correct marriage, and applied for the certificate (see p. 15).

Unfortunately, in the early years of civil registration exact ages were frequently not given on marriage certificates – only 'of full age'.

Death Certificates. The English death certificate (see p. 16) is not very helpful genealogically, but will often yield a useful address for looking up in census returns. Moreover, if the cause of death is at all unusual, it may provide the vital clue for discovering a full report in a local newspaper (see pp. 42 and 62). Age at death is given in the indexes only from 1866. From 1970 the index gives the exact date of birth.

Separate registration systems. It is important to remember that the St Catherine's House indexes cover only England and Wales, and not Scotland, Ireland, the Channel Islands and the Isle of Man, which have their own systems. (See pp. 117, 153.)

TRUE EXTRACT FROM DUPLICATE OF REGISTER OF
BIRTHS IN THE MUNICIPAL LIMITS OF KARACHI.

Serial No.	10416
Date and hour of Birth	27th September 1936 8-20 am
Registration Division	Saddar
Quarter	Frere Town
Road, Street or Lane	Bath Island
Number of House	3
Name of Child	Ronald Gordon Honeycombe
Name of Father and Grand Father	Gordon Samuel Honeycombe
Occupation of Father	Merchant
Caste	European
Sex of Child	Male
Whether born alive or stillborn	Alive
Whether since dead	
No. and date of duplicate Register of vaccination certificate	
No. and date of vaccination Register	Vaccinated by Dr ... on 24/1/37 ... 29.1.37

105 *Remember, not everybody's birth certificate will be found at St Catherine's House.*

The main series of St Catherine's House indexes do not include British people born abroad, and this involves a great many people. Thus Gordon's own birth, in 1936, is not recorded at St Catherine's House, since he was born in British India. [105].

Separate indexes at St Catherine's House. When searching the main series of indexes don't overlook the supplementary indexes at St Catherine's House of:

(i) Births and deaths at sea from 1st July, 1837 to 31 Dec 1874. (Births and deaths at sea after 1874 are held by the Registrar-General for shipping and seamen, Llandaff, Cardiff, Wales.)

(ii) Consular returns of births, marriages and deaths of British citizens abroad from 1 July 1849.

(iii) Army returns of births, marriages and deaths from 1761.

(iv) RAF returns of births, marriages and deaths from 1920.

Adoptions. Indexes of adoptions from 1927 are on the open shelves at St Catherine's House, but it must be remembered firstly that children are listed under the surname of their *adoptive* parents, and secondly that adoption might take place many years after birth. However, the index may well clear up why an individual cannot be found in the main index of births and a certificate can be obtained on completion of a special form. This will give date of birth, adoptive parents' names, court of adoption and adoption order date.

Under the new adoption laws, an adopted person over eighteen can obtain information on his or her true parents but application must be made in person.

Divorces. If a person remarried, apparently in the lifetime of the first wife, divorce is a more likely explanation than bigamy. Until 1857, divorce was possible only by special act of Parliament. However, in that year an act made divorce a practical possibility for most people. The register of divorces is still kept at Somerset House in the Probate and Divorce department but is not open to the public. On payment of a fee, Somerset House staff will search the register and send details, but this usually takes a few days.

VII Scottish Civil Registration

General. Scottish Civil Registration books are kept at New Register House, Princes Street, Edinburgh. They date from January 1855 and are extraordinarily thorough. Unfortunately, the system was found too cumbersome to keep up, and at the end of that year many details were dropped from birth, marriage and death certificates. Even so, all three types of certificate still contain more information than their English counterparts. In addition, Scottish registration has one tremendous advantage over the English. Although unlike St Catherine's House there is a charge (currently £5.25 per day) for searching the *indexes*, the *original entries* identified from the indexes may then be consulted without further charge, making it economic to follow up collateral branches. Between April and September a queue system operates by which access to the registers is limited to a period of thirty minutes at any one time, though additional periods can be secured by rejoining the queue.

The Society of Genealogists holds a microfilm copy of all 1855 registers and of the *indexes* 1855 to 1920.

Birth certificates.

Information given. The Scottish birth certificate, as that for Gordon's father shows [106], contains one important detail that the English one lacks – the date and place of the parents' marriage. This spares the searcher the task of having to work back systematically, quarter by quarter from the birth of the child, until he finds the parents' marriage.

1855 certificates. The 1855 birth certificates also gave parents' ages and birthplaces, and the number of other issue living and deceased. These details, together with the date and place of parents' marriage, were dropped in 1856, but the latter was restored in 1861.

Marriage certificates.

Information given. The Scottish marriage certificate too, gives more information than the English one. It is interesting to compare the certificate for Henry's first marriage in England [107] with that for his second marriage in Scotland [108]. In the former, only the fathers are given, in the latter, both parents.

An interesting point about Henry's second marriage is that it took place in an Episcopal Church, and Henry described himself as 'Bachelor'. In fact, he was divorced, and his remarriage in church would not have been possible had the church authorities known of this.

1855 certificates. The 1855 marriage certificates also gave the places of both present and usual residence, details of any former marriages, and the number of children by each former marriage, living and deceased.

Death certificates.

Information given. By naming both parents of the deceased, the Scottish death certificate will take you much further back than any English one. For example, one of Gordon's great-great-grandparents on his mother's side, Robert Reid, a farmer of Irvine, died

No.	Name and Surname.	When and Where Born.	Sex.	Name, Surname and Rank or Profession of Father. Name, an Maiden Surname of Mother. Date and Place of Marriage.	Signature and Qualification of Informant, and Residence, if out of the House in which the Birth occurred.	When and Where Registered, and Signature of Registrar.
917	Gordon Samuel Honeycombe	18 98 July Twenty third 3 h 25 m a m 5 Duke Street	M	Henry Honeycombe Manager Refreshment Dept Mary Honeycombe m.s. Spers 1897 September 15ᵗ Fields	(Signed) H. Honeycombe Father Present.	18 98 August 11ᵗʰ At (Signed) John R. McLaren Registrar.

106 *Extract from Scottish birth certificate. The place and date of the parents' marriage are given.*

English and Scottish marriage certificates. The latter give both parents of each of the parties. It is interesting that Henry, although a divorcee is described as 'bachelor' and was married in church. Did the bride and minister know of his previous marriage?

in 1868, aged eighty-one. So he was born about 1787. The death certificate gives his parents as William Reid, farmer, and Mary Gray, both deceased. William and Mary would be born about 1762. However, the names of parents of the deceased are not always accurate. In this case, *Mary* Gray should almost certainly have been *Elizabeth* Gray.

1855 certificates. The 1855 certificates also gave the place of birth, details of marriages, burial place (often helpful in locating a tombstone) and a list of all issue living and deceased. Unfortunately, this superb degree of detail was found too complicated to keep up.

Maiden names. Another great advantage of Scottish registration is that a woman never completely loses her maiden name. Thus not only are both parents given in the death certificate, but it is the mother's *maiden* name which is given. Married women appear in the indexes under both their married name and their maiden name – and also under their previous surname if they have been married before. Here, for example, is the death certificate of Gordon's grandmother, Mary Spiers. It can be seen that after Henry's death, in 1915, Mary married again, a foreman baker called William Elder. In England, Mary's death would have appeared in the indexes only under 'Mary Elder'. In Scotland it appeared under Mary Spiers, Mary Honeycombe and Mary Elder.

Supplementary indexes at New Register House

Marine register of births and deaths (from 1855). Births and deaths on British registered merchant vessels at sea if the child's father or the deceased person was a Scottish subject.

Air Register of births and deaths (from 1948). Births and deaths in any part of the world in aircraft registered in the United Kingdom where it appears that the child's father or the deceased person was usually resident in Scotland.

Service records (from 1881): (i) army returns of births, deaths and marriages of Scottish persons at military stations abroad (1881–1959); (ii) service department registers of births, marriages and deaths of service men and their families from 1959; (iii) marriages by army chaplains outside the UK where one of the parties was Scottish and at least one party was serving in HM Forces (from 1892).

War Registers. South African War, 1899–1902; World Wars I and II.

Consular returns of persons of Scottish descent or birth. (Births and deaths from 1914, marriages from 1917).

High Commissioners' returns. From some Commonwealth countries (from 1964).

Births, marriages and deaths in foreign countries. Information supplied by parties (1860–1965).

Foreign marriages. Certified copies of certificates (from 1947).

1861 – 1965

Extract of an entry in a REGISTER of DEATHS

Registration of Births, Deaths and Marriages (Scotland) Act 1965

No.	1 Name and surname, rank or profession and whether single, married or widowed	2 When and where died	3 Sex	4 Age	5 Name, surname, and rank or profession of father, Name and maiden surname of mother	6 Cause of death, duration of disease, and medical attendant by whom certified	7 Signature and qualification of informant, and residence, if out of the house in which the death occurred	8 When and where registered and signature of registrar
46	Mary ELDER (Married to 1st Henry Honeycombe Hotel Proprietor 2nd William Elder Baker (Foreman)	1950 July Fourth 8h.35m. P.M. 54 Caledonian Road, Stevenston	F	74 years	William Spiers Fruit Merchant (Deceased) Jane Spiers m.s. Laing (Deceased)	Coronary Embolism As cert by John Daly LRCP&S	*Signed* William Elder Widower (Present)	1950 July 6th At Stevenston *Signed* E.W. Donaldson *Registrar*

The above particulars are extracted from a Register of Deaths for the .... District .... of .... Stevenston ....

in the .... County .... of .... Ayr

Given under the Seal of the General Register Office, New Register House, Edinburgh, on   18th August 1978

The above particulars incorporate any subsequent corrections or amendments to the original entry made with the authority of the Registrar General.

It is an offence under section 53(3) of the Registration of Births, Deaths and Marriages (Scotland) Act 1965 for any person to pass as genuine any copy or reproduction of this extract which has not been made by the General Register Office and authenticated by the Seal of that Office.

Any person who falsifies or forges any of the particulars on this extract or knowingly uses, gives or sends as genuine any false or forged extract is liable to prosecution under section 53(1) of the said Act.

RXD3 (T)
March 1974

109 *Scottish death certificate. Note the inclusion of both parents of the deceased and of previous marriage.*

VIII Census Returns and Directories

The censuses for which the Enumerators' Returns are open to the public were held on 7 June 1841, 30 March 1851, 8 April 1861, 2 April 1871 and 3 April 1881. The 1891 census will become available on 1 January 1992. Before consulting microfilms of the returns at the Public Record Office annexe at Portugal Street, London WC1, it is necessary to apply well in advance for an annual reader's ticket from the Keeper of the Records, Chancery Lane, London WC1. No fee is payable.

Scottish census returns are kept at New Register House, Edinburgh, and may be consulted up to 1891. Unlike England, there is a charge for searches, currently £3.75 a day. The Irish ones before 1901 were destroyed in 1922. (See p. 153.)

Copies held locally. Most record offices and some reference libraries have copies for their own localities. Some have been transcribed and indexed by local family history societies. A useful list of local microfilm copies has been compiled by J.S.W. Gibson (see p. 164), and a second booklet, *Marriage, Census and Other Indexes for Family Historians* shows what indexes have been made or are in progress.

Information Given

1841 *Census* [see pp. 50, 82]. The 1841 Census gives the householder's name followed by his dependants, but relationships are not given. However, the marks made by the enumerators are extremely important. A single line marks the end of a household, a double line the end of a building. In the towns, as many as ten different households may be found at one address. However, the exact address is rarely given – only the name of the street. The numbers which appear at first sight to be house numbers are enumeration numbers and these run on from street to street.

Ages in the 1841 Census are exact for children up to 14, thereafter in five-year groups (15 = 15–19, 20 = 20–24 and so on).

Occupations are given, but not exact places of birth, only 'whether or not born in the same county' indicated by a Y (Yes) or an N (No).

1851–1881 Census (see pp. 58, 60). These Censuses include exact addresses, ages and birthplaces, and relationships to the head of the household.

Later censuses. General Register Office, St Catherine's House, 10 Kingsway, London WC2B 6JP, will release information from censuses from 1891 to 1901 providing an exact address is given, the consent of descendants has been obtained and a declaration signed that the information will not be used for litigation. Searches are conducted by GRO staff on payment of a fee of £10.00.

Earlier Censuses. The statistical returns compiled from the 1801, 1811, 1821 and 1831 Censuses may be consulted at major libraries, but the original enumerators' returns were not kept. However, most county record offices have a few isolated returns for particular districts where unofficial duplicates were made.

Abbreviations. Most are self-explanatory. The most common are M.S. or F.S. (Male or female servant) and Ag. lab. (Agricultural labourer).

Errors. Care must be taken with the age groupings in the 1841 Census, and ages in later censuses are often unreliable. Errors in birthplaces, relationships and occupations are not uncommon. For example, in the 1861 Census for St Helier, Jersey, William Honeycombe's daughter, Margaretta, was described as his wife. Corroboration of details in a census should always be sought.

Making a search.

Urban areas. Here, if you are to avoid a lengthy search, you need a precise address. This may be discovered from oral evidence, from birth, marriage or death certificates for any member of the family near the census date, from contemporary directories or from a will.

It is important to remember, however, that street names and house numbers may have changed between the date of one of these records and a census, or between censuses. If a family cannot be found, directories or censuses should be compared to see whether the three or four neighbours on either side can be located. If they were still at the same addresses, the family you seek had doubtless moved. Otherwise, the whole block of entries may be found with different numbers or under a different street name.

At the Public Record Office, there are street indexes for most of the larger towns, a list of which is included in Gibson's booklet mentioned above. A useful flow-chart for census searching is to be found in the *Family Tree Magazine* (Vol 1, No 2, Jan–Feb 1985).

Rural areas. Here even if you have an exact address, it is still worth searching the whole district as other relatives are likely to be found.

A comprehensive search. The experienced family historian will not confine his extracts to one surname. Having prepared a list of all surnames of wives and married daughters, he will abstract *all* entries for those names. Not only does a daughter not cease to be part of the family when she marries, but occupations of in-laws will sometimes throw light on the family history. In Scottish census returns, a widow – or even a wife whose husband is away – may well be listed under her maiden name.

It is helpful to note down the neighbours as well, so that you have some idea of the kind of environment in which your relations lived.

In the past, census returns were largely the preserve of the genealogist. In recent years historical demographers have discovered them and have used them to make all kinds of exciting discoveries about Victorian social life. However, many family historians do not adopt a really historical approach and still confine their searches to abstracting the barest genealogical data. Yet census returns have perhaps more to offer the family historian in terms of an understanding of the total environment than almost any other source.

Directories. London and many other towns have directories dating back to the eighteenth century. County directories are found from the early nineteenth century. Local libraries usually have a local collection. A fine series is in the Guildhall Library, London.

As well as area directories, occupational lists and directories can be very useful, e.g., Crockford's Clerical Directory and the army, navy, law and medical lists. The Society of Genealogists has a good collection.

Like Census Returns, directories tend to be scanned for references to a particular surname. However, as we saw in the case of the Northfleet Honeycombes (see p. 43), directories may prove useful in building up a picture of the extended family in its local context.

CALSTOCK, within the port of Plymouth, is an extensive parish, township, and village, 5 miles east from Callington, 14 north-east from Liskeard (Poor-law Union town), and 6 south-west from Tavistock (post town), in the Middle division of East Hundred, Liskeard Union, rape of East Devon, deanery of Cornwall, and archdeaconry and diocese of Exeter. It is situated on the beautiful river Tamar, which divides it from Beer Alston, in Devon, and on the Callington and Tavistock turnpike road. The church of St. Andrew, which stands on a commanding eminence, is an old stone building in the perpendicular style, with nave, aisles, chancel, porch, embattled tower with pinnacles and 6 bells. The living is a rectory, worth £440 yearly, with residence and 60 acres of glebe land, in the gift of his Royal Highness the Prince of Wales; the Rev. Frederick Thomas Batchelor is the incumbent. There are chapels and Sunday schools for Baptists and Wesleyan Methodists. There is a National school for boys and girls, also a Sunday school. There are many copper and tin mines. Brickmaking is carried on. There are breweries, an iron and brass foundry, and a tannery. Large quantities of coals, timber, and manure, are imported at the quays, from which tin and copper ores are exported. The population, in 1851, was 4,536, whereas in 1841 it was 2,553; and the acreage is 6,133. The soil is light, and the subsoil is granite and clay slate.

Wesleyan Methodists and Bible Christians. A Sunday school is attached to each. There is also a day school for boys and girls. An extensive granite quarry supplies large quantities of stone to the Keyham works, the Plymouth, Stonehouse, and Devonport Commissioners, and the new Westminster and Saltash bridges. A market is held here every Saturday for provisions, and a cattle fair yearly, on the first Monday after the first Friday in May. Here are several copper and tin mines.

HAREWOOD HOUSE, the seat of Sir William L. S. Trelawny, Bart., is half a mile east from Calstock. It is a handsome building, erected on one of the most delightful spots on the banks of the Tamar. Cotehill House, the seat of Earl Mount Edgcumbe is 1½ miles west of Calstock; it is one of the most ancient and curiously constructed mansions in England; it is situated on an eminence on the western bank of the Tamar, but being almost surrounded with wood, the river can only be seen from some of the upper windows. There is no account when this mansion was erected, but from the style of architecture it is supposed to have been built about the time of Henry VII.

COTEHILL QUAY is 2 miles south-west from Calstock. Large quantities of coal, timber, and manure are imported; tin and copper ores are exported.

HONEYCOOMBE, the seat of Edward Williams, Esq., is 2½ miles west-north-west from Calstock, and is pleasantly situated.

110 *Directory entry for Calstock. As well as pinpointing ancestors and identifying their neighbours, directories may provide useful information on local industries, schools and places of worship.*

IX Monumental Inscriptions

Monumental inscriptions may be found in churches, on tombstones in churchyards, non-conformist burial grounds and civil cemeteries, and on war memorials. Even when information on a family is believed to be fairly complete, every effort should be made to locate relevant inscriptions. Different surnames appearing on a stone may indicate married daughters or other relatives, and may be extremely valuable in clarifying identity and relationships. Thus one tombstone in St. Cleer churchyard bears inscriptions to *Grace wife of William Honeycombe of this parish* who died in 1840, and to *John Henwood 'stepbrother to the above William Honeycombe'* who died in 1838. This was our only source for identifying William as the son of a John Honeycombe and Jane Henwood married at Bodmin 1780.

Relatives need not, of course, be on the same stone but people did tend to be buried near their relations. So whenever copying an inscription it is always worthwhile noting those on neighbouring tombstones.

The northern part of the churchyard was often used for burying paupers, the unbaptised, the excommunicated and suicides.

Two notes of caution are necessary. Firstly dates may be inaccurate, as a stone was often put up many years after the death of the first person mentioned.

Secondly, the inclusion of a name on a stone does not necessarily mean that the person was buried there. The Honeycombe family tombstone in Northfleet churchyard includes Gordon's great-grandparents, Samuel and Emma Honeycombe, their son William Thomas and Samuel's sister, Margaretta. Surprisingly it also includes Gordon's grandfather, Henry, who died at Bridge of Allan, Stirlingshire, in 1915, aged 65. Henry is buried, however, in Bridge of Allan, where he has his own stone and is helpfully described as 'of Northfleet' which he had left as a young man.

Cemeteries. Burial grounds were started by the noncomformists in the 17th century and considerably increased throughout the 18th. Public cemeteries were started in London in 1827 (Kensal Green) and, soon after, in other towns and cities. An act of 1850 empowered the General Board of Health to establish cemeteries and to close any of the old churchyards. Gradually civil cemeteries were established almost everywhere, and many of the nonconformists preferred to be buried in these rather than in the parish churchyard. This was certainly the case at St Cleer, where the General Cemetery was started in 1864. The registers and a very detailed plan were located in private hands. The plan gives the owner of the plot and reference numbers to the register entries of those buried there. In this way we may pick up entries for related families. Thus in the register, Elizabeth Honeycombe, who died in 1878 is numbered 626, and there is the grave reference Sec. A, Slip 18 Grave 13, which we find on the plan is William Honeycombe's plot. In turn the plan gives 626 and 1558 for this grave. The second reference is to the register entry of her husband William, who died in 1908. The plan shows that neighbouring graves are occupied by their son and daughter-in-law, and by William, Anne and George Udey, three infant children of another daughter. It is worth noting that the plan gives register numbers for many graves for which no tombstones survive, if indeed they ever existed.

Tombstones are disappearing at an alarming rate as churchyards are grassed over for ease of upkeep. Even without the help of man, weathering and subsidence mean that tombstones have only a limited life. So, like the oral evidence, finding the tombstones of your ancestors is a matter of urgency. They may not be there next year. You may, however, be fortunate in finding a copy of the inscriptions at a local library or record office, or at the Society of Genealogists in London. Such copies should be searched even when the churchyard is apparently intact, as they may include inscriptions which have become illegible since the copy was made.

III   *The tombstone of Elizabeth Honeycombe in the Civil Cemetery at St Cleer together with her entry in the burial register and on the cemetery plan. Note that the latter reveals five other members of the family for whom no stones survive.*

112

113

X Photographs

Photographs make the past live in a way that no other document can, and one reason for contacting distant relatives is that most of them have a small photographic collection. Portraits of relatives may turn up in the most unlikely places. Margaret Honeycombe, a daughter of Samuel, the St Helier Town Crier (see p. 84), emigrated to Salt Lake City in 1894. Her elderly daughter lent Gordon a large album of family portraits. When he looked through this, he was astonished to find a picture of his own grandfather, Henry Honeycombe, as a young man [114]. How it got to Salt Lake City is a complete mystery.

The sad thing about this album was that none of the pictures were endorsed with names, dates or places. Alas, this was typical of old collections of photographs. Whilst it is often too late to recover these details, there may be somebody alive who can tell you – another good reason for talking to relatives before it is too late. In 1980 I visited Margaret Honeycombe's 85-year-old daughter, Florence Fones in Tooele, Utah, and she was able to identify a fair proportion of the photographs. A few months after my visit Mrs Fones died. Had I not gone to a great deal of trouble to see her, the identity of many individuals in those albums would have been lost beyond recall. If you suspect an unidentified person may have come from a particular locality, *any* elderly resident may be able to make an identification – he or she does not have to be a relative.

If no-one can identify a picture, there are often clues which may lead to identification. A military uniform, for example, can be identified as belonging to a particular regiment [115]. The photographer's name and address may also give a useful lead.

Family photographs may sometimes be dated by the photographic process used (Daguerreotypes 1840s, Talbotype or Calotype 1840s and 1850s, Ambrotype c.1848–78, gelatine dry plate c. 1871–88, celluloid from 1880s) or by the backdrop (1880s balustrade, column and curtain, 1870s, rustic bridge and stile, 1880s hammock, swing and railway carriage, 1890s palm trees, cockatoos and bicycles, and early twentieth century, motor cycles and side cars).

Photographs are invaluable in that your ancestors become so much more real when you know what they looked like, but the majority are inevitably studio portraits, pictures of special occasions such as weddings or snapshots of holidays. They seldom record the family in its everyday setting at home, or at work. However, family photographs can nearly always be complemented by pictures from other sources. In local and national archives there are hundreds of thousands of views of almost every town and village in Britain. Often, you can find photographs of particular streets or work places connected with the family.

Apart from such very specific quests, it is relatively easy to find books with pictures which are evocative of social life and working conditions in any period from 1860s to the present. Picture researching is, perhaps the most neglected aspect of family history.

114. *Gordon's grandfather, Henry, as a young man: a picture discovered in an album sent from an American Honeycombe.*

116

115. An unnamed photograph from the album sent from America. But who is he? His uniform shows he was a major in the Royal Irish Regiment.

116. An early photograph of Calstock, Cornwall, showing the use of sailing barges. The railway viaduct had yet to be built.

117. Liskeard, Cornwall, c. 1914. A picture very evocative of the period. Note the hatter's shop and the absence of traffic.

118. Thomas le Breton (left), husband of Margaret Honeycombe, working on the construction of the Mormon temple in Salt Lake City. A photograph provided by a descendant.

118

XI Newspapers and periodicals

Newspapers. Local libraries very often have fine runs of local papers – sometimes extending way back into the eighteenth century. Full details of the dates when newspapers began, ended or were taken over, will be found in the works listed on page 179. The most accessible source is probably John West's *Town Records* (Phillimore, 1983).

The British Library, (Formerly called the British Museum Library and still housed in the British Museum) has a fairly comprehensive collection of British newspapers. Pre-nineteenth century London newspapers are in the Reading Room in London, as are also an incomplete file of *The Times* and the complete series of the *London Gazette*. All 19th and 20th-century newspapers and provincial and foreign papers before 1800 are at the special newspaper library at Colindale, North London (see p. 161).

Public libraries and newspaper offices often have copies of their local papers. Thus the details of the accident on page 42 were found in the microfilm copy of the *Gravesend Reporter* in Gravesend Public Library.

If a person was well-known locally, like Samuel George Davey Honeycombe, there will usually be a fair number of references to him in newspapers – you will probably be able to locate an obituary which may well give clues to earlier accounts (see p. 29).

Because of their interest in the sensational, newspapers may well be the source of some of the most poignant stories in the family history (see pages 42 and 62). Perhaps the most interesting accounts are those of trials which may be extremely detailed, particularly if the accused was sentenced to death for some relatively trivial offence – until 1828 theft from a dwelling house of goods worth more than 40 shillings carried the death penalty.

However, more recent magazines should not be overlooked. National monthlies and weeklies are perhaps most useful for providing general background rather than information about ancestors and relatives, but the religious (especially parish) magazines and sports and hobbies journals which exist in great profu-sion may well mention relatives. Nearly all occupations, trade unions, regiments, clubs and societies produce their own magazines, and have sometimes been doing so for more than a century.

Advertisements These can be almost as useful as reports. Here, for example, is an advertisement for the ship which almost certainly carried John Symons Honeycombe, the author of the *Brief Abstract*, and his relatives to the New World.

FOR QUEBEC AND UPPER CANADA.
TO Sail from Plymouth, 22d APRIL, the fine fast-sailing Ship
ROSLIN CASTLE,
MONDAY, Master, 750 Tons burthen.
This favourite Ship is well-known in the Quebec trade has made some of the best voyages. She is of great h between decks, with excellent ventilation, and has superior a modations for both Cabin and Steerage Passengers; and, the arrangements that are made, she will be found to be desirable conveyance for Passengers to Quebec, the Canada the United States. She will be despatched under the dire of her Majesty's Emigration Officer.—For further partic apply to
RICHARD HOCKING & SONS, Whitehall, Stonehouse JOSEPH SCALES, 9, Parade, Plymouth.
☞ *The Vessel is now in the Sound.*
Dated April 20th, 1855.

Periodicals. The most useful old periodical for the family historian is the *Gentleman's Magazine*, started in 1731, which includes many references to the middle as well as the upper classes. Each annual volume is indexed, (though by surname only) and there are cumulative indexes for 1731 to 1786, and 1786 to 1810. Also, marriages have been indexed up to 1768 and biographical and obituary notices to 1780. (See p. 179.)

Beyond any doubt, newspapers and periodicals contain material relevant to every family history. All too often, however, the searcher overlooks them, deterred by the apparent immensity if the task, the smallness of the print, and the time taken to find his way around. The more he uses them, however, the easier becomes the task and the greater the rewards.

XII Maps

Parish maps. The very useful County Maps published by the Institute of Heraldic and Genealogical Studies, Northgate, Canterbury, Kent, show parish boundaries, probate jurisdictions, starting dates of registers and the location of parish churches [**132**].

Large scale Ordnance Survey maps. These can be very informative with regard to communications and local industries and it is helpful to find on a map the residences given in parish registers and census returns, and look for patterns and explanations. In urban areas, the locality in which a family lived usually reflected their wealth and status. A change of address can sometimes indicate increased prosperity, somesimes the reverse. A large-scale map will also help in showing which churches, schools or work places relatives would most likely have attended.

The first twenty-five inch to the mile survey (from which the 6 inch to the mile maps were produced by reduction) was 1853–93, although Lancashire and Yorkshire had a six inch to the mile survey between 1840 and 1854. A second edition, or first revision, was produced between 1891 and 1907, a third between 1906 and 1922, which covered most of the country.

For urban areas, there are very large-scale Ordnance Survey town plans, produced between 1843 and 1894. These show not only individual buildings but features as small as lamp posts and horse troughs. The first of them – St Helens – was published on a scale of five feet to one mile and during the next half century, three main series of town plans were prepared on scales of five feet to one mile (1/1056), ten feet to one mile (1/528) and 10.56 feet to one mile (1/500). In 1894, the large-scale town plans were discontinued, although in 1911 a new series of fifty inch to one mile town plans was inaugurated for provincial towns. These have now been replaced by a series produced between 1943 and 1967 which covers all major towns.

Very useful nineteenth-century town plans will often be found in town histories and guides.

One inch to the mile series. For periods before 1853 (except for Lancashire and Yorkshire) the one inch to the mile, which began publication in 1805, is the only Ordnance Survey series available. The 'Old Series' or first edition consisted of 110 sheets, published between 1805 and 1873. Publication began with South-East England, and the Ordnance Survey have

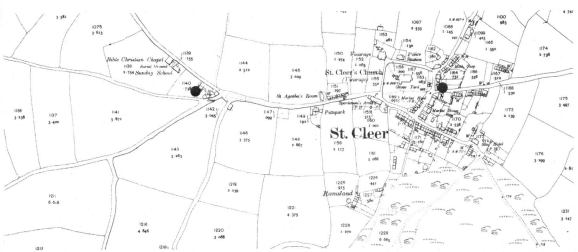

120 *Detail from an Ordnance Survey 25-inch to one-mile map 1907.*

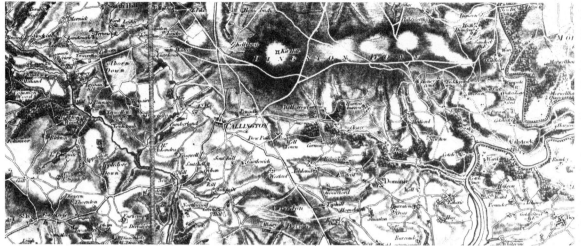

122 *First edition one-inch to the mile Ordnance Survey map showing places associated with the Honeycombe family.*

republished their 1810 map of the Southampton area. The whole series has been reprinted (though with the railways added) by David and Charles, Newton Abbot, Devon [**122**].

Enclosure maps. These show the redistribution of land as a result of the enclosure of land by private act of Parliament in the late eighteenth and early nineteenth century. Although they indicate the land allotted to each landowner, they do not, of course, show the fields into which he may have subsequently divided up his holding. Besides the enclosure map (if it survives), there will be a copy of the act, a schedule showing the new owners and the acreage of their holdings and various associated documents. These often include a map of the parish as it was before enclosure.

Tithe maps. These were made between 1838 and 1854 after the Tithe Commutation Act of 1836 converted the tithe in kind into an annual fixed payment. In many counties all parishes were covered. In others there may be awards for only a third or less of the parishes. Often no tithe award was necessary in the remainder, since enclosure acts had extinguished the tithes at the same time as the land was redistributed. The tithe maps usually show fields with each field numbered. The schedules are the key to the maps and

show the names of each landowner and occupier, the field names, the descriptions of land or premises, the stage of cultivation and the acreage, and the rent charged.

Enclosure and tithe maps are usually very big and some record offices cannot photocopy parts of them, but if prior arrangements are made with the archivist, you may be able to trace that part of a map which shows an ancestor's holding. When the tracing is finished an excellent reproduction can be made by putting it in a photocopier with a piece of white paper on top of it. The resulting photocopy can be shaded to indicate different landowners.

Estate maps. Estate maps are sometimes found dating from the second half of the sixteenth century. However, they are not common for another century, and in some counties not until well on in the eighteenth century. There may be a whole series for some estates. They are usually on a large scale, and show field boundaries [**124**]. Some resemble tithe maps.

Other maps. Very useful nineteenth century town plans will often be found in town histories and guides. Most County Record Offices and major libraries also have useful collections of older maps, sometimes extending back to the sixteenth century.

NAME OF PROPRIETOR OR CLAIMANT.	DESCRIPTION OF CONVENTIONARY TENEMENT IN THE LAST ASSESSIONAL GRANT THEREOF.			PARTICULARS OF LANDS CONSTITUTING SUCH TENEMENT.		
	Name of Tenement.	Number.	Article.	Name of Field.	No. of Field on Map.	Statute Measure.
						A. R. P.
Hockin, John, Charles Hockin, and Frank Hockin,	Metherill,	74	2 3	House and Orchard, ... *	1854	1 11
Hocking, Elizabeth	Calstock Town, ...	88	16	Orchard, ...	2555	2 23
	Calstock Town, ...	95		House and Garden, ... *	2605	15
Honeycombe, Ann	Northwood, ...	30	2	House, ... *	817	5
Honeycombe, John	Calstock Town, ...	88	14	House, ... *	2606	1
Honeycombe, Matthew	Calstock Town, ...	88	10	House and Garden, ... *	2606b	2

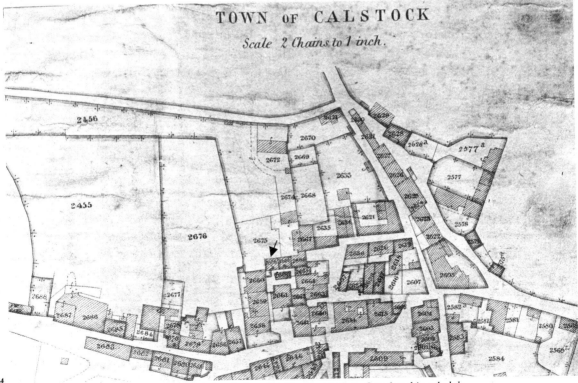

TOWN OF CALSTOCK

Scale 2 Chains to 1 inch.

123, 124. Duchy of Cornwall: Manor of Calstock Assessionable Award Map 1845–6 and its schedule.

XIII School Records

Most major (and many minor) public and grammar schools have extensive records, some of which may have been published.

Many of our older schools within the state system have registers going back to the 1850s, when a great many National and British schools were built for the Church of England or the nonconformist denominations by private benefactions and public subscriptions. The 1879 Education Act ordered the setting up of Local School Boards to 'fill in the gaps' and within the next twenty years innumerable 'Board Schools' were built all over the country. Increasingly, their log books and other records are being deposited in record offices. Many, however, are still held either by the schools or by local education offices.

School log books. Almost every log book will provide information about attendances, accidents, punishments, illnesses, the health and discipline of the school, the competence of the teachers and inspectors' reports (see p. 45). In church schools, there would also be visits from diocesan inspectors.

Most log books yield vivid accounts of tussles between teachers and children, parents and teachers, teachers and School Board, Board and Inspector.

School registers. At first sight, the information contained in school registers does not, perhaps, seem very promising. However, as with the log books, a closer scrutiny will often reveal a great deal of indirect evidence about the children's families [125].

NAME.	Index number.	DATE. 1856	Age. Y	M	RESIDENCE.	Parent's occupation.	Means of previous Instruction.	TIME previously under Instruction. Y	M
Sloane Eliza	1	July 7th 1856	6	1	Pearl Court	Cabinet maker	Infant School	1	
Alder Annie	2	7 1856	6	—	Hosier's Street	Shoe maker	Infant School	2	4
Brown Maria	1	—	6	—	Thorn Street	Butcher	—	—	6
Hunt Harriet	1	—	6	—	Brook Street	Sawyer	—	—	4
Kent Rosa	1	—	6	—	Sand Place	Painter	—	—	5
Knight Mary Jane	2	—	7	—	Somerset Place	Shoemaker	—	—	—
Loder Mary Ann	1	—	12	2	Cherry Court	Labourer	Trinity School	—	8
Marsbridge Ellen	1	—	6	—	Pike Court	Fuller & mason	Infant School	2	—
Morris Mary	2	—	6	2	Brook Street	Shoe maker	—	—	—
Painter Elizabeth	3	—	7	—	Chatham Street	Gardener	Trinity School	—	2
Savage Louisa	1	—	6	—	Hosier's Street	Labourer	Infant School	2	—
Smith Caroline	2	—	6	—	Friar Street	Shoemaker	—	1	6
Tindell Julia	1	—	6	—	Brook Street	Labourer	St Giles School	—	4
Smith Emma	3	14th 1856	8	—	Hosier Square	Baker	Infant School	—	6
Bolton Emma	2	21st 1856	6	2	Somerset Place	Shoe maker	—	—	3
Webb Sarah	1	21st 1856	7	3	Coley Terrace	Butcher	—	—	9
Mann	2	1856	7	11	Lavender Street	Upholsterer	Private School	1	4

125 *A Church of England school admission register, 1856. Many of the children are quite old by the time they start school. An extreme example is Mary Ann Loder (number 7) who entered school aged 12 years 2 months. The withdrawals register shows that Mary Ann left school three months after her arrival to go into service.*

XIV Secondary Sources

General works. Wide background reading is essential at every stage of your investigations and there are many bibliographies which will enable you to locate relevant books and articles. These may usually be obtained from your local library through the inter-loan system.

With regard to more general browsing, history is not well served by the Dewey system in use in most libraries. Because every subject has a history, only the most general works tend to find their way onto the 'history' shelves. The books you will find helpful are much more likely to be shelved with the history of religion, transport or architecture. It is advisable, therefore, to acquire some knowledge of the Dewey system and to have frequent recourse to the subject index.

More detailed works. In background reading, as with picture researching, the general should be complemented by the specific. For example, in the case of the Salonika campaign, it might be best to start with a general history of the First World War before moving on to the greater detail of the relevant regimental history, which will often give the names of officers and men involved in a particular engagement. The industrious family historian could also unearth reports from Salonika in *The Times* and other newspapers.

Memoirs, diaries and letters. You can also draw upon a wealth of memoirs, diaries and letters of others who shared some of the experiences of your ancestors. You may not be as lucky as Gordon was in having inherited a diary but you will be unfortunate if you cannot find a relevant published one.

Novels. The family historian should not disparage the novel. In their very different ways, E. M. Forster's *A Passage to India*, John Masters' *Bhowani Junction* and Paul Scott's *Raj Quartet* achieve more in recreating the texture of Anglo–Indian life, than a whole shelf of histories. Similarly, the novels of H. G. Wells, Arnold Bennett or R. F. Delderfield bring out the foibles as well as the fabric of Edwardian life.

Local histories. A major library in your vicinity will probably have the *Victoria County History* of the county in which you are interested. Begun towards the end of the nineteenth century and still in progress, this series includes both general historical material on the county and a history of each place. Volumes completed more recently give much more emphasis to social history than the older ones.

The simplest way to discover what other local histories have been written is by looking up the place name in the *British Library Catalogue*, available in most major libraries. Although mainly an author catalogue, in this respect it acts like a subject index. More recent books will not be in the main index but in the various supplements.

A note of caution. Although secondary sources can be very useful in providing background information for the family history, it is important to remember that they are not evidence. The books you have used should always be cited, and wherever possible checked against primary sources.

Published Source Material. Libraries are not merely useful for secondary material. Many have records, maps and photograph collections as well. Also, much primary source material has been published (see Primary Sources, p. 187). You would therefore be well advised to see if you can make arrangements to visit your nearest university library or, on occasion, armed with a ticket and a list of books or articles you cannot easily locate elsewhere, one of the six statutory libraries which are entitled to a free copy of every publication. (See p. 165.)

Unpublished Personal Name Indexes. Many record offices and libraries have very useful place and name indexes. Some are very large – the Burnett Morris index in the West Country Studies Library, Exeter, contains over a million cards. The list of record repositories (pp. 161–167) gives some indication of these. For further details you will need the appropriate Gibson guide. (See p. 164.)

XV Parish Registers

General.

Parochial Records Measure. On 1 January 1979 the Parochial Records Measure came into force, compelling the deposit of church records in diocesan record offices (usually the appropriate County Record Office) when incumbents cannot meet very stringent safety and preservation requirements. As a result, nearly all church records have been deposited. The measure also gives one the right to ask for parish records still with the incumbent to be placed on loan at the diocesan record office for a period of up to twelve months. Deposited registers are listed in the *Phillimore Atlas and Index of Parish Registers* (see p. 173) and lists are often available from County Record Offices.

Fees. Record offices holding parish registers may either charge no fees or charge according to regulations they devise themselves. In practice most record offices allow registers to be consulted free of charge, but a few charge a day search fee for use of the record office.

Incumbents holding registers are legally obliged to allow access to their registers but are still entitled to charge the full fees laid down in 1972 – 30p for the first year and 15p for each subsequent year for marriages up to 1837 and for all baptisms and burials (i.e., 90p for the first year and 45p for each subsequent year for a comprehensive search of all three registers). Most incumbents are, however, willing to agree to a reasonable figure when extensive searches are involved.

Starting dates. Parish registers were begun in 1538 but most start much later. The maps published by the Institute of Heraldic and Genealogical Studies (see p. 139) show not only parish boundaries but also the starting dates of registers.

Searching. It is important to note gaps or illegible portions of registers both in order to search the bishop's transcripts (see below), and also to assess the probability of relevant entries being lost.

Scotland. Parish registers for the whole of Scotland have been deposited at New Register House, Princes Street, Edinburgh. At the time of going to press they may be searched for a fee of £4.00 per day.

Ireland. The majority of Irish parish registers were destroyed when the 'Four Courts', the Irish Public Record Office, was blown up in 1922. Surviving registers may be consulted in the Public Record Office in Dublin.

Bishop's transcripts. Started in 1598, bishop's transcripts (known as 'BTs') normally run from Lady Day (25 March) to Lady Day and are now usually in County Record Offices (except for Wales, where all of them are in the National Library of Wales). They may be useful not only when the original register has been lost but also when it survives intact, for in many cases they include information not in the parish register. They may have been copied independently from the clerk's rough register, or have actually *been* the rough register – copied into the parish register and then sent off. Most series of bishop's transcripts are defective either because the returns were not made, or because they were subsequently destroyed at the Bishop's Registry or elsewhere. Sometimes, the transcripts of a whole diocese were lost, as with those for the diocese of London when St Paul's Cathedral was destroyed in the Great Fire of London in 1666. It is therefore a matter of luck which years have survived and which have not.

At the Devon County Record Office, Exeter, there are bishop's transcripts for St Cleer for the following years before the first surviving parish register begins in 1678. 1597–1602, 1614, 1617, 1633–35, 1663, 1664, 1665 or 6 (date missing), 1667, 1668, 1670, 1672, 1673.

It can be seen that there is a gap during the Civil War and Commonwealth period. This partly reflects the fact that when bishops were abolished, there were obviously no bishop's transcripts! However, there is usually a gap like this in the original registers. There was a great deal of disruption in the churches caused by the war, by the replacement of clergy with strong 'Anglican' views by Puritans, and by the institution of civil registration in 1653.

Full details of which record repositories hold bishop's transcripts can be found in the indispensable

Gibson guide *Bishop's Transcripts and Marriage Licences, Bonds and Allegations; a guide to their location and indexes.* (See p. 164.)

Modern copies of parish registers. A large number of parish registers have been copied and many of these have been printed. There is usually a copy at the Society of Genealogists (see p. 158). Other copies are in local libraries and record offices.

In locating these copies, the two booklets published by the Society of Genealogists will be found extremely useful. (See page 161.)

The largest group of printed registers is the Phillimore Marriages series. W.P.H. Phillimore, the founder of the publishing company (whose great-grandson, incidentally is married to a Canadian Honeycombe, descended from the Jersey branch), started the series in 1895, and in the following twenty or thirty years, the marriage registers of many parishes were printed. Among these was St Cleer, and there could scarcely be a better example of the folly of relying on such transcripts. Phillimore's marriage registers are often criticised for their many errors. However, apart from a few relatively minor mistranscriptions, the St Cleer copy is fairly virtuous in this respect. What is disastrous is not its errors but its omissions. These fall under four categories:

(i) *Bishop's transcripts not used.* Firstly, although the parish register starts in 1678, Phillimore ignores the bishop's transcripts which exist back to 1597, and so the user has been robbed of some very important early entries.

(ii) *Banns entries not transcribed.*

(iii) *Names of witnesses not recorded.*

(iv) *Signatures and marks.* No indication was given whether or not a person could sign.

The significance of these omissions will be discussed under *Marriages* below. Suffice it to say at this point that the omissions actually made it impossible to prove Gordon's pedigree from the printed copy alone.

Mormon microfilms. Because in many dioceses they have met with religious objections from bishops and clergy, the Mormons have been able to microfilm only about one third of the pre-1837 registers of England and Wales, although they have been allowed to film all the Scottish ones. These microfilms are kept near Salt Lake City, where the Mormons have hollowed out the inside of a granite mountain to house them. Positive copies of the microfilms are lent to branch libraries throughout the world. (For British branch libraries, see pp. 165–166).

The International Genealogical Index (IGI). The IGI, formerly called the Computer File Index (or CFI) (see p. 69), is rapidly revolutionizing genealogical research and must now be your first port of call after you have obtained all the information you can from civil registration. Microfilm copies of the Index for particular counties, the whole of the British Isles or, in some cases, the whole world, are increasingly being obtained by county record offices, libraries and family history societies. The very useful booklet *Where to Find the International Genealogical Index* by Jeremy Gibson and Michael Walcot, published by the Federation of Family History Societies, gives you full details.

When using the IGI, very few genealogists take any notice of the reference numbers. However, the batch number gives us an important piece of information as there are *two* main types of entry in the Index: records of whole parishes put in under what is called 'Controlled extraction' programme, which have batch numbers beginning P,C,M or 725, 745 or 754; and entries for single families submitted by private individuals since 1969, which have a third digit number smaller than 4, e.g., 7309309.

It is very important to know what parishes you have searched by using the IGI and for what years. The convenient way of discovering this is to consult the *Phillimore Atlas and Index of Parish Registers* edited by C. R. Humphery-Smith (see p. 165). Also, at the front of each county, the IGI itself includes a list of parishes. If you get a print-out of this, not only will you have more details on which parishes are covered, but it will enable you to identify errors in the IGI. Thus the marriage of Gordon's probable ancestor, Matthew Honeycombe, was ascribed to *Scilly Islands Parish*, which was highly unlikely. A quick check on the list showed that batch number–5929–1 – covered the parish of Morval. The register of this parish was examined and the entry found [128].

With regard to the Devon list, the batch number 7309309 for the marriage at Stoke Damerel of William and Dorothy, the parents of Samuel George Davey Honeycombe told us two things. Firstly, it was only chance that this entry was in the IGI and it did not mean that by searching the IGI we had covered all the marriages of Stoke Damerel. Secondly, it meant that the entry was there because someone else had been interested in it, most probably a relative. Mormon records at Salt Lake City would show the address of this person at the time the entry was submitted. Take care! Many entries have been submitted from imperfect printed or manuscript transcripts, and many more from entries for single families submitted by private individuals, the accuracy of whose work cannot be guaranteed. Although the IGI would have enabled Gordon to find the marriage date of Samuel's parents quite easily, it would not have been as helpful for finding the baptisms of his brothers and sisters – the Stoke Damerel baptisms are only in the IGI up to 1801 and no 'casual' later Honeycombe baptisms have been included.

For those researching Welsh genealogy, the IGI is something of a mixed blessing as after 1813 a person's surname is assumed to be the name given in the surname column of a baptismal register, but before *1813* the father's Christian name is assumed to be the child's 'surname', e.g. William (son of), even for English-type surnames. The Welsh situation is extremely complex, and no-one should use the Welsh counties of the IGI until they have studied the article by Chris Pitt-Lewis in Gibson and Walcot's booklet mentioned above.

The extreme Welsh special case illustrates the more general principle which has already been emphasised (see p. *69*). One must always remember that the IGI is a finding aid, not a source. Not only will the original entry often give more information, but it may well reveal a transcription or other error in the IGI.

Marriage indexes. In the 1930s, Percival Boyd, a Fellow of the Society of Genealogists compiled *Boyd's Marriage Index*, a gigantic national marriage index with seven million names, subdivided by county and then by period. Mainly compiled from printed registers, it may be consulted at the Society of Genealogists. Care must be taken in using it, as surname variants are grouped together according to Boyd's own system and some volumes include both brides and grooms, others one or the other (see p. 173, Steel).

Relatively few of the entries in Boyd are in the IGI (which is mainly baptisms) so Boyd has not yet been superseded, though it may be eventually. In recent years, Boyd has been supplemented by a number of county marriage indexes, most of them compiled by local family history societies. Details will be found in Gibson's *Marriage, Census and other Indexes for Family Historians* (see p. 164). There is also the massive Pallot Index, especially strong on London marriages 1780–1837, held by the Institute of Heraldic and Genealogical Studies, Canterbury.

Baptisms.

Information given. Up to 1812, baptism registers consisted of blank leaves on which the parish clerk wrote an account of each baptism [126]. From 1 January 1813 registers consisted of volumes of printed forms with ruled columns for date of baptism, Christian names of the child, parents' Christian names, father's surname, father's abode and profession and by whom the ceremony was performed [127].

Delay between birth and baptism. It is important to remember that until 1837 you are nearly always dealing with baptisms and not births. The delay between birth and baptism varied at different times. In the seventeenth century, three days was probably about the norm. By 1813, however, it might well be several weeks. Some baptisms are not of children at all but of adults. Thus the second Honeycombe baptism Gordon came across at Stoke Damerel was of Philip (C13), son of William and Mary, baptised on 22 July 1812 but born on 6 February 1788.

Missing baptisms. When you have taken down a series of baptisms from a parish register, you must never assume that you have a complete record of the family. There are all kinds of reasons why baptisms may be missing. The parents may have come to the parish with several children, or left it before others were born. They may have become nonconformists, with the baptisms performed elsewhere, or, in the case of

A pre-1813 register of baptisms from St Cleer, Cornwall. Note the year change on 25 March. William Honeycomb was baptised on 12 March 1750 but we would call it 1751. 1751 was the year the calendar was changed, so had only ten months.

Post-1813 baptismal register from St Cleer. Note that eight children of William and Louisa Honeycombe were baptised on the same day.

128 *A seventeenth-century marriage at Morval, Cornwall, discovered with the help of the IGI (see page 133). This discovery disproved an identification previously made by Gordon.*

Quakers, not at all. Very often, the first child was baptised in the mother's parish, as it was common for the young wife to go to her mother for her first confinement. The parish clerk may have been negligent and the entry never recorded. Lastly, some children were never baptised at all, as religion gradually lost its hold on the labouring population. Sometimes you will find several children baptised together. This might either be because the vicar had a baptismal round-up or because the parents decided to baptise one infant and then have older children 'done' at the same time [127].

Marriages

Information given. Up to 1753, entries of marriages were written on blank pages [128]. From 1 January 1754 printed forms were used. This was one of the results of the 'Hardwicke' Marriage Act of 1753, so called because it was passed largely at the instigation of Lord Hardwicke, the Lord Chancellor. Called 'an act for the better prevention of clandestine marriages' it laid down that all marriages, except those of Quakers and Jews, must henceforth be in the parish church and must be by banns or by licence.

The printed forms of the 'Hardwicke' marriage registers show the parishes of the parties and their status (bachelor or spinster) and the occupation of the groom. If one or both parties was a minor (i.e., under twenty-one) this is stated, and with the consent 'of parents' or 'of her father' or 'of her guardian' added thereby indicating whether both, one or no parents were alive at the time of marriage. Both parties signed, or – if they were illiterate – made a mark.

Witnesses. Two witnesses (occasionally three), also signed or made their marks. The printed registers in Phillimore's marriage series never include the names of witnesses. However, these are often the most valuable part of the entry and their names should always be noted, for often they were relatives. In the case of the Phillimore and other similar copies this means that the original must be examined, for time and again the father of at least one of the parties is a witness, and this may provide the only evidence of parentage. For example, on 10 August 1760 the Phillimore copy gave *William Honicombe and Sarah Bowden, lic.* The original register showed that one of the witnesses was a Jonathan Honicombe. This made it almost certain that the William married in 1760 was the William (H9) baptised in 1735, the son of Jonathan Honicombe (H7) which in fact, turned out to be crucial in proving Gordon's pedigree. The best example of all, however, of the value of witnesses was the marriage of the grandparents of John Symons

Banns of Marriage *Between William Honicombe and Mary Pitt both of this Parish were Published the 16th 23d and 30th days of June 1776 by one John Jope Cur.*

No 164 *The said William Honicombe* of *this* Parish

and *Mary Pitt* of *the*

Parish *aforesaid* were

Married in this *Church* by *Banns*

this *Seventh* Day of *July* in the Year One Thousand Seven

Hundred and *Seventy Six* by me *John Jope Cur:*

This Marriage was solemnized between Us { *The Sign of ° William Honicombe* / *Sign W Mary Pitt* }

In the Presence of *Saml Kingdon —*

Samuel Sibly

129 *Post-1754 'Hardwicke' marriage register from St Cleer, combining banns and marriages in the same entry. Note the difference in spelling from William's baptism in 1750/1. (126) and the marks. Samuel Sibly was the parish clerk.*

Honeycombe in 1805. The marriage of John Honicombe, mason (D10) and Joanna Davey (D11) was witnessed by Peter Davey and Samuel Honeycombe. Here, the clerk had actually added the word 'fathers'. Even this remarkable piece of information was omitted in the Phillimore copy.

Just as important as noting the names of witnesses is checking to see whether they appear in other entries. In this way the parish clerk and other 'regulars' can be distinguished from relatives and friends. If a totally unfamiliar name is not a 'regular', it might save years of searching, as wills of that surname might well turn up something. But if a 'regular' is not identified, a great deal of time can be wasted in looking for a non-existent connection.

Signatures. It can be most useful to know whether or not a person could sign his name, and in the case of Gordon's pedigree there were several occasions where the use of a mark or a signature was the crucial factor in a correct identification. Once again, there was no indication in the printed register.

Banns. The Hardwicke Marriage Act of 1753 ordered that all marriages must be by banns or licence and that registers of banns must be kept. There were three types of banns registers:

(i) separate registers;

(ii) in the marriage register but in a different part of the volume;

(iii) combined entries for banns and marriage.
The St Cleer register belongs to the third type [129].

The Phillimore transcriber ignored all banns entries, including those not followed by a marriage at St Cleer. In a way, banns entries for marriages elsewhere are *more* important than those of marriages in the parish, for they lead you directly to the 'missing' marriages which did not take place in the parish which it might be virtually impossible to discover otherwise. Where the bride and groom came from different parishes, it was usual to marry in the bride's parish and in the St Cleer marriage register, there are quite a number of banns entries where the marriage took place in another parish. For example, in 1781 we have 'Banns of Marriage between John Honicombe, of this Parish and Jane Henwood, of the Parish of Bodmin, were published the 28th October, and the 4th and the 11th of November, 1781.' This provides the mother's maiden name for a William, son of John and Jane Honeycombe, baptised in 1783. Apart from filling a 'gap' in the family tree, such information might be indispensible genealogically in that it might enable us to consult the wills of the Henwoods which mentioned Honeycombe relatives and clarified the pedigree.

Christian Horrill was Buried 18 of August
Elizabeth May was Buried 9 of September
... May ... was Buried 10 of September
Jone Lyple was Buried the 17 of October
Matthew ... was Buried 26 of October
John Kraft was Buried first of November
... was Buried 4 of December

130 *A pre-1813 burial register (St Cleer, 1693). Burials of children are not distinguished from those of adults, making identification difficult. Matthew was four years old.*

Even when the marriage took place in the parish church, the banns part of the entry might give additional information. For example Phillimore gives 'Ezekiel Johns, sojourner & Joan Roberts *lic* 17 Nov. 1775'. The marriage entry gives 'Ezekiel John sojourner ye lawful time in ye parish & Joan Roberts (sig Robarts) were married by Licence. Both sign. (He signs Ezekiel Joh*n*). The marriage is witnessed by John Robarts and Samuel Sibly. Samuel Sibly was the parish clerk.'

The banns give 'Banns of Marriage between Ezekiel John of the Parish of Redruth, a sojourner in the Parish of Linkinhorne, and Joan Roberts, of this Parish, were published the 10th 17th and 24th of September, 1775.'

Here, the banns entry gives Ezekiel's parish of origin and his parish of residence, (which was *not* St Cleer) and the witness to the marriage is probably his bride's father. All three vital pieces of information are missing in the Phillimore copy.

Checking for widows and widowers. With every marriage, it is important to seek the baptismal entry for the wife. If it is within a few years of the husband's the identifications are probably correct. What many people forget, however, is the frequency of remarriages, so one must also bear in mind each time the possibility that the wife was a widow or the husband a widower.

Child marriages. Up to 1754, boys could be married at fourteen and girls at twelve, so a seemingly im-

possible identification could be correct. Such child marriages were, however, relatively rare and uncanonical marriages under these ages even rarer.

Burials.

Information given. Before 1813, most frequently only the name of the deceased is given, sometimes with some short description such as 'widow', 'wife of X' and occasionally with an occupation. Parentage is normally given in the case of infants or children, but not always – there is no indication in the case of earlier entries at St Cleer [130].

After 1813, in the printed registers there are columns for 'name', 'abode', 'when buried', 'age' and by whom the ceremony was performed [131].

Burials in woollen. To assist the wool industry the government passed laws in 1666 and 1678 compelling burial in woollen shrouds, and the vicar had to make an affidavit to that effect.

The calendar change of 1752. Until 1 January 1752 the year began on 25 March. So January 1750 followed December 1750. To avoid confusion, both the old and new style dates should be given, e.g. February, 1750/1, 24 March 1750/1, but 25 March 1751 [126].

The same Act of Parliament replaced the Julian Calendar by the Gregorian Calendar introduced in 1582 by Pope Gregory XIII. This was more accurate that the Julian Calendar but by 1582 was eleven days

BURIALS solemnized in the Parish of STOKE-DAMEREL, in the County of DEVON, in the Year of our Lord God 1820				
Name.	Abode.	When Buried.	Age.	By whom the Ceremony was performed.
Samuel Philip Davey No. 426 Honeycombe	Devonport Marlboro' St	31	4 years 5 months	J. Jacob Officiating Minister

131 *Post-1813 burial register. Until the late nineteenth century most families lost at least one child under five.*

132 *Parish map of Cornwall published by the Institute of Heraldic and Genealogical Studies, Canterbury, showing parish boundaries, probate jurisdictions, starting dates of registers and the location of churches.*

ahead of it. To bring Britain into line, it was necessary to decree that the next day after 3 September, 1752, would be 14 September. So 1751 had only approximately nine months, starting on 25 March and ending on 31 December, and 1752 was eleven days short.

Days of celebration were left unchanged. So not only was Christmas Day left on 25 December, but Guy Fawkes Day, for example, was left on 5 November, even though it was no longer a true anniversary of the 5 November 1605. The bankers, conservative as ever, refused either to change their date or to have a year eleven days short. So the financial year went on until 5 April, eleven days after 25 March, and has done ever since.

Spelling. In most of the earlier Honeycombe entries, the name is spelt *Honicombe* rather than *Honeycombe*. In his *Brief Abstract*, John Symons Honeycombe makes a great deal of this archaic spelling of the name which he uses to substantiate its etymology from his Norman warrior's nickname *Honi à Combat*. However, there was no real consistency – until the nineteenth century, spelling was, in fact, very flexible, As most people were illiterate, the clerk spelt the name the way he thought most appropriate. The genealogist, therefore, never discounts an entry because the spelling is different [126, 129].

By the mid nineteenth century, most families had settled upon a particular spelling and this may be a help in relating people to a particular branch. For instance, nineteenth century entries in St Cleer registers with the spelling *Honeycomb* were invariably for the descendants of Philip Honeycomb (G12) and it is the spelling used by his descendants in America.

Demographic data. Counts of baptisms, marriages and burials can be very useful in establishing basic demographic trends against which to set the events in your own family. In establishing years of good and bad harvests, the harvest year is reckoned from August to July. A moderately high death rate may indicate a bad harvest, a very high one, a plague or smallpox epidemic.

As with Census Returns, most family historians still use Parish registers solely as a source for genealogical data, and have scarcely begun to assemble the data which will set the family in its local and social context.

XVI Other Parish Records

Poor law records.

Overseers' accounts. Detailed overseers' accounts are available in most parishes (including St Cleer) from the latter part of the eighteenth century. See page 73.

Poor rate books. These record the collection of the poor rate, the forerunner of our present day rates. Though sometimes they give only totals, they often record individual payments, thus acting as a kind of directory of the more prosperous parishioners. None survives for St Cleer.

Settlement certificates. The parents of William the sawyer (c8) – William Honeycombe (c1) and his wife, Mary (nee Pitt) (c2) – certainly moved to Liskeard around 1784-6 and may even have gone on to Devonport. Yet, if our identification is correct, it was at St Cleer that Mary drew poor relief after her husband's death in 1815 (see p. 70). There is a simple explanation for this. By an Act of 1662, each parish was responsible for the relief of people who had a legal *settlement* there. By this Act you gained a settlement by being born in a place, by renting a tenement of £10 per annum, or by finding security to discharge the parish of your adoption from all expense it might incur in providing relief for you. An act of 1691 laid down other ways by which you could obtain a legal settlement; by serving a parish office, paying a parish rate, being apprenticed by indenture to a parishioner, or by serving a year in service. Either William was working for himself or was not in continuous work, and so never achieved the year in service which would have given him a settlement in Liskeard.

Up to 1743-4, since birth in a parish gave a legal settlement, pregnant women were hastened on from parish to parish so that the baby would become somebody else's responsibility. This inhumane practice was ended by an Act of 1743-4 by which a bastard child of a vagrant woman took the mother's place of legal settlement.

Settlement and removal gave rise to a vast amount of documentation which means that fortunately there are many exceptions to the generalisation that parish register entries are the only evidence for a move.

A temporary stay in another parish (e.g. at harvest) necessitated a certificate from your own parish agreeing to take responsibility for you, and an Act of 1696-7 introduced the issue of settlement certificates for a permanent stay – your own parish would still pay for you if you needed relief.

If you arrived without a settlement certificate, you were liable to be removed forthwith and sent back to the *last* parish where you had gained a legal settlement – the parishes where you had previously obtained a settlement were irrelevant. You could be removed whether or not you actually became chargeable. The settlement system very tightly controlled the movement of people and in many cases inhibited it altogether.

Examinations and removal orders. The whole system resulted in enormous expense and endless litigation. However, it has left the family historian knowing a great deal about any ancestors or relatives who were 'removed', for prior to removal, the unfortunate pauper was brought before the magistrates to establish the last legal place of settlement. Then a removal order was granted. Copies of the examinations and removal orders may survive either with the parish documents of the unwilling host parish or with the County or Borough Quarter Sessions records, now usually deposited at a County Record Office [134].

The examinations are almost invariably very informative, giving a complete biography of the unfortunate pauper. Fortunately for the Honeycombes, though less fortunately for us, we have not yet found any record of any of the Honeycombes being 'removed'.

Bastardy Papers. When an unmarried girl gave birth to a bastard, she was examined to ascertain the identity of the father. When, as was often the case, she was reticent, considerable pressure was exerted. Once identified the father was usually compelled to make weekly payments towards the maintenance of the child. So too was the mother if she were working [133].

In St Cleer in 1829, a distant relative of Gordon, John Honeycombe, a labourer, having got Margaret Wills with child, failed to answer the summons to

COUNTY OF Cornwall **The** Order of *John Butler and William Jope Esquires* two of his Majesty's Justices of the Peace in and for the said County, one whereof is of the Quorum, and both residing next unto the Limits of the Parish Church within the Parish of *Saint Cleer* in the said County, made the *twelfth* Day of *December* One Thousand Eight Hundred and *twenty nine* concerning *a female* Bastard Child — lately born in the Parish of *Saint Cleer* aforesaid, of the Body of *Margaret Wills* single Woman.

Whereas it hath appeared unto us the said Justices, as well upon the Complaint of the Churchwardens and Overseers of the Poor of the said Parish of *Saint Cleer* as upon the Oath of the said *Margaret Wills* that she the said *Margaret Wills* on the *Eighth* Day of *November* now last past, was delivered of *a female* Bastard Child — at *Ononhill* in the Parish of *Saint Cleer* in the said County, and that the said Bastard Child *is become* chargeable to the said Parish of *Saint Cleer* — and further that *John Honeycombe* — *of the said Parish* in the *of Saint Cleer Labrover* did beget the said Bastard Child — on the Body of her the said *Margaret Wills* And whereas the said ~~~~~ ~~hath appeared before us, in Pursuance of our Summons for that Purpose, but hath not shewed any sufficient Cause why he the said John~~ ~~Honeycombe~~ ~~shall not be the reputed Father of the said~~ ~~Bastard Child~~ We therefore, upon Examination of the Cause and Circumstances of the Premises, as well upon the Oath of the said *Margaret Wills* as otherwise, do hereby adjudge him the said *John Honeycombe* to be the reputed Father of the said Bastard Child — And thereupon we do order, as well for the better Relief of the said Parish of *Saint Cleer* — as for the Sustentation and Relief of the said Bastard Child — that the said *John Honeycombe* shall and do forthwith, upon Notice of this our Order, pay or cause to be paid to the said Churchwardens and Overseers of the Poor of the said Parish of *Saint Cleer* or to some or one of them, the Sum of *Two Pounds fifteen Shillings Twenty eight* for and towards the Lying-in of the said *Margaret Wills* and the Maintenance of the said Bastard Child — to the Time of making this our Order, and for the Charges and Expences incurred prior to the said Order of Filiation being made, and incident to the obtaining of the said Order, as ascertained on Oath. And we do also hereby further order, that the said *John Honeycombe* shall likewise pay or cause to be paid to the Churchwardens and Overseers of the Poor of the said Parish of *Saint Cleer* for the Time being, or to so meor one of them, the Sum of *One Shilling and eight pence* weekly and every Week from this present Time, for and towards the Keeping, Sustentation, and Maintenance of the said Bastard Child — for and during so long Time as the said Bastard Child — shall be chargeable to the said Parish of *Saint Cleer* And we do further order, that ~~the~~ the said *Margaret Wills* shall also pay or cause to be paid to the said Churchwardens and Overseers of the Poor of the said Parish of *Saint Cleer* — for the Time being, or to some or one of them, the Sum of *Two Pence* weekly and every Week, so long as the said Bastard Child — shall be chargeable to the said Parish of *Saint Cleer* in Case she shall not nurse and take care of the said Child — herself. Given under our Hands and Seals the Day and Year first above written.

J Butler

W Jope

It has been duly proved to us upon Oath that the said John Honeycombe has been duly summoned to appear before us the said Justices to the end that we might examine into the cause and circumstances of the premises, and Whereas the said John Honeycombe has neglected to appear before us according to the said Summons.

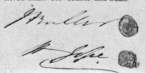

Langston and Harker, Mercury Office, Sherborne.

133

appear before the magistrates. In his absence he was ordered to pay £2 15s 8d towards her lying in and 1s 8d a week. Margaret was to pay 10d a week [133].

Churchwardens' accounts. These deal with the regular purchase of necessities such as communion wine, with payments for jobs such as cleaning the church, or the washing of surplices, and with the rather more expensive work connected with the maintenance of the church (see pp. 87–91).

Vestry minutes. These chronicle the civil administration of the parish. There were two kinds of vestry – an *open vestry*, attended by all the parishioners and a *select* vestry, which only the wealthier parishioners attended. No vestry minutes survive for St Cleer for the eighteenth century. The nineteenth century ones give the impression of a select vestry. All kinds of information may be found in vestry minutes, including assistance given to individuals to emigrate, though this does not seem to have applied to St Cleer.

Other accounts. Other accounts not found for St Cleer but available elsewhere are those of the Parish Constable and the Surveyor of the Highways. Like the churchwardens and overseers these were all honorary positions to which people were elected each year.

Enclosure and tithe awards and maps. See p. 128.

Records of parish charities. None appears to survive for St Cleer.

Church seating plans. See p. 96.

The other records in the parish chest have yet to receive the attention from genealogists that parish registers have had. However, not only are they almost the only source before the 19th Century for putting poor rural families in context, but they may be indispensable for proving the genealogy itself. Gordon's ancestor, William (C1) could be differentiated from two other Williams only by reference to the Overseers accounts (see pp. 70–71) and the Churchwardens' accounts provided vital evidence for proving an earlier stage of the pedigree (see pp. 87–88). Most interesting of all, however, they demonstrated in no uncertain terms just how far the Honeycombes really were from the Manor House of St Cleer!

UPON the Complaint of the Church-Wardens and Overseers of the Poor of the Parish of *Saint Cleer* aforesaid in the said County of *Cornwall* unto us, whose Names are hereunto Set and Seals affixed, being two of His Majesty's Justices of the Peace in and for the said County of *Cornwall* and one of us of the Quorum, that *William Bonnett Jane his Wife and their two Children, to wit, William aged about two years and quarter and Mary aged about eight Weeks* have come to inhabit in the said Parish of *Saint Cleer* not having gained a legal Settlement there, nor produced any Certificate owning *them* to be settled elsewhere, and that the said *William Bennett Jane his Wife and William and Mary their Children* are likely to be chargeable to the said Parish of *Saint Cleer* We the said Justices upon due Proof made thereof, as well upon the Examination of the said *William Bonnett* upon Oath, as otherwise, and likewise upon due Confideration had of the Premises, do adjudge the same to be true: And we do likewife adjudge, that the lawful Settlement of the said *William Bennett Jane his Wife and William and Mary their Children* is in the said Parish of *Saint Ive* in the said County of *Cornwall* We do therefore require you the said Church-Wardens and Overseers of the Poor of the said Parish of *Saint Cleer* or some, or one of you to convey the said *William Bonnett Jane his Wife and William and Mary their Children* from and out of your said Parish of *Saint Cleer* to the said *Parish of Saint Ive* and to deliver to the Church-Wardens and Overseers of the Poor there, or to some, or one of them, together with this our Order, or a true Copy thereof, at the same Time shewing to them the Original; and we do also, hereby require you the said Church-Wardens and Overseers of the Poor of the said Parish of *Saint Ive* to receive and provide for *them* as — Inhabitant*s* of your said Parish. Given under our Hands and Seals the *Twenty feconsd* Day of *June* in the *Eleventh* year of the Reign of his said Majesty King GEORGE the Third. *and in the year of our* 1771

134 *Removal order, St Cleer, 1771. The Bennetts were removed not because they were chargeable, but because they were likely to become chargeable, i.e. they had arrived without a settlement certificate.*

XVII Wills and Inventories

There are three closely related types of record. *Wills* are normally signed by the deceased and witnessed; *letters of administration* (usually referred to as *admons*) are grants to the next of kin to administer the property of someone who died intestate; and *inventories* are lists of personal and household goods left by the deceased.

Pre-1858 wills.

Probate jurisdictions. A will was normally proved in the Court of the archdeaconry in which the testator died. If however he held property in two archdeaconries, the will had to be proved in the bishop's court (known as an *Episcopal Consistory Court*); if in two dioceses to the *Prerogative Court of Canterbury* (PCC) or *York* (PCY); if in two archdioceses to the Prerogative Court of Canterbury. PCC wills are in the Public Record Office, London, and PCY wills at the Borthwick Institute, York.

However, people with any pretentions of status tended to use a higher court than was necessary. The wills of most people who held land or any substantial property are therefore to be found in PCC or PCY, particularly the former.

From 1653 to 1660 *all* wills were proved by PCC.

Peculiars. Another complication is that there were a large number of *peculiars*. These were groups of parishes exempt from the archdeacon's and usually also the bishop's authority. Thus in Cornwall twenty-two parishes were peculiars of the Bishop of Exeter and four more of the Dean and Chapter of Exeter. Wills for all these parishes were kept in Exeter, and were destroyed by enemy action in 1942. Three parishes were in the Royal Peculiar of St Buryan, but wills for these are in the Cornwall Record Office with those of the Consistory Court of the Archdeaconry of Cornwall.

Two excellent guides to the various jurisdictions and to the location of wills are A. J. Camp's *Wills and their Whereabouts*, and J.S.W. Gibson's *Wills and Where to Find Them* (see p. 162). All ecclesiastical jurisdictions are shown on the parish maps produced by the Institute of Heraldic and Genealogical Studies (see p. 127) [132].

Nun-cupative wills. A nun-cupative will was a will made orally, usually by a testator on his death bed. This was written down and sworn by the witnesses but not signed by the deceased. Thus, in 1647, we have the following deposition in the Cornish County Record Office at Truro.

The voluntary deposition of Mark Berry of Plymstock, mariner given at the Admiralty Court of Cornwall held at Croft Hole the eighteenth day of October, 1647. This deponent saith that he was a cabin mate with Daniel Honicombe deceased, in the voyage that the said Honicombe died in being then in the Cat of Millbrook (whereof John Trenaman was master) and that he heard the said Honicombe advisedly and . . . say words to this effect: vide: that his old father Ambrose Honicombe should have his voyage and all else that he was owner of. And this deponent further asking him whether he had not made his will before he come away, the said Daniel answered him that he had made no will; but that his will was that his father should have all that he had as aforesaid. And this deponent is sure he made no other will afterward because he was constantly with him until he died.

There was a second deposition to the same effect. There is a note 'Mem to inquire for the will of Daniel Honicombe de Millbrook 5 or 6yr 8yr and to get a processo ad proband etc', and in fact a will by Daniel Honicombe had already been proved in the PCC in 1638/9.

Making Searches

Delay between death and probate. It is wise to search the indexes for at least three years after the date of a relative's death as there was sometimes a delay in proving a will.

Bequests. One cannot assume that all children are mentioned, and omissions are rarely because the children were out of favour. For example, Samuel George Davey Honeycombe (A3) mentions only his daughter, Emma (A11) – there is no mention of his son Henry (A9) or his family, or of his married daughters

Margaret (A6) and Eleanor (A12). It may be that Samuel had made gifts to them during his lifetime, or felt he had so little to leave that he gave it all to his unmarried daughter who had looked after him for many years (see p. 18).

Wills of relations on the female side. It is very important to abstract not only wills of the surname you are tracing but also those of relatives on the female side. Most individuals were in close touch with many relatives on their mothers' and grandmothers' side and many married aunts and cousins. On average, therefore, wills of bearers of the surname you are seeking will account for only a quarter of the total number of wills mentioning members of the family. Thus in 1822, Peter Davey, yeoman of St Cleer gives 'unto my daughter Joanna, the wife of John Honicombe, the sum of fifty pounds'. John (D9) and Joanna (D10) were the grandparents of John Symons Honeycombe (D19). See Table D, p. 71.

Since few wills have been comprehensively indexed for all names mentioned in them, the difficulty is in locating relevant ones. There are two possible approaches. One is to look up the wills of all surnames of families into which your family married, make mini family trees of the wives to find out what families *their* sisters and nieces married into and study wills of these surnames also. The other is to examine *all* wills of the parishes where your family lived. Both methods are very time-consuming but may yield information which could not be obtained anywhere else.

Estate Duty Office Registers of abstracts and indexes. From 1796 abstracts, and from 1812, copies of all wills and administrations in England and Wales had to be deposited at the Estate Duty Office. Most full copies were recently destroyed – an almost unparalleled act of archival vandalism approved by the Lord Chancellor and carried out despite the offer of the Society of Genealogists to house them. The only exceptions allowed were those relating to Devon, Cornwall and Somerset, the originals of which were destroyed during the war. These were sent to the appropriate County Record Office. The *registers of abstracts* for the whole country 1796–1857 are now in the Public Record Office. They record the date of probate, all beneficiaries, details and value of the property and the duty paid, and may now be searched right up to 1857.

From 1796 to 1812, the registers of abstracts are arranged in three groups: PCC wills, PCC administrations and 'County Court' wills, and administrations arranged court by court. A list of the volume numbers for each court is given in *The Genealogists' Magazine* Vol 15 No. 11 (Sept 1967) pages 394–7. The indexes to PCC wills (PRO ref IR 27/1–16) are in yearly volumes, those for PCC Admons (IR 27/17–20) contain several years and those for the County Courts (IR 27/67–93) several years and courts.

Unfortunately, these indexes are not strictly alphabetical but by initial letter and the first vowel in the surname. e.g. HA, HE, HI, HO, HU. In the case of H this results in approximate alphabetical order, but BA for example would not only include *Baxter* but *Blatch* and *Bradford*, BI not only *Bilston* but *Britton*.

From 1812, all wills are indexed in one consolidated series, whatever the court. There is a second index for PCC administrations and a third for all administrations from the County Courts. These post 1812 indexes are arranged by three letter groups, e.g. HOG to HON.

PCC wills. Except for 1853–8, when there is a proper printed index at the PRO, the indexes to PCC wills are arranged by year and then by first letter of the surname only, so searching can be a lengthy process. However, as we have seen, from 1796 it is more convenient to search them through the Estate Duty Office indexes, except perhaps for 1853–8 when there is a proper printed index.

Indexes to PCC wills have been published for 1383–1700 and 1750 and to PCC Admons 1559–1660. Details are given in the Gibson guide *A Simplified Guide to Probate Jurisdictions* FFHS 3rd edn, 1985, page 2.

The Society of Genealogists holds a card index of PCC wills 1750–1800 and publication is in progress.

So, in effect one needs to search the inadequate PRO indexes only for the period 1701–1749.

Wills proved locally. Except for 1653 to 1660 when all wills were proved by the PCC, for the period before 1796 it is necessary to conduct searches locally (usually in the county record office). Indexes have been published for many jurisdictions and the Society of Genealogists holds microfilms of many others.

Comprehensive searches
When undertaking a comprehensive search of pre-

1858 will for a particular surname a logical sequence of searches would be:

(i) Published PCC Indexes 1383–1700, 1750, especially 1653–1660 which covers all wills
(ii) Society of Genealogists card index of PCC wills 1750–1800 (by special application)
(iii) Estate Duty Office consolidated index 1812–1857 (PRO)
(iv) Estate Duty Office separate indexes for PCC wills PCC admons and all relevant local courts 1796–1812 (PRO)
(v) Society of Genealogists microfilm copies of indexes of relevant local courts
(vii) Other indexes held by local record offices
(viii) PRO indexes of PCC wills by first letter of surname 1701–1750
(ix) PCY wills at Borthwick Institute, York

Post 1858 wills. All post 1858 wills are at Somerset House, Strand, London WC1 where the indexes may be consulted free. Care must be taken in using them, as up to 1870 the indexes to wills and administrations are in separate volumes, and these are often not very clearly labelled on the spine. So it is easy to think you have searched the indexes to wills for a year, when in fact you have done only the administrations. Registered copies of wills will be produced for a fee of 25p each. You may also ask for the *original* wills which, of course, include the actual signatures. Printed indexes to post-1858 wills are also to be found in many county record offices and libraries.

Post 1858 wills may not only clarify relationships but may provide addresses which can be looked up in census returns. These addresses can, in fact, be obtained from the indexes free of charge.

Wales. Welsh pre-1858 wills are at the National Library of Wales, post 1858 at Somerset House.

Scotland. Scottish wills (or *testaments* as they are always called in Scotland), prior to 1823 are in the Scottish Record Office, Old Register House, Princes St, Edinburgh. Since then, they have been proved locally by the Sheriff Courts. They may either still be held locally by the relevant Sheriff Clerk or voluntarily deposited at the Scottish Record Office, which also holds a consolidated calendar of confirmations for the whole of Scotland since 1876.

Ireland. Irish wills were practically all destroyed in 1922 (see p. 153), though many lists of them (and some extracts) survive.

Inventories. Before the middle of the eighteenth century, most rural inventories – even those of craftsmen – mention farm animals and those of farmers usually mention both animals and crops for there was little specialisation, except that dictated by local conditions. Thus in 1644, John Honicombe of Callington [135] left four and a half acres of wheat in the earth (£5), two acres of barley in the earth (40s), seven acres and a half of kale (£5', corn threshed and unthreshed (£20), two steers of four years old (£14), one yearling steer and two steers of two years old (40s), one yearling heifer, four heifers and five calves, fourteen ewes and fourteen lambs (£7), thirty-five wethers and barren ewes (£6), and six pigs.

There were frequent mentions of beds and bedclothes. Tables were most commonly referred to as table boards and were boards on trestles. A cupboard was formerly just a side table (a cup board), but by the seventeenth century, had acquired an extra shelf and doors. Chairs were mentioned in many of the inventories but there were more stools and forms, for chairs were normally used only for the head of the household and important visitors. Kitchen utensils and equipment were usually mentioned – brass pots and pans, pewter dishes, iron spits and bars, pothooks and pot-hangers – there were no ovens and all cooking and boiling was done over (or in front of) the open fire. Troughs and tubs figured prominently – they were used for salting (with the shortage of winter feed this was the only way of ensuring a food supply for the winter) and for boulting (sieving the flour to separate it from the bran).

In many counties, the inventories listed each room in turn. Unfortunately, this rarely seems to apply to the Cornish ones.

135. Will of John Honicombe of Callington, 1644, from the Archdeaconry of Cornwall wills in the Cornwall County Record Office. It seems likely that Christian was 19 and Agnes 18. John and two of the three witnesses made marks in the form of initials. One of the witnesses was a woman.

XVIII Other Ecclesiastical Records

As well as the parish, the diocese and the archdeaconry both kept records and these are now usually to be found in County Record Offices. Wills we have dealt with elsewhere. The other main classes of records are:

Marriage licences. The jurisdictions for marriage licences were similar to those for wills (e.g. if the parties came from two dioceses, the licence must be granted by the Archbishop of Canterbury or York and if two provinces, by the Archbishop of Canterbury). So relevant marriage licences will usually be found in the same repository as relevant wills.

Strictly speaking, the term 'marriage licence' is incorrect, for what are held are normally not the actual licences (which were given to the parties to present to the vicar, and are sometimes found among the parish records) but the *allegations* and *bonds* which preceded the granting of the licences. These often record the father of one or both of the parties, as well as the groom's occupation. Thus the marriage licence for William, the son of Jonathan Honicombe in 1760 describes him as *yeoman*, our only clue that his branch of the family was engaged in agriculture.

Other licences. As well as marriage licences, diocesan and archdeaconry records may include licences to schoolmasters, surgeons, midwives, parish clerks and curates, licences to incumbents for non-residence and licences to eat meat during Lent.

Act books. The act books of Bishop's and Archdeacon's courts are less accessible to the family historian since they are usually in Latin up to 1731. They deal with any matters brought to the attention of the bishop or archdeacon, particularly concerning the clergy (see pp. 90–91).

Penances. Presentment to the Archdeacon's court for fornication or slander normally resulted in an order for penance to be publicly performed in church.

Here is one for a Richard James of St Cleer and his wife Margaret, dated 28 October 1741.

Whereas you have been presented in the Archdeaconry Court of Cornwall for the crime of fornication each with other before marriage, and whereas you have confessed . . . therefore you are enjoyned and required . . . to doe and perform the penence following that you shall on the next Sunday after the receipt hereof in the forenoon in time of Divine Service in the Chancel of the parish church of St Cleer say and repeat the words following We Richard and Margaret James doe humbly confess and acknowledge that we have highly offended Almighty God by committing the sin of fornication each with other before marriage and being therefore so great a scandal to the Church and Christian religion we do therefore hereby declare our hearty sorrow and penitence for the same in the presence of Almighty God and you present, promising by God's assistance amendment of life for the future . . . And of your performance hereof you are to bring to the said Court an authentick certificate under the hands of the Minister and Churchwardens and two of the principal inhabitants of St Cleer aforesaid at or before the sixteenth day of November next.

The Vicar and churchwardens certified that the penance had been carried out on 8 November.

Excommunications. Severe misdemeanours (such as persistent refusal to attend church or the court) might result in excommunication, and these books too can be very interesting.

Churchwardens' presentments. In most dioceses (though not for Exeter) there survive not only the books of penances and excommunications, but also the actual churchwardens' presentments by which the churchwardens presented parishioners to the Bishop's or Archdeacon's Court for fornication, adultery, slander and many other misdemeanours. Between about 1660 and 1760, there are extensive presentments for non-attendance at church, the vast majority being of nonconformists, particularly Roman Catholics and Quakers.

XIX Migration

Recent demographic research has shown that from the sixteenth to the eighteenth century people were much more mobile than was once thought. Few families were in one place for many generations. However, before the Industrial Revolution, migration tended to be short-distance.

London attracted people from all over the country, so that the population grew rapidly despite a very high death rate. Places of birth of Londoners may often be found in the apprenticeship records of the City companies, most of them in the Guildhall Library, London.

Migration in Family History. Perhaps the most interesting aspects of migration are the reasons for it. These have been discussed elsewhere (see pp. 33, 65–68, 77–81).

Migrants going any distance almost invariably went in the first instance to relatives or friends. It is also important to remember that the permanent migration of a family might be preceded either by seasonal migration or by the permanent settlement of the breadwinner only, his wife and children following later.

Hints for searching. From the piecing together of the story of the Jersey masons (see pp. 76–81) we can draw a number of points of wide application:

1. *Always commence your search of a parish register a substantial period before the date when you think you might start finding entries.* The *Brief Abstract* says John Honeycombe III (E25) went out to Jersey in 1825. So Gordon started his parish register searches in 1824. However, you need a much bigger 'margin' than this. If you think the family arrived in a place in 1825, start your parish register search a generation before – say 1800. There may be no entries of the surname you are interested in, but you may well find entries of relatives on the female side, for people often went where they had relatives. Such entries could be a clue providing an explanation for the move.

Of course, in the case of large parishes with huge registers, you may have to settle for much less than the ideal (unless they are in the International Genealogical Index). Though perhaps unavoidable, this can be dangerous – William the sawyer married in Devonport in 1811 and as far as was known he was the first member of the family to go there. However, as we have seen, there were earlier Honeycombe entries, and a William was witnessing a marriage there in 1802.

2. *Search records for all surnames which appear on the family tree for the last two or three generations, including the maiden names of wives and the married names of daughters.* As has been pointed out elsewhere, the occupations and connections of inlaws will help to build up the total family context, and throw light on the nature of the community in which the family were living.

3. *Analyse the annual number of baptisms, marriages and burials over a period to look for trends,* e.g. a sudden rise in the baptisms and marriages, pointing to substantial immigration.

4. *Note any other parishes mentioned.* When Ann Honeycombe married John Montgomery in 1826, she was described as 'of Devonport'. How many other entries were there with parishes in South-West England and when did such entries start?

5. *For the nineteenth century, analyse occupations and places of birth in the census records to look for a pattern.* Your ancestor may have died in 1849, but the 1851 Census could give an indication of the areas where workers were recruited.

6. *Do as much background reading as possible on the area, and search other records (e.g. newspapers) which will help to explain what was going on.* We have seen how knowing something of the various building projects going on in Jersey was necessary before we could begin to provide any explanation of the move to St Helier. The complementary search – a study of the Plymouth papers looking for advertisements for masons – has yet to be done.

7. *Formulate theories to explain the data you have found.* The historian is never satisfied with raw data. He is always looking for an *explanation*.

XX Manorial Records

Copyhold tenure. In the Middle Ages, there were two main kinds of tenants of the manor – the free tenants and the villeins or 'bondmen'. The free tenants paid rent, and were free of any services to the lord. The villeins were granted land in return for working on the lord's land or *demesne*. There were two main kinds of services: *week work*, a number of hours to be put in regularly each week; and *boon work*, help at special times such as harvest. Early in the fourteenth century, lords were finding it increasingly convenient to commute some or all of the villein's services to a money payment with which he hired labourers. This was not really rent for the land as it was with leasehold tenure, but a 'quit-rent' or payment to be quit or free of services. This kind of tenure was called *customary tenure* because the land was held according to the custom of the manor. Because the tenant theoretically held a copy of the entry in the manorial roll commuting the services to a money payment, he was most commonly known as a *copyholder* and the tenure as *copyhold*.

In the early days of copyhold tenure, the tenants were still theoretically villeins and their chattels all became the lord's on their death. This practice gradually died out. However, the lord continued to charge fines when one tenant died, before his heir succeeded to the property. The value of money kept fairly steady for centuries. Then, in the sixteenth century for various reasons, of which the influx of gold and silver from the New World was one, there was massive inflation. During the 'Price Revolution' as it is now known, the value of copyhold quit rents became very low and since these were fixed, the landowners tried to recoup by charging ever larger fines. In the sixteenth century, many cases came to the Court of Chancery which were appeals against fines which it was claimed were inequitable. Copyhold tenure was not finally abolished until 1925.

The conveyance of copyhold land had to be noted in the manor court rolls although it need not necessarily have taken place in the manor court. So when they survive the rolls have almost complete coverage.

Court rolls. In the fifteenth century, the manorial court became divided into two: the *court leet*, or *court customary* for customary tenants, and the *court baron* for free tenants. These terms were, however, very loosely applied. Even when they were held separately, it was not unusual in the sixteenth century for a so-called 'court baron' to exercise all the functions of a customary court. By the sixteenth century, the functions themselves had changed. The *court leet and view of frankpledge* elected the manorial officers such as the constable and the haywards and dealt with the enforcement of the laws and customs of the manor and the punishment of petty misdemeanours and offences. The *view of frankpledge*, which became combined with the court leet, dated back to Saxon times and was concerned with the maintenance of law and order. The *court baron* was mainly concerned with changes in tenancy in copyholds, with minor infringements of property rights and with the organisation of the open fields, meadows and commons. By the end of the seventeenth century the increasing power of the county justices and parish vestries made the court leet redundant and in the eighteenth century, there was, in most cases, once again only a single court. By the nineteenth century, periodical courts were largely abandoned, the business hitherto dealt with being transacted in the office of the steward of the manor, invariably a lawyer.

The Duchy of Cornwall manors were organised rather differently from the rest of the country. Not only were there no open fields in Cornwall, but there was no copyhold tenure either, rents being assessed every seven years. However, the details of tenancies in the Calstock assession rolls are similar to those we find in court baron rolls elsewhere and we can follow the successive transfers of small pieces of land. Thus in 1528, Thomas Honeycombe, freeman, took one messuage and twenty-two acres which Walter, his father, held before. The rent was 4s 6d and, in addition, on taking up the tenancy he had to pay a fine of 25s od. Walter Honycombe and Robert Webbe stood as sureties.

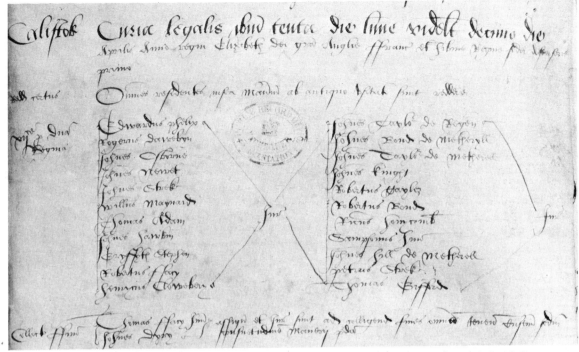

136 *Court Leet roll from Calstock, 1559, the first year of Elizabeth's reign, showing the* homage *or jury which includes a Richard Honycomb.*

Gradually, the tenement got divided. Thus in 1570, we have:

Stephen Honycombe, from the surrender of James Honycombe from the surrender of the said Thomas Honycombe his father for a half, Sampson Grilles from the surrender of the said James Honycombe and from the surrender of the above Thomas Honycombe his father for the other half took 1 messuage and 22 acres.

Before the start of parish registers, manorial records are almost the only detailed genealogical source we have for the bulk of the population. However, as entries like this show, they are no mere substitute but have greater precision with regard to identification.

In Calstock, the manor court and court leet rolls come to an end in 1648, though the assession rolls continue to the middle of the eighteenth century.

Format. Most manorial rolls begin with the *homage* or jury, followed by the *essoins* or apologies for absence.

Non-appearance at the court usually incurred a fine so many paid rather than lose a day's work.

Latin. Up to 1653, court rolls were written in Latin with a complicated system of abbreviations. English was used during the commonwealth period, but in 1660 Latin was restored and was used until 1732.

Location. Manorial rolls may be almost anywhere – in the County Record Office, in the Public Record Office, in the British Museum or still in the possession of the lord of the manor. In the case of Calstock, the rolls were divided between the Public Record Office and the Duchy of Cornwall office. Rolls for Calliland Manor (around Callington) were among the Additional Charters at the British Museum. St Cleer was divided among many manors but apart from a few small items in the Cornwall County Record Office, their records have not been located. A substantial but still incomplete list of manorial records and their location is held by the National Register of Archives, Quality Court, Chancery Lane, London WC2.

XXI Palaeography and Latin

Palaeography. This is the study of old handwriting, which is beginning to pose problems by the time you get back to the seventeenth century. However, sixteenth- and seventeenth-century handwriting is a much less formidable hurdle than you might imagine when you first try and read a document which, for all you can decipher, might be written in a foreign language. A few hours practice will work wonders.

It is essential to practice on copies of documents for which there is a transcript available, like those printed in Emmison's booklet (see p. 164). Try and decipher a document without the help of the transcript and then check for errors and omissions. You will find you very soon recognise the vast majority of the letters and the number of your gaps will decrease very rapidly.

Latin. The 'dog' Latin of the clerks is very easy to pick up and within the reach of anyone who studied Latin at school. Eileen Gooder's *Latin for Local History* is an invaluable guide as all the examples and exercises are taken from the kind of documents you are most likely to be using.

The easiest way to approach the problem of reading manorial records before 1732 is to study very closely the format and wording after 1732 and work backwards. Usually the post 1732 wording is a straight translation of that in use for centuries.

What seems at first sight the most formidable problem – the extensive use of abbreviations, so that the endings rarely appear on words, is in fact a help. Very often the scribe who wrote the record may not have been sure of the correct endings himself! In effect, the Latin of a medieval document is Latin without the inflections. Once one is used to its strangeness it is an easier variety of Latin altogether.

[137] *Handwriting guide, reproduced by kind permission of the Society of Genealogists.*

XXII Channel Islands, Manx and Irish Sources

Channel Islands. In *Jersey*, parish registers were kept from the 16th century (earliest register 1584). In 1842, registration became compulsory, but no new registers were started – it merely meant that henceforth, parish registers were in the custody of the local Parish Registrar, as is still the case. The Superintendant Registrar of Jersey has a copy of *all* parish registers, but neither indexes nor registers for *any* period are open to public inspection. He will conduct post-1842 searches, but all pre-1842 searches and many post-1842 are undertaken for enquirers by the Société Jersiaise, 9 Pier Road, St Helier, Jersey.

In *Guernsey*, registers have also been kept on a parish basis. A separate civil registration system was started in 1840 with the registers deposited centrally, but this was comprehensive only for births and deaths. Roman Catholic and Anglican marriages were held by the churches, the Registrar recording only non-conformist and civil ones until 1919, when the system became comprehensive. The centralised index of births dates from 1840, that for marriages from 1919 and the index for deaths only from December 1963. Before these dates, marriages or deaths are indexed by parishes. In the parish indexes of deaths before 1963, married women are indexed only under their maiden names. However, the indexes *and* the actual registers are open to the public on payment of a very modest search fee. The microfilms of the 1841–1881 censuses are also on hand.

Civil registration began in *Alderney* and *Sark* only in 1924, with duplicates kept in Guernsey. Earlier parish registers are still held locally.

Isle of Man. The General Registry is in Douglas (Tel: 0624 73358). Civil registration of births and deaths was effected in 1878, and of marriages in 1884. Prior to these dates, you are entirely dependent upon parish registers, though the marriage registers did start to give more detail in 1849. Some parish registers are held at the General Registry.

Ireland. Research in Ireland is beyond the scope of this volume. Irish family history has been rendered infinitely more difficult by the destruction of the Four Courts in Dublin (the Irish Public Record Office) in the 1922 civil war. In that building were housed all census returns and wills, and most of the parish registers and marriage licences. Little survived.

Civil registration. Fortunately, records of births, civil marriages and deaths were not destroyed and can be consulted at the General Register Office, Custom House, Dublin 1. They cover the whole of Ireland from 1864–1921 and Eire from 1921. The information given is similar to that on English certificates. There are registers of Protestant and mixed Protestant-Catholic marriages from 1845. The Northern Ireland General Register Office, Oxford House, 49–55 Chichester St, Belfast ET1 4HL holds births, marriages and deaths from 1921.

Church registers. A few Church of Ireland registers survived the civil war. These are listed in LEADER, M. *Church registers in Ireland* in BURCHALL, 1986. Roman Catholic registers were not destroyed as they were kept by parish priests. These have been microfilmed and are available in the National Library of Ireland; however, few start before 1800. Just under half the Presbyterian registers of Ulster have been filmed by the Public Record Office, 66 Balmoral Ave., Belfast BT9 6NY. Many are available at the Presbyterian Historical Society's library, Church House, Fisherwick Place, Belfast 1. For Quaker registers, try the Friends Meeting House, Eustace St, Dublin, Eire.

Other sources before 1865 are the *Betham Extracts* – (from destroyed wills proved in the Prerogative Court of Armagh 1536–1800), the Register of Deeds in Henrietta Street, Dublin, (with information on all land transactions since 1708), and newspapers.

XXIII Surnames

Place names. When a family and a place have the same name, the former is nearly always derived from the latter, and not *vice versa*. The 'combe' in Honeycombe is a very common place name element in the South-West. It means 'valley'. Honeycombe might mean what it seems – 'honeyed valley' or 'sweet valley', or it could be derived from the Anglo-Saxon name Huna. Ekwall's *Concise Oxford Dictionary of English Place Names* does not give *Honeycombe*, but it gives *Honeychurch*, 'Huna's church'; *Honeywick*, 'Huna's dwelling', *Honeychild*, 'Huna's spring' and *Honiton*, 'Huna's homestead'. Was this an ubiquitous Saxon warrior rampaging through Devon and Cornwall to suppress the Celts! Or was Huna a fairly common Anglo-Saxon name? Quite often, the spelling of the surname has stayed the same, though the spelling of the place has changed. Thus, Bristol used to be called Bristow, and that is how the surname is still spelt. A variation on the place name theme is the 'locative' surname derived from features found in most villages, such as *Church, Green, Brooks, Rivers, Hill*, or *Field*. Clearly no one would expect all people of these surnames to be related.

Occupational names. Occupations have, in fact, given rise to many surnames – some are instantly recognisable such as *Butcher*, or *Baker*; others like *Chandler* (candle-dealer) are less so. Some are totally unrecognisable, for the occupations have completely disappeared, like *Fletcher* (arrowmaker).

Patronymics. The third main source of surnames is the patronymic – (taking one's father's name). There tend to be three forms of these – with the full 'son' (*Johnson*), with the possessive 's' (*Johns*), or the Christian name alone (*John*). A lot of surnames are derived not from full Christian names but from shortened forms of them, or nicknames. *John* has given rise to some odd ones. A medieval diminutive ending was 'cock'; the old form of John was *Johan* – so putting the two together, we get *Hancock*. In the Middle Ages, people went in for rhyming names. A few of these still survive, like *Bill* for William, *Bob* for *Robert*; *Peggy* for *Margaret* (*Mag-Meg-Peg-Peggy*), *Polly* for *Mary* (*Mary-Molly-Polly*). But in the Middle Ages, there were a lot more of them. So *Roger*, for example, has given rise to the surname *Rogerson, Rogers*, and *Roger*; in its shortened form to *Rudge*. But *Rodge* rhymes with *Hodge* and *Dodge*, so we have names like *Hodge, Hodgeson, Dodd, Dodds, Dodgeson*, all derived from ancestors called *Roger*.

Nicknames. Many surnames are derived from nicknames or from some characteristic of the person, e.g. *Short, Wise*. Of course, we cannot be sure they were truly descriptive. They might have been used jokingly, as with Robin Hood's Little John. The first Mr Wise might have been the village idiot. Some names in this class are quite strange. For example, the Scottish name *Cameron* is derived from the Gaelic *cam schron* – crooked nose. However, one must always beware of such derivations. *Courtney* is not derived from *court nez*, 'short nose' but from a French place name. Similarly, *Honeycombe* could not come from *Honi à Combat*. Norman knights just did not have names like that – and the non-sounding of the final consonant in French only goes back a few centuries. *Honi*, in fact, does not mean evil, it is the past participle of the Old French verb *honir*, and means 'disgraced' or 'dishonoured'. Correctly translated, *Honi à Combat*, means 'Dishonoured in battle', an odd nickname for a Norman knight to perpetuate.

There is, in fact, no proven male-line descent from anyone who fought at Hastings. The story of Honi à Combat is reminiscent of the fanciful derivations of the names of famous families that were dreamed up in the eighteenth and nineteenth centuries – such as *Percy*, from 'Pierce-eye' (an ancestor pierced someone's eye) or *Napier* (an ancestor fought so well in battle that the King of Scotland said with an impeccable Scottish accent, 'That Knight has nae peer!').

Unfortunately, myths die hard and all too often the will to believe them persists despite the most overwhelming evidence.

Reference Section

XXIV Family History Societies

Local Family History Societies. The majority of English and Welsh counties have one society, often with various local branches. In some counties, such as Greater London or Surrey, several societies have agreed on their respective 'spheres of influence'. In other cases, however, major societies overlap or groups operate within an area covered by a county society. There is also the complication that several societies operate on the basis of the new counties created in 1974 or the new London boroughs created in 1965. To help you to locate societies which take an interest in at least part of the ancient county where your ancestors lived, all English pre-1974 counties have been listed here, whether or not they correspond to modern ones. When societies are based on towns, the county has been added in brackets, but does not, of course, form part of the name of the society. If in doubt, you would be wise to contact all the societies which might have an interest in your area. Scottish societies have a regional rather than county coverage.

Since the secretaries of societies change quite frequently, their addresses have not been given here, but you can write off for details of the Federation and a list of its member societies (which includes the names and addresses of the current secretaries) to the Administrator, Federation of Family History Societies, 31 Seven Star Road, Solihull B91 2BZ, enclosing a foolscap stamped addressed envelope (UK) or three international reply coupons (overseas).

ENGLAND

Avon: *Bristol and Avon FHS: Weston-super-Mare FH Workshop.*
Bedfordshire FHS.
Berkshire: *Berkshire FHS; Windsor, Slough & District FHS.*
Birmingham & Midland Society for Genealogy and Heraldry.
Bristol & Avon FHS.
Buckinghamshire: *Buckinghamshire FHS; Windsor, Slough & District FHS.*
Cambridgeshire: *Cambridgeshire FHS; Peterborough FHS.*
Central Middlesex FHS.
Cheshire: *FHS of Cheshire; North Cheshire FHS.*
Cleveland FHS.
Cornwall FHS.
Cumberland: *Cumbria FHS.*
Derbyshire FHS.
Devon FHS.
Doncaster (South Yorkshire) *Society for FH.*
Dorset: *Somerset & Dorset FHS.*
Durham: *Northumberland and Durham FHS; Cleveland FHS.*
East of London FHS.
East Surrey FHS.

East Yorkshire FHS.
Essex Society for FH.
Essex Society for FH.
Folkestone (Kent) *& District FHS.*
Gloucestershire: *Gloucestershire FHS; Bristol & Avon FHS.*
Hampshire Genealogical Society.
Herefordshire FHS.
Hertfordshire Family & Population History Society.
Huntingdonshire: *Peterborough & District FHS.*
Kent: *Kent FHS; Folkestone & District FHS; North-West Kent FHS; Woolwich & District FHS.*
Lancashire: *Lancashire FH and Heraldry Society* (formerly called the Rossendale Society for Genealogy and Heraldry); *Manchester & Lancashire FHS; Liverpool & District FHS.*
Leicestershire FHS.
Lincolnshire: *Society for Lincs. History and Archaeology (FH section).*
Liverpool and District FHS.
London & Middlesex. The following societies cover the Greater London area: *Society of Genealogists* (see below); *East of London FHS; Central Middlesex FHS; North Middlesex FHS; West Middlesex FHS; East Surrey FHS; Essex FHS; Hertfordshire Family & Population History Society; North-west Kent FHS; Waltham Forest FHS; Woolwich & District FHS.*
Manchester & Lancashire FHS.
Middlesex: (see London and Middlesex).
Monmouthshire: see Wales below.
Norfolk & Norwich Genealogical Society.
North Cheshire FHS.
North Middlesex FHS.
North-west Kent FHS.
Northamptonshire FHS.
Northumberland & Durham FHS.
Nottinghamshire FHS.
Oxfordshire FHS.
Peterborough & District (Cambridgeshire, formerly Huntingdonshire) *FHS.*
Rossendale (Lancashire) *Society for Genealogy and Heraldry*, now renamed the *Lancashire FH and Heraldry Society.*
Rutland: *Leicestershire FHS.*
Sheffield & District (Yorks) *FHS.*
Shropshire FHS.
Somerset & Dorset FHS.
Staffordshire: *Birmingham & Midland Society for Genealogy and Heraldry.*
Suffolk Genealogy Society.
Surrey: *West Surrey FHS; East Surrey FHS.*
Sussex Family History Group.

Waltham Forest (London, formerly Essex) *FHS.*

Warwickshire: *Birmingham & Midland Society for Genealogy and Heraldry.*

West Middlesex FHS.

West Surrey FHS.

Westmorland: *Cumbria FHS.*

Weston-Super-Mare (Avon – formerly Somerset) *FH Workshop.*

Wiltshire FHS.

Windsor, Slough & District (Berkshire, Slough formerly Buckinghamshire) *FHS.*

Woolwich (London) *& District FHS.*

Worcestershire: *Birmingham & Midland Society for Genealogy and Heraldry.*

York FHS.

Yorkshire: *Yorkshire Archaeological Society Family & Population Studies Section; East Yorkshire FHS; York FHS; Sheffield & District FHS; Doncaster Society for FH; Cleveland FHS.*

ISLE OF MAN AND CHANNEL ISLANDS

Isle of Man FHS.

Channel Islands FHS.

WALES

The Welsh societies are organised on the basis of the new post-1974 counties. The old counties covered by each area have been added in brackets. Addresses of secretaries may be obtained from the Federation of Family History Societies (see above).

Clwyd FHS. (Flintshire, Denbighshire and the Edeyrnion District from Merionethshire)

Dyfed FHS. (Carmarthen, Cardiganshire, Pembrokeshire)

Glamorgan FHS. (Whole of old county of Glamorgan, now subdivided into North, Mid and South Glamorgan).

Gwent FHS. (Identical with old Monmouthshire with minor border changes).

Gwynedd FHS. *(Caernarvonshire, Merionethshire, Anglesey).*

Powys FHS. *(Montgomeryshire, Brecknockshire, Radnorshire).*

SCOTLAND

Scottish Genealogy Society, 21 Howard Place, Edinburgh, Scotland EH3 5JY. Library at 9 Union St, Edinburgh.

The Scottish regional societies with the ancient counties covered by each are as follows. The addresses of secretaries can be obtained from the *Federation of Family History Societies*, (see above), or from the *Scottish Genealogy Society* (see above).

Aberdeen & North East Scotland FHS. (Roughly the Grampian region – Aberdeenshire, Kincardineshire, Banffshire, part of Morayshire).

Glasgow & West of Scotland FHS. (Roughly the Strathclyde region – Argyllshire, Bute, Dunbartonshire, Stirlingshire (part), Ayrshire, Lanarkshire, Glasgow City, Renfrewshire).

Highland FHS. (Highland region covers Inverness-shire, part of Morayshire, Caithness, Sutherland, part of Argyllshire, Nairn, Ross and Cromarty).

Tay Valley FHS. (Tayside region covers Angus, Dundee City, part of Perthshire).

There are no family history societies at present for the Borders (Berwickshire, Selkirkshire, Roxburghshire, Peebles), Fife, Central Region (Clackmannan, part of Perthshire, part of Stirlingshire), Lothian (E. Lothian, Midlothian, City of Edinburgh), Orkney, Shetland or the Western Isles (Barra, Harris, North Uist and South Uist from Inverness-shire and Lewis from Ross and Cromarty), though the *Scottish Genealogy Society*, of course, takes an interest in all of them, and in effect acts as the local society for the Lothian area. For the Western Isles, you would be well advised to join the *Society of West Highland and Island Historical Research*. This publishes *Notes and Queries* three times a year which contains genealogical information.

NORTHERN IRELAND

North of Ireland FHS. An ordinary family history society catering for family historians living in Northern Ireland. Address of secretary can be obtained from the Federation of Family History Societies (see above).

Ulster Genealogical & Historic Guild, c/o Public Record Office of Northern Ireland, 66 Balmoral Avenue, Belfast BT9 6NY. A daughter-organisation of the Ulster Historical Foundation (see Professional Help, below). In effect a subscription book-club concerned particularly with those living overseas. Publishes a newsletter, but has no meetings.

Irish Genealogical Association, 164 Kingsway, Dunmarry, Belfast BT17 9AD (0232 629595). Formed in 1981 to encourage and assist overseas people who wish to visit Ireland to trace their family history, and to provide a personalised research service for those unable to do it themselves. Close links with the Northern Ireland Tourist Board.

REPUBLIC OF IRELAND

Irish Family History Society Secretary: Michael Byrne, Convent View, Tullamore, Co. Offaly, Republic of Ireland.

OVERSEAS-BASED IRISH SOCIETIES

England: *Irish Genealogical Society of Great Britain* Secretary: F.B. Peyton, Glenholm, High Oakham Rd, Mansfield, Notts. The society has a library at the Challinor Club, 59/61 Pont St, London SW1, but any arrangement to visit this must be made through the secretary.

U.S.A.: *The Irish Family Names Society*, PO Box 2095, La Mesa, California 92041, USA.

The Irish Genealogical Society, 99 Ash Street, New Bedford, Minnesota 02740, USA.

Irish Family Research Association, Inc. President: Mrs Richard G. Champ, 9411 Hunters Creek Dr., Dallas, Texas 75243, USA.

Joining a Family History Society

You would be advised to join:

(a) *the society in the area in which you live.* This will increase your knowledge of the subject and enable you to meet others who share your interest.

(b) *the societies in the areas from which your ancestors came.* Not only will their journals keep you in touch with the local record situation, but most family history societies keep a record of the families in which members are interested, and many have published directories of these.

Projects. The majority of family history societies are engaged on projects of various kinds, especially the transcription of monumental inscriptions and the compilation of marriage and census indexes. The Federation of Family History Societies has published a Directory of Family History Projects Co-ordinators.

Federation of Family History Societies. This co-ordinates the activities of local family history societies. It publishes the half-yearly *Family History News and Digest* which gives an indication of the principal articles in the journals of member societies, many of general rather than local interest, as well as numerous other publications, especially short guides to records. For a list of publications, or to order any individual publication, contact the Federation of Family History Societies, 31 Seven Star Road, Solihull B91 2BZ, marking your envelope 'Publications'.

Society of Genealogists, 14 Charterhouse Buildings, Goswell Road, London EC1M 7BA. When you have made a certain amount of progress, you might like to consider joining the Society of Genealogists. It has the best library on the subject in England, containing much material not duplicated elsewhere. (For holdings see National Repositories, p. 161.) This is open to non-members for day searches, but if you are going to use the library more than a few times, you would be well advised to join. Members receive the quarterly journal, the *Genealogists' Magazine*, an important vehicle for keeping up to date with the subject.

The Institute of Heraldic and Genealogical Studies, Northgate, Canterbury, Kent CT1 1BA, runs full-time, part-time, correspondence and residential courses in all aspects of family history, and supports other organisations and projects in the fields of heraldry, genealogy and family history, as well as post-graduate research. Associate members have the use of the splendid library in the medieval buildings owned by the Trust. (For holdings see National Repositories, p. 161.)

Specialised Family History Societies. There seem to be few 'specialist' family history societies. The Society of Genealogists has a computer group (Secretary: David Hawgood, c/o the Society – address as above), but the only independent special interest family history society, other than one-name societies, would appear to be for English Catholic Family History (Secretary: Leslie Brooks, Hill House West, Crookham Village, Aldershot, Hants).

One-name societies. Many one-name societies have been founded in recent years, and numerous family historians, while not having launched a formal society, are interested in all occurrences of a given surname. The *Register of One-name Studies* (1985), published by the Guild of One-name Studies, c/o Box G, 14 Charterhouse Buildings, Goswell Rd, London, EC1M 7BA, lists about 800 surnames covered either by properly constituted societies, or by individual family historians who are members of the Guild. There are, however, many other individuals interested in all occurrences of a surname, and these may usually be located by reference to the various directories of family historians' interests (see p. 187). If you are interested in all occurrences of a surname you are strongly advised to join the Guild by writing to the above address. If there is no one-name society for your surname in existence you might like to consider starting one – see the booklet *Forming a One-name Group* published by the Federation of Family History Societies. Note should also be taken of the many American organisations interested in particular surnames. Most of these tend to be family associations rather than one-name societies, i.e. they are concerned with all descendants of a single ancestor, often an immigrant, rather than with all occurrences of a surname. A large number of such organisations appear in J. Konrad (ed.) *Family Associations, Societies and Reunions: a Comprehensive Listing*, Summit Publications, P.O. Box 222, Munroe Falls, Ohio 44262, 6th edn, 1985.

Local History Societies. Family historians might also like to consider joining local history societies in the areas from which their ancestors came. As noted above (see p. 36), the local knowledge of members will do much to help to put ancestors in their local, social and economic context, and in many cases societies have substantial information on local families and can put enquirers in touch with other people with related interests. The majority of local history societies are listed in *Local History Societies in England and Wales: A List*, Standing Conference for Local History (1978), or in the *Environmental Directory* (6th edn, 1985), published by the Civic Trust, 17 Carlton House Terrace, London SW1. If there is no society listed there, or the address is out of date, you can try the local libraries or the British Association for Local History, The Mill Manager's House, Cromford Mill, Matlock, Derbyshire DE44 3RQ.

WALES The Honorable Society of Cymmrodorion, 118 Newgate St, London EC1A 7AE, publishes material on Welsh history and culture.

SCOTLAND As noted above, in Scotland the Society of West Highland and Island Historical Research publishes *Notes and Queries* three times a year which contains much genealogical information.

NORTHERN IRELAND Ulster local history societies are associated in the Federation for Ulster Local Studies.

Denominational Societies and Military and Naval Historical Societies see under Record Repositories (pp. 161–167).

Specialised Societies. There are societies for almost every kind of specialised interest. If your ancestor was a millwright or worked on the railway, or even if he had an unusual occupation, it is highly probable that there is some society which will be able to help you. Often a national organisation will be able to put you in touch with a local branch, either where you live or where your ancestor worked. You may well be able to locate the national secretary from the publication *Directory of National Organisations*, Standing Conference for Local History (1978). Some societies of particular interest to family historians are:

Local Population Studies Society, Tawney House, Matlock, Derbyshire.

Heraldry Society, 44–45 Museum St, London WC1.

Historians' Medical Information Bureau, Wadham College, Oxford OX1 3PN. To put historians who have a problem involving medicine in touch with the appropriate specialist. In the initial letter, the nature of the problem should be explained as concisely as possible.

Society for the Social History of Medicine, c/o Adrian Wilson, Clare Hall, Cambridge CB3 9AL.

Manorial Society of Great Britain (See National Repositories, p. 161).

Business Archives Council, Dominion House, 37–45 Tooley St, London Bridge, London SE1 2QF. Will help to trace records of firms.

Business Archives Council of Scotland, c/o Loanhead Transport Ltd, Johnstone PA5 8UD.

British Records Association, Master's Court, The Charterhouse, Charterhouse Square, London EC1M 6AU. Works for the preservation and indexing of records. See article by B.C. Redwood, *Amateur Historian*, vol. 3, no. 7, p. 283, Spring 1958.

Council for British Archaeology, 112 Kennington Park Rd, London SE11.

Professional Help. Amateurs are often reluctant to employ a professional, believing that it will cost more than they can afford. However, it is often cheaper to ask a professional to undertake a particular search than to visit a distant repository yourself. See BROWN, M. S., 'Choosing professional help' *New Zealand Genealogist*, vol. 8 no. 71, Jan–Feb 1977.

In the case of obtaining certificates from St Catherine's House, it is very much cheaper to employ a London agent than to pay the high General Register Office charges for certificates obtained by post, and cheaper still to use the services of the North Middlesex Family History Society (hand-collected cost of certificates plus £1.50 which includes a search of up to 2 years).

Genealogists. A number of firms are prepared to tackle cases in any part of the country. These tend to advertise in the *Genealogists Magazine*, the journals of local family history societies, the annual volumes of the *National Genealogical Directory*, the Australian-based *Genealogical Research Directory*, and overseas magazines and journals, particularly *The Genealogical Helper*, Everton Publishers Inc, P.O. Box 368, Logan, Utah 84321, USA. You would be wise not to confine yourself to a single edition of any particular journal, for few firms advertise in every number of a journal but prefer to spread their advertising more thinly over a larger number. So it is best to search back numbers for about two years. Once you have compiled a shortlist of possible firms or individuals, send as much information as you can, stating exactly what you would like the professional to do, and asking for estimates not only of the cost, but of the time the task is likely to take. Many firms have more cases than they can adequately handle; others sub-contract work to searchers who also have more than they can cope with. Factors such as this make it not unknown for clients to be waiting up to a year for their first report. Of course, the quality of the work when you get it may well justify the long wait, but this is a factor which you should know and take into account when making your initial decision. Since professionals vary so much in price, quality and speed of delivery, once a firm or individual has presented a report, you would be wise to ask other members of your family history society how these factors compare in your case with their experience.

SPECIALIST HELP. Rather than use a general firm, it is often better to use a searcher who is a specialist in the area, occupation, religious group or type of record in which you are interested. Many local agents and the majority of specialists are members of the *Association of Genealogists and Record Agents* (AGRA) whose secretary, Mrs Jean Tooke, 1 Woodside Close, Caterham, Surrey CR3 6AU, will supply a list of members with their specialisms on receipt of (at the time of going to press) 55p (UK) or five international reply coupons.

SCOTLAND The major firms will also undertake research in Scotland. There is also *The Scots Ancestry Research Society*, 20 York Place, Edinburgh EH1 3EP (031–556 4220). This is a non-profit-making trust set up in 1945 by the then Secretary of State for Scotland to assist people of Scottish descent to trace their ancestors.

A list of Scottish researchers will be found in JAMES, A.

Scottish Roots (Macdonald, 1981). A fuller list may be obtained from the Secretary, *Scottish Association of Genealogists and Record Agents*, 106, Brucefield Ave., Dunfermline KY11 4S7, Scotland.

NORTHERN IRELAND *Ulster Historical Foundation*, c/o P.R.O. of Northern Ireland, 66 Balmoral Ave., Belfast BT9 6NYY (0232 661621). This was formerly called the Ulster Scot Historical Society, but it has long been concerned with Protestant and Catholic genealogy equally. It is an organisation owned by the Department of the Environment, but run by Trustees, mainly academics, and was set up in 1956 to deal with the flood of genealogical enquiries which come into the Northern Ireland Public Record Office. It also engages in valuable transcription and publishing work. See the article 'The Ulster Historical Foundation', *Genealogical Journal* vol. 7, no. 3, Sept 1978.

Irish Genealogical Association, 164 Kingsway, Dunmurry, Belfast BT17 9AD (0232 629595) is particularly concerned with research for overseas people of Northern Irish descent. Publishes an attractive magazine *Irish Family Links*.

Irish Genealogical Services, c/o David McElroy, 60 Ivanhoe Ave., Carryduff, Belfast BT8 8BW, Northern Ireland (0232 813142).

John McCabe, 12F South Link, Belfast BT11 8GX, Co. Antrim, Northern Ireland.

REPUBLIC OF IRELAND There are very few professional genealogists and searchers residing in the Irish Republic and consequently long delays are not uncommon. One regular advertiser is:

Henry McDowell, Celbridge Lodge, Celbridge, Co. Kildare, Ireland (Dublin 288347).

UNITED STATES Relatively few British family historians seem to use professional help to trace overseas branches. But a modest outlay can produce rich dividends, particularly in the United States where most censuses are indexed. Lists of certified or accredited genealogists may be obtained from:

Board for Certification of Genealogists, 1307 New Hampshire Ave., Washington D.C. N.W., 20036, USA.

The Genealogical Society of Utah, 50 East North Temple St, Salt Lake City, Utah 84150, USA.

Many American genealogists (and some in other countries) belong to the *Association of Professional Genealogists*, 19W South Temple, Suite 761, Box 11601, Salt Lake City, Utah 84147, USA.

Specialist Publishers and Booksellers

UNITED KINGDOM *Phillimore & Co., Ltd*, Shopwyke Hall, Chichester, Sussex (0243 787636) are the principal genealogical publishers in Britain, and every serious family historian should get on the mailing list for their catalogues to keep abreast of publications in this fast developing field. They are also the principal UK booksellers for genealogy.

The Federation of Family History Societies (Administrator, 311 Seven Star Rd, Solihull B91 2BZ – mark envelope 'Publications') has a growing list of publications, in particular the twice-yearly *Federation News and Digest* and the series of guides by Gibson and McLaughlin. These are obtainable direct or through individual family history societies. The FFHS also stock some books by other publishers.

The Society of Genealogists, 14 Charterhouse Buildings, London EC1M 7BA, has published many guides to records and has two major series in progress: the *National Index of Parish Registers* and *An Index to Wills Proved in the Prerogative Court of Canterbury 1750–1800*. All publications are listed in their free Leaflet No. 1: *Publications List*. Also maintains a small bookshop.

The Institute of Heraldic and Genealogical Studies, Northgate, Canterbury, Kent, has many useful publications, including their fine series of county maps.

Heraldry Today, 10 Beauchamp Place, London SW3 (01-584 1656) and Parliament Piece, Ramsbury, Marlborough, Wiltshire (0672 20617). Specialises in reprints.

Pinhorns Write to BCM Pinhorns, London WC1V 6XX. Guides to records, usually reprints from journals.

A very useful list of antiquarian booksellers can be found in BEARD, T. F. and DEMONG, D. *How to find your family roots*, pp. 362–366, McGraw-Hill Book Co., New York (1977).

REPUBLIC OF IRELAND *Heraldic Artists*, Trinity Street, Dublin 2, Ireland.

The Genealogy Bookshop, 3 Nassau St, Dublin 2, Ireland.

UNITED STATES A very useful list of American specialist genealogical publishers will be found in EAKLE, A. and CERNY, J, *The Source*, Ancestry Publishing Company, Salt Lake City, Utah (1984).

A massive list of American genealogical books in print and where they may be obtained is SCHREINER-YANTIS, N. ed. *Genealogical books in print*, published by the editor, 6818 Lois Drive, Springfield, Virginia 2215, USA.

XXV Record Offices

National Repositories

Note: A map showing the location of national repositories in London is given in GIBSON, J. and PESKETT, P., *Record Offices and Where to Find Them*, Federation of Family History Societies, 3rd edn (1985).

General Register Office: St Catherine's House, 10 Kingway, London WC2B 6JB (01–242 0262). For birth, marriage and death certificates. 8.30–4.30. See CHAPMAN, C. 'St Catherine's House – Inside Out' *Journal of Beds FHS* vol. 4, no. 8, Winter 1984.

Public Record Office: This is now in three buildings. All 9.30–4.45. A list of classes of records at Chancery Lane and Kew appears in *Family History News and Digest* vol. 1, no. 1, Summer 1977, p. 27. A reader's ticket should be applied for in advance.

(1) Chancery Lane: London WC2A 1LR (01–405 0741). Records here include central legal records, noncomformist registers of births, marriages and deaths (including non-authenticated ones), PCC and Estate Duty wills (see pp. 144–146) and old taxation records, i.e. most of the records described in Vol. 1 of the *Guide to the Contents of the Public Record Office*. Over half of UNETT, J. *Making a Pedigree* David and Charles, 2nd edn (1971) is devoted to PRO sources, mainly 17th century and earlier.

(2) Kew Repository: Ruskin Ave., Kew, Richmond, Surrey (01–876–3444). This holds Army and Navy records, Foreign and Home Office papers, Board of Trade and Inland Revenue records and old maps. See COX, J. and PADFIELD, T. *Tracing your Ancestors in the Public Record Office* HMSO, 3rd edn (1984), and *Guide to the Contents of the P.R.O.*, Vols 2 and 3. LEESON, F. 'A visit to Kew', *Genealogists' Magazine* vol. 19, no. 5, March 1978, p. 172, and LEESON, F. 'How to order by computer at P.R.O. Kew', *Genealogists' Magazine*, Vol. 19, no. 7, Sept 1978, p. 249.

(3) Census Search Room, Portugal Street, London WC2A 1LR (01–405 3488). This holds only Census Returns. Reader's ticket necessary, but day searchers' tickets are obtainable. See MCLAUGHLIN, E. *The Censuses 1841–1881* (A McLaughlin Guide) FFHS, 2nd edn (1985). A practical guide to using the PRO Census Room and its indexes, and interpreting the information. GIBSON, J.S.W. *Census Returns 1841–1881 on Microfilm: a Directory to Local Holdings*. 4th edn, updated (1984) may make a journey to Portugal Street unnecessary, and GIBSON, J. *Marriage, Census and Other Indexes for Family Historians*, FFHS, updated (1985) may lead you to an index.

Society of Genealogists: 14 Charterhouse Buildings, Goswell Rd, London EC1M 7BA (01–251 8799). (Charterhouse Buildings is a cul-de-sac at the junction of Goswell Road and Clerkenwell Rd, about 500 yards north of Barbican Underground Station, on the Circle and Metropolitan lines.) Mon closed. Tues, Fri and Sat 10.00–6.00, Wed & Thurs 10.00–8.00. As noted above, this is the major British library for genealogical material. Holds a large collection of family histories and of printed and manuscript copies of parish registers, Boyd's *Marriage Index* (an index of marriages in parish registers, including over seven million names), and *Boyd's Citizens of London* – 238 volumes of information on Londoners, mainly of the 16th and 17th centuries. It is one of only a handful of repositories in Britain to have the IGI for the whole world. There is also the *Great Card Index* with some three million slips, and a microfilm of *Bernau's Index* with four and a half million slips, where you may encounter all kinds of information about people bearing your surname. The Society also houses the *National Pedigree Index*. (See *Family History News and Digest*, vol. 2, no. 2, Autumn 1979.) Free to members, the library is open to non-members on payment of a search fee. See the Society's booklet *Using the Society of Genealogists, 1984*, and *WILLIS, A.J. and TATCHELL, M. *Genealogy for Beginners* Phillimore, 5th edn (1984) which has a useful section on the Society's collection, including checklists of the main items.

The British Library: Department of Manuscripts and Map Room, Great Russell St, London WC1B 3DG (01–636 1544). See GILSON, J.P. *A Student's Guide to the MSS of the British Museum* (Helps for Students of History, no. 31) SPCK (1920), NICKSON, M.A.E. *The British Library: Guide to the Catalogues and Indexes of the Department of Manuscripts ...* (1975), and *Catalogue of Printed Maps, Charts and Plans* British Library Reference Division (1978). Detailed calendars are available of most of the manuscript collections.

Reading Room: Great Russell St, London WC1B 3DG (01–636 1544). Includes London newspapers before 1800.

Newspaper Library: Colindale Ave, London NW9 5HE (01–205 6039, 01–205 4788). All other newspapers. See PROBERT, R.A. 'British Museum Newspaper Library', *Origins* (Journal of Bucks FHS), vol. 1 no. 1, Winter 1976, p. 8.

Principal Registry of the Family Division: Somerset House, Strand, London WC2R 1LP (01–405 7641, ext. 3959). Post-1858 wills. See p. 146 and Post-1858 Wills, below.

House of Lords R.O.: House of Lords, London SW1A 0PW (01–219 3073). Holds the Protestation Returns of 1641 (see p. 93). See BOND, M.F. *Guide to the Records of Parliament* HMSO (1971), BOND, M.F. *The Records of Parliament* Phillimore, 1964, reprinted from *The amateur historian*, vol. 4 no 8, Winter 1959–60 to Summer 1960 and EDWARDS, L.W.L.

Protestation returns of 1641–2: a checklist. Society of Genealogists, Leaflet no. 8, 1977, also printed in *Genealogists' Magazine*, vol. 19 no. 3, Sept 1977. p. 84.

National Register of Archives: Housed at the Royal Commission on Historical Manuscripts, Quality House, Quality Court, Chancery Lane EC2A 1HP. Includes the Manorial Documents Register (list of known manorial records and their location) and Tithe Documents Register.

Manorial Society of Great Britain: 104 Kennington Road, London SE11 (01–735 6633). Comprehensive index of manors, lords and stewards. Searches made by staff.

Borthwick Institute of Historical Research: University of York, St Anthony's Hall, Peasholm Green, York Y01 2PW (0904 59861). Holds archives for the Archdiocese of York, including Prerogative Court of York (PCY) wills and marriage licences granted for the whole province of York, as well as most of the bishop's transcripts, wills and marriage licences of the diocese of York. Appointment essential. See WEBB, C.C. *A Guide to Genealogical Sources* in the Borthwick Institute of Historical Research, University of York, Borthwick Institute (1981).

Lambeth Palace Library: London SE1 7JU (01–928 6222). The Faculty Office granted marriage licences anywhere in England and Wales. The Vicar General granted them within the province of Canterbury. Both series of records are in Lambeth Palace Library.

College of Arms: Queen Victoria Street, London EC4V 4BT (01–248 2672). Records of armigerous families and much other useful material. Not open to public. Searches made by college staff by arrangement. Obtain estimate. Visits by arrangement. See WAGNER, Sir ANTHONY, *Records and Collections of the College of Arms*, Burke's Peerage 1952, (reprinted 1974).

Kensington Central Library: Phillimore Walk, London W8 7RX (01-937 2542). Specialises in genealogy and family history, and non-members of the Society of Genealogists will find there many rarer printed works to consult which they would, of course, have to pay at the Society.

The Guildhall Library: Aldermanbury, London EC2P 2EJ (01–606 3030), also has a good collection of genealogical material, particularly relating to London. Exceptionally strong on directories. See *Guide to Genealogical Sources in the Guildhall Library* Corporation of London 2nd edn, (1981), JONES, P.E. and SMITH, R. *A guide to the Records in the Corporation of London Records Office and the Guildhall Library Muniment Room* (English Universities Press, 1951), and JONES, P.E.H. 'Genealogy and the City of London records', *Genealogists' Magazine*, vol. 11, pp. 134, 167, Dec 1951, March 1952).

Institute of Heraldic and Genealogical Studies: Northgate, Canterbury, Kent (0227 462618). (See above, p. 158.) The library contains a wide collection of printed books on genealogy and family history which is especially strong on S.E. England. It holds the *Pallot Marriage Index* (a massive index of marriages *c.* 1780–1840 covering a very high proportion of London marriages), an index to some 20,000 researched family histories, a Catholic Marriage Index, and the Andrews Index of Britons dying overseas (mainly 19th/20th century). It also has one of the best heraldic collections in the country.

Kelly's Directories: Quadrant Picture Gallery, IPC Business Press Ltd, Quadrant House, The Quadrant, Sutton, Surrey (01–661 3336). Appointment essential. Half-day or day fee includes 20 photocopies.

Society of Antiquaries of London: Burlington House, London W1V 0HS (01–734 0193/9954). Not open to the public.

Post-1858 Wills

Post-1858 wills are kept at the Principal Registry of the Family Division, Somerset House, Strand, London WC2R 1LP (01–405 7641, ext. 3959). Copy wills will be produced for a fee of 25p a will and photocopies cost 25p a page. (See MCLAUGHLIN, E. *Somerset House Wills after 1858*, Federation of Family History Societies (1985).

Sets of the printed indexes to post-1858 wills are now available locally. So it is a relatively simple and inexpensive matter to identify all the wills in which you are interested, and arrange with a London record agent to get photocopies from Somerset House. (On these indexes see GIBSON, J.S.W. 'Printed indexes to probate records after 1850'. *Local Historian*, vol. 15, no. 4, Nov 1982.) The location of the indexes is given in GIBSON, J.S.W. *A simplified guide to probate jurisdictions: where to look for wills*, FFHS, 3rd edn, 1985. Some are still in local probate registries but increasingly they are being transferred to county record offices.

Denominational Societies and Repositories

ROMAN CATHOLICS

English Catholic Ancestor (The Society for Promotion of English Catholic Family History): Secretary: L. Brooks, Hill House West. Crookham Village, Nr Aldershot, Hampshire GU13 0SS. Journal (*English Catholic Ancestor*) twice a year. Also members' interests.

Catholic Record Society: Miss R. Rendel, Flat 5, Lennox Gardens, London SW1X 0BQ.

NONCOMFORMISTS

Doctor Williams's Library, 14 Gordon Square, London WC1H 0AG (01–387 3727). The principal reference library for nonconformity generally. Some manuscript material, but note that it does not hold the Register of Births started in 1748; this is in the Public Record Office (Chancery Lane site – see p. 161). It does, however, now hold the Unitarian Historical Society's collection and the archives formerly deposited at the Congregational Library. Guide.

Baptist Union Library, 4 Southampton Row, London CW1B 4AB (01–405 9803). Records being transferred – see below.

Regent's Park College, Pusey Street, Oxford OX1 2LB (0865 59887 or 53452). Baptist records are in process of being transferred from the Baptist Union Library to the College.

Baptist Historical Society, 96 Palmerston Rd, Buckhurst Hill, Essex (01–505 6009).

United Reformed Church History Society, 86 Tavistock Place, London WC1H 9RT (01–405 7611). Mainly Presbyterian archives, but is now equally interested in the history of both denominations, and is increasingly receiving deposits from ex-Congregational churches.

Methodist Archives, The Methodist Connexional Archivist, Division of Property, Central Buildings, Oldham St, Manchester M1 1JQ (061–236 5194).

Wesley Historical Society, General Secretary: Mrs E.D. Graham, 34 Spiceland Rd, Birmingham N31 1NJ (021–475 4914).

Society of Friends Library, Friends House, Euston Rd, London NW1 2BJ (01–387 3601). Holds comprehensive digests of registers for whole country and much other useful material.

Unitarian Historical Society, 6 Ventnor Terrace, Edinburgh EH9 2BL (031–667 4360). Library at Dr Williams's Library (see above).

Huguenot Society, The Secretary, c/o Administrative Secretary, University College, Gower St, London WC1E 6BT. Written enquiries only. Holds a library, but this is not open to the public except by special arrangement with the secretary.

MORMONS
Genealogical Society of Church of Jesus Christ of Latter-day Saints, Mr J. Packe, 65 Severn Rd, Ipswich, Suffolk IP3 0PU.

JEWS
Jewish Historical Society of England, Dr J. Israel, 33 Seymour Place, London W1 (01–723 4404).

Anglo-Jewish Archives, The Mocatta Library, University College, Gower Street, London WC1E 6BT (01–387 7050). As well as primary source material, this holds three substantial collections – The Sir Thomas Collyer-Fergusson collection (mainly will abstracts, M.I.'s, newspaper cuttings etc), the collection made by Albert M. Hyamson, an amateur genealogist, and the Jewish Museum collection made by R.J. D'Arcy Hart and others.

The Anglo-Jewish Association, Woburn House, Upper Woburn Place, London WC1. (The same address houses the Jewish Museum, but this now has no original records.)

Army, Navy, R.A.F., Merchant Navy and East India Company – Repositories and Societies

Army Museums Ogilby Trust, Connaught Barracks, Duke of Connaught Road, Aldershot GU11 2LR (0252 24431). Acts as a clearing-house for information about regimental and other military museums.

Society for Army Historical Research, c/o The Library, Old War Office Building, Whitehall, London SW1 (01–218 9000).

Army Records Centre, Bourne Ave., Hayes, Middlesex. Recent records.

Military Historical Society, Duke of York's Headquarters, Chelsea, London SW3 (postal enquiries only).

National Army Museum, Department of Records, Reading Room, Royal Hospital Rd, Chelsea, London SW3 (01–730 0717). Locations of regiments, biographical index for Indian army officers.

Liddell Hart Centre for Military Archives, King's College, Strand, London WC2R 2LS (01–836 5454).

Peter Liddle's 1914–1918 Personal Experience Archives. St Mary's Building, Sunderland Polytechnic, Chester Road, Sunderland SR1 3SD. Records of personal experience of the First World War – diaries, letters, memoirs, photographs, tape-recordings etc.

National Maritime Museum, Greenwich, London SE10 9NF (01–858 4422). Lloyds Registers. Guide.

Naval Personnel Records, Room 20077 0S9 (a), Ministry of Defence, Empress State Building, London SW6 1TR.

Navy Records Society, c/o Royal Naval College, Greenwich, London SE10 (01–858 2154). Publishing society only. No library or records.

Department of Documents, Imperial War Museum, Lambeth Rd, London SE1 6HZ (01–735 8922). No personal records but excellent for background material such as diaries, letters, memoirs. Post-1914 records only. Especially strong on the two World Wars.

Dept of Archives and Aviation Records, Royal Air Force Museum, Hendon, London NW9 5LL (01–205 2266).

R.A.F. Personnel Management Centre, Eastern Ave., Barnwood, Gloucester GL4 7AN.

Registrar General of Shipping and Seamen, Llantrisant Rd, Llandaff, Cardiff GL4 7AN.

India Office Library, Foreign and Commonwealth Office, 197 Blackfriars Rd, London SE1 8NG (01–928 9531). Guide.

Some Other Specialised Repositories

Fawcett Library, City of London Polytechnic, Old Castle St, London E1 7NT (01–283 1030, ext. 570). Specialised library on the suffragettes and women's rights.

Modern Records Centre, University of Warwick Library, Coventry, W. Midlands CV4 7AC. Social and economic archives, especially Trade Union records (including major unions such as the National Union of Railwaymen and the Transport and General Workers Union.) See DRUKER, J. and STOREY, R. 'The Modern Records Centre at Warwick and the Local Historian' *Local Historian*, vol. 12, no. 8, p. 394, Nov 1977.

Post Office Archives, Freeling House, 23 Glass Hill St, London SE1 0BQ (01–261 1145).

Photographic, Print and Portrait Collections

Details of 1,580 photographic collections will be found listed in WALL, J., *The Directory of British Photographic Collections*, Heinemann, London 1977. Some of the most important open to the public are:

The Victoria and Albert Museum, Dept of Prints, Drawings and Photographs, South Kensington, London SW7 2RL (01–589 6371). 300,000 prints and photographs, especially of Victorian daily life. Catalogue.

The National Portrait Gallery, 2 St Martin's Place, London WC2H 0HE (01–930 8511).

The Imperial War Museum (see above) has two million photographs.

The National Monuments Record, Fortress House, 23 Savile Row, London W1X 1AB, has 800,000 photographs and 20,000 drawings.

Institute of Agricultural History and Museum of English Rural Life, University of Reading, Whiteknights Park, Reading RG6 2AG (0734 85123, ext. 475). Has 400,000 photographs.

Greater London Council Photograph Library, Room B66, County Hall, London SE1 7PB 0AB (01–633 3255). 250,000 photographs.

Guildhall Library and Art Gallery, Aldermanbury, London EC2P 2EJ. 100,000 prints and photographs of London.

Local History Library, Manchester Central Library, St Peter's Square, Manchester M2 5PD (061–2366 9422, ext. 265). 115,000 photographs.

Birmingham Reference Library, Birmingham B3 3HQ (021–235 4219). 20,000 photographs and 20,000 negatives.

Beamish Open Air Industrial Museum, Beamish Hall, Stanley, Co. Durham DH99 0RG (0207 31811). 20,000 photographs.

If you require pictures for publication, the following major collections are also open to you:

Radio Times Hulton Picture Library, 35 Marylebone High St, London W1M 4AA (01–580 5577). Six million pictures, including historical prints, portraits, photographs.

Mansell Collection, 42 Linden Gardens, London W2 4ER (01–229 5475). Two million photographs, prints, engravings. Very good on local pictures and portraits.

Mary Evans Picture Library, 1 Tranquil Vale, Blackheath, London SE3 0BU (01–318 0034). Emphasis on living and working conditions. One million prints and engravings. Some photographs.

Local Repositories

Record Offices. The addresses of most record offices are in GIBSON and PESKETT *Record Offices: how to find them*, below. Others, including more specialised ones, are in the works listed on p. 172. Many record offices hold parish registers,

wills, bishop's transcripts and marriage licences for the whole of the county. In other counties, these records are divided between different repositories. For example, in the case of Berkshire, although the county record office is the diocesan record office as far as parish records are concerned, the bishop's transcripts up to 1836 were held until relatively recently by the diocesan record office at Salisbury, and then transferred to the Wiltshire County Record Office. The post-1836 transcripts, held until recently by the Bodleian Library, Oxford, have been transferred to the Oxfordshire County Record Office. This kind of situation arises because most archivists prefer to keep an archive group together; Berkshire was part of the diocese of Salisbury until 1836, and then the diocese of Oxford.

Many boroughs have their own record offices, and in some cases these have been designated diocesan record offices. The series of record guides, compiled by J.S.W. Gibson (some with collaborators) and published by the Federation of Family History Societies, are invaluable in locating original records, copies and indexes, not only in repositories, but held privately or by societies. These (by Gibson unless otherwise stated) are:

1 *Record offices: how to find them*, compiled by GIBSON, J.S.W., and PESKETT, P. (1985). Street maps showing the location of most record offices, with the nearest car parks and railway and bus stations.

2 *A simplified guide to probate jurisdictions*, 3rd edn 1985. Where to look for wills.

3 *Bishop's transcripts and marriage licences*, 2nd edn (1983, updated 1985). These are found in diocesan record offices, usually, but not always, county record offices.

4 *Census returns 1841–1881 on microfilm: a directory of local holdings*, 4th edn (1983, updated 1984). Many held in libraries as well as record offices.

5 *Marriage, census and other indexes for family historians* (1984, updated 1985). Mainly indexes held by family history societies or individuals.

6 *Where to find the International Genealogical Index*, ed. GIBSON, J.S.W. and WALCOT, M. (1984, updated 1985). Location of microfiche copies of the IGI including which repositories have print-out facilities.

7 *Unpublished personal name indexes in record offices and libraries* (1985). County by county, this lists known card indexes, whether general (e.g. the one million cards in the Burnet Morris index in the West-Country Studies Library, Exeter), on a particular place (e.g. West Bromwich inhabitants) or source (e.g. York Apprenticeship Records).

8 *The hearth tax, other later Stuart tax lists and the associaltion oath rolls* (1985). Records mainly in the PRO, Chancery Lane, but some held in local record offices. This also lists published records and locally held microfilm copies of returns in the PRO.

9 *Land Tax Assessments, c.1690–c.1950*. ed. GIBSON, J.S.W. and MILLS, D. (1983, updated 1984).

10 *Quarter sessions records for family historians: a select list*, 2nd edn (1983, updated 1985).

In preparation: *Local newspapers before 1920*, comp. by GIBSON, J.S.W. and WEST, J.

To these guides may be added the equally valuable:
HUMPHERY-SMITH, C.R. (ed.). *The Phillimore Atlas and Index of Parish Registers*, Phillimore (1982). Compiled by the Institute of Heraldic and Genealogical Studies, and incorporating their series of parish maps, this also includes for each ancient county in England a map first published in 1834. It lists all parishes in England and Wales and indicates the date of deposited original parish registers, nonconformist registers at the PRO, the coverage of the IGI (see above), copies in the Society of Genealogists, Boyd's Marriage Index (see p. 134), the Pallot Marriage Index held by the Institute, local marriage indexes, and copies of registers at the Society of Genealogists.

Visiting a Record Office. Before visiting a record office, it is wise to ring and make an appointment, and at the same time check on the opening hours – many have recently restricted their hours because of financial cut-backs. Although most record offices will admit searchers without an appointment, a few (e.g. Cornwall) can be visited only by appointment – and even then it is often difficult to get in. The use of ballpoint or other pens is not allowed in record offices, so remember to take a pencil. A useful list of do's and don'ts in visiting record offices is given in Gibson and Peskett's *Record Offices: How to Find Them* referred to above. Some record offices (e.g. Devon, Gloucestershire) now make a small charge, and this practice is likely to increase.

Libraries. Some libraries hold archival material, either because they are the official repository of a borough, or because the county record office has established a branch there. Many others have a substantial local collection, including microfilms of census returns, the IGI, local newspapers, maps and directories, a useful array of local books and a substantial picture collection. Whether or not they appear in a guide as holding source material, you should make every effort to visit all the local libraries of the area in which you are interested, and find out exactly what each of them has. If it has nothing of genealogical importance, it is more than likely that you will find there general background material relevant to your family history. But more often than you might suppose, you strike real gold!

For rare books – or even just for the convenience of having a lot of books on one topic together in one place – it is sometimes very useful to visit a really major library. Six libraries are entitled to a free copy of every work published. These are the British Library, the National Libraries of Scotland and Wales, the Bodleian Library, Oxford, Cambridge University Library and Trinity College, Dublin. If you wish to visit one of these, it will be necessary to obtain a ticket in advance. However, it should be remembered that most of the other university libraries, whilst not being as comprehensive as any of these, are usually more comprehensive than any other library in the vicinity, and probably have most of the publications you want, including runs of record series, parliamentary papers, obscure journals and the like. Many are particularly strong on locally relevant published (and sometimes manuscript) material. It is usually possible to visit them for reference purposes. Borrowing facilities are a different matter, but special visitors' tickets are occasionally granted for a particular purpose. Usually not included on the lists, but in some cases almost as extensive, are the libraries of polytechnics (many of which are now very strong in the history area, especially social and economic history), colleges of higher education and colleges of education. All these libraries are listed in COLTHORPE, M. (ed.) *Libraries in the United Kingdom and Republic of Ireland*, Library Association, 1985. Very few people indeed will find that they live too far away from good reference facilities if they take the trouble to explore all the possibilities.

Research in libraries: a strategy. The best way to use these libraries is probably to go armed with a long list of books and articles culled from bibliographies, and to look at as many as possible. Some will not be helpful at all, but from others you will be able to take notes on the spot or to photocopy appropriate pages. Some, however, will need detailed study, and to save time, the best idea is not to get bogged down with these, but to restrain your enthusiasm until you can obtain them from your local library through inter-library loan.

Journals of family history societies. The Bibliography includes references to articles in journals of family history societies in all parts of the country and, indeed, abroad. At first sight this may seem unrealistic – if you live in Somerset you might suppose you are not very likely to see the journal of the Northumberland and Durham Family History Society, still less the *New Zealand Genealogist*. But you would be wrong, for nearly all local family history societies exchange journals with other member societies of the Federation, making a wealth of information available to you locally. As noted above, twice a year the Federation produces the *Family History News and Digest* which lists the more significant articles in journals. Some societies take bulk orders for this, and find they sell well, for people like to keep informed not only about articles they would never otherwise find, but about general developments on the family history scene. If it does not appear to be available regularly in your society, approach the officers about it. As a last resort you can always order directly from the Federation.

LDS (Mormon) branch libraries. These are branches of the

library of the Genealogical Society of Utah, in Salt Lake City, Utah, USA, financed by the Church of Jesus Christ of Latter-Day Saints to provide access to the enormous store of genealogical material microfilmed by the Church – parish registers, wills and an almost infinite array of other material. They are, of course, private libraries belonging to the Church, but through the kindness of the Mormons are open to the public without charge. However, since most librarians work part-time, libraries are usually open only at certain times, and there is often great pressure on space, under no circumstances should a searcher arrive without an appointment.

The value of these libraries is immense. Many of them hold a copy of the IGI not just for the whole of Britain, as most other major genealogical repositories do, but for the whole world. Where a specific item of microfilmed material is not available on the spot, the branch librarian will obtain a copy for you from another branch library or from Salt Lake City. There may well be a delay of up to three months, and written permission may be required from the owner of the record. But it is often more convenient to wait and consult a record locally than to travel to a distant repository. Mormon branch libraries and their facilities are described in SMART, P.F. 'More genealogical libraries in Great Britain', *Local Population Studies*, no. 21, Autumn 1978.

The addresses of the majority of the branch libraries will be found in GIBSON and WALCOT's booklet (see above), *Where to find the International Genealogical Index*. It is planned to increase the number of libraries in the UK from 24 to 40 by the end of 1986, so that each stake (i.e. Mormon diocese) has its own library. If the booklet does not list one near you, or you wish to check what edition or coverage of the IGI is held by a particular library, contact the Mormon British Isles Microfilm Ordering Centre 993 at 751 Warwick Rd, Solihull, West Midlands B91 3DQ (021–705 6731) for the latest position.

The International Genealogical Index (IGI). As well as the Mormon branch libraries, an increasing number of record offices, libraries and family history societies have obtained copies of the IGI (see p. 133), a fair proportion of them for the whole country. These are listed, with their holders, in GIBSON, J.S.W. and WALCOT, M. *Where to find the International Genealogical Index*, listed above. In case of difficulty, the current secretary of the society can be obtained from the Federation as described on p. 156.

Whenever you visit a repository to consult the IGI, you should always write or telephone to book a reader in advance. Remember to specify that it is a micro*fiche* reader and not a micro*film* reader that you require.

Other Countries. Eleven Mormon branch libraries have the whole world, but only two British family history organisations – the Society of Genealogists and the Institute of Heraldic and Genealogical Studies. Though two other societies have some

of the English-speaking countries, most family history societies have only the British Isles or less, rather surprising in view of the fact that the IGI is quite a major source in tracing overseas branches or even, at times, in locating elusive relatives who turn out to have been born abroad.

The list of those repositories known to hold the whole world is as follows (MBL = Mormon Branch Library):
Society of Genealogists, London; Institute of Heraldic and Genealogical Studies, Canterbury, Kent; Huddersfield MBL; Sunderland MBL; Leicester MBL; Hyde Park, London MBL; Southampton MBL; Bristol MBL; Liverpool MBL; Manchester MBL; Preston MBL, Rawtenstall; Norwich MBL; Staines MBL.
(For addresses of the Society of Genealogists and the Institute, see pp. 161 and 162, and for those of the Mormon branch libraries (MBL), see GIBSON and WALCOT, above.)

Those holding more than the British Isles, but less than the world are:
Hampshire Genealogical Society (British Commonwealth and former British Empire); *Bedfordshire FHS* (British Isles, Australia, New Zealand, Canada, USA); *St Mary Jersey MBL* (British Isles and Southern Europe, i.e. Albania, Andorra, Cyprus, Italy, Malta, Portugal, Yugoslavia, Rumania); *Maidstone, Kent MBL* (Central and Southern Europe).

Edition variations. It is important to check on the edition of the IGI held by a particular society or repository. The 1981 edition did not group surname variants together. This was remedied in the 1984 edition.

Scotland. Coverage for Scotland is far from comprehensive, and the earlier editions of the IGI treat Scotland as a whole like a single English county. A *Scottish Old Parochial Register Index* similar to the IGI has been prepared by the Registrar General, Scotland, in association with the Mormons. Progress on this is far advanced, and copies of the parts completed at the time of writing (mainly the North of Scotland) are available at New Register House, Edinburgh, the Society of Genealogists and the Manchester and Lancashire FHS. Though the completion of this project will be an immense boon to those interested in Scottish registers, if the area of Scotland from which the family came is not known, you would still do best to consult the earlier editions of the IGI to try to locate the areas where the surname was common, before using the new SOPRI to try and locate the individual in one or more counties.

Print-outs. Print-out facilities are important in three ways. Firstly, each county in the IGI has a list of places and dates covered. Unless you have a copy of *The Phillimore Atlas and Index of Parish Registers* or a local reference work which lists the places in the IGI, such as Hugh Peskett's *Guide to the Parochial and Non-parochial Registers of Devon and Cornwall* (Devon and

Cornwall Record Society, 1979), you will need a print-out to know which places you have covered by searching the IGI, and which still need to be searched.

Even if you have a suitable reference work, a check on the county microfiches of the current edition of the IGI may reveal that further parishes have been covered. You would be wise to go through the county print-outs, shading parish maps obtained from the Institute of Heraldic and Genealogical Studies, and seeing what blanks are left. But be careful to note parishes which are in the IGI only for certain periods – it is very easy to miss 'infilling', particularly if most of the registers are included.

Secondly, unless you have a very common surname, you would be wise to obtain a print-out for your surname for the counties in which you are interested. Not only will this save a great deal of valuable time in a repository (as well as freeing a reader for someone else) but in working on these at leisure, you will often find you can get almost a complete overview of the family. You also have the print-out available for constant reference to try and identify individuals who turn up in other records.

Thirdly, print-outs of surnames of related families can often be useful in building up mini-trees of relatives on the female side, which you would normally not have the leisure to pursue, and in this way they may help to locate useful wills.

Only a minority of the societies or repositories which hold a copy of the IGI have print-out facilities, but the number is growing steadily. Only two LDS branch libraries (Hyde Park, London and Romford, Essex) have printers. In addition, the LDS microfilm ordering service at Solihull has a printer, but this is available only by filling in an order form at a branch library, and pressure on it is intense. Repositories with printers can be located from GIBSON and WALCOT's *Where to find the International Genealogical Index*. This also gives prices, though, of course, these do change. You would do well to shop around, perhaps doing your research in one repository, but ordering your print-outs from elsewhere. Of course, some of the cheaper repositories may well not have the county you require, so you must obviously study carefully not only their prices but their holdings as well. Almost incredibly, there seems to be no printer in the whole of Wales, Scotland, Northern Ireland and the Republic of Ireland.

Parish microfilms by surname. If a register is in the IGI, and hence has been microfilmed by the Mormons, it is usually possible to obtain a microfilm of it arranged under surnames through a branch library. This is a little known and hence little used facility.

XXVI Bibliography

Abbreviations

AH   *Amateur Historian (*the forerunner of the present *The Local Historian)*

FFHS   Federation of Family History Societies

GJ   *Genealogical Journal* (of the Utah Genealogical Association)

GM   *Genealogists' Magazine*

LH   *Local Historian*

LPS   *Local Population Studies*

MA   *Midland Ancestor*

NZG   *New Zealand Genealogist*

NIPR   *National Index of Parish Registers*

R & B   *Root and Branch* (journal of the West Surrey FHS)

Titles marked with an asterisk are general books to which later references are made under specific headings. Such references are by author only, or by author and title in cases of ambiguity, and indicate the general books considered most helpful on that topic.

I FAMILY HISTORY, GENEALOGY AND ARCHIVES

'How to do it' Guides

ABBOT, J.P. *Family patterns: a personal experience of genealogy* Kaye and Ward, 1971. op. A 'how I did it'.

BURNS, N. *Family tree: an adventure in genealogy* Faber, 1962. op. An entertaining 'How I did it.'

CAMP, A.J. *Tracing your ancestors* Gifford, 3rd rev. edn, 1970. A good and inexpensive general introduction.

COLLINS, R.P. *A journey in ancestry* Sutton Publishing Ltd, 1984. In two sections, the first a genealogical 'How I did it', the second an East Anglian family history in which the ancestors are set in their full historical context. Useful as an example of good practice by an enthusiastic amateur.

*COLWELL, S. *The family history book: a guide to tracing your ancestors* Phaidon Press, 1980. Well-presented, attractively illustrated survey, both of genealogical sources and historical background.

COLWELL, S. *Tracing your family tree* Faber, 1984. A slim general introduction, but interesting as, being based on three families from Grasmere, Westmorland (including the Wordsworths), it provides a northern contrast to the Honeycombes. Useful chapters on the army, navy and other professions, and on 'school and work'.

*CURRER-BRIGGS, N. ed. *A handbook for British family history: a guide to methods and sources* Family History Services, 1979. op. Information on basic records, census, map and photographic holdings of libraries, and origins of surnames.

Especially useful on adoption and illegitimacy, on migration and for its checklist of over 70 sources.

CURRER-BRIGGS, N. and GAMBIER, R. *Debrett's family historian: a guide to tracing your ancestry* Debrett, 1981. A sumptuously (some might say excessively) illustrated general introduction. The number and size of the pictures keep the text to a minimum, but there are interesting sections on genetics, graphology, land records, emigration and heraldry. Re-issued as a paperback entitled *Debrett's guide to tracing your ancestry* Macmillan, 1982. Unchanged except that there is a much improved Chapter 12 on emigration to Australia and New Zealand written by Hugh Peskett.

FIELD, D.M. *The step by step guide to tracing your ancestors* Hamlyn, 1982.

*HAMILTON-EDWARDS, G.K.S. *In search of ancestry* Phillimore, 4th edn, 1983. For long a standard work, now completely revised. Strong on Army and Navy, Scotland, East India Co. Extensive bibliography.

HARVEY, R. *Genealogy for librarians* Bingley, 1982.

HUMPHERY-SMITH, C. *Introducing family history* Institute of Heraldic and Genealogical Studies, 1983. A short introduction.

IREDALE, D. *Discovering your family tree: a pocket guide to tracing your English ancestors* Shire, 3rd edn, 1977. A good and inexpensive general introduction.

*MANDER, M. *Tracing your ancestors* David and Charles, 1976. Reissued in paperback as *How to trace your ancestors* Mayflower Books, 1977. Another good general guide with more emphasis on the poor and the social context than most of the others.

MATTHEWS, C.M. *Your family history and how to discover it* Lutterworth Press, 2nd edn, 1982. A comprehensive and enjoyable guide to tracing your ancestors. Particularly good on ancillary topics such as surnames and old handwriting. Despite the title, there is little on family history as against genealogy.

PELLING, G. *Beginning your family history* FFHS, 3rd edn, 1984. An excellent introduction very clearly explained with the beginner in mind.

ROGERS, C.D. *The family tree detective: a manual for analysing and solving genealogical problems in England and Wales 1538 to the present day* Manchester University Press, 1983, new edn in preparation. A really first-rate tool-kit.

SOCIETY OF GENEALOGISTS. Leaflet No. 6 *Note for Americans tracing their British ancestry.*

*UNETT, J. *Making a pedigree* David and Charles, 2nd edn, 1971. op. Strong on Medieval sources, manorial records, Chancery proceedings and other public records. Complements most of the above.

*WILLIS, A.J. and TATCHELL, M. *Genealogy for beginners* Phillimore, 4th edn, 1979, repr. 1984. A.J. Willis's classic guide, first published in 1955 and now thoroughly revised and updated by Molly Tatchell. Particularly good on record repositories and includes a fascinating 'How I did it' section.

General Guides to Sources

DUNNING, R., *Local history for beginners* Phillimore, 1980.

EMMISON, F. G. *Introduction to archives* Phillimore, 1978.

EMMISON, F. G. *Archives and local history* Phillimore, 1978. A general survey of local history sources. Equally useful for the genealogist and family historian.

*FITZHUGH, T.V.H. *A dictionary of genealogy: a guide to British ancestry research* Alpha Books, 1985. Descriptions and locations of records, explanations of terms, lists of family history societies and records for English counties.

*HOSKINS, W. G. *Local history in England* Longman, n.e. 1973. Most sources discussed are relevant to family history.

*IREDALE, D. *Enjoying archives* Phillimore, 1980. Another excellent general survey.

MACFARLANE, A. *et al.* *Reconstructing historical communities* CUP, 1977. op.

MACFARLANE, A. *A guide to English historical records* CUP, 1983. Surveys records created by state, church and landlord. Based on a computerised project which analysed all surviving records for two parishes, one in Westmorland and the other in Essex.

*MARKWELL, F. C. and SAUL, P. *The family historian's enquire within* FFHS, 1985. A mini-encyclopedia of terms and sources used by the family historian. Crammed full of useful information. Gives Chapman county codes.

MASSEY, R. 'A genealogical check list' *Berkshire Family History Society Journal,* vol 1, no 2. Apr 1976. p. 38. List of 81 common sources with their availability.

MUNBY, L. M. ed. *Short guides to records* Historical Association, 1972. Collection of articles originally published in *History.* An example is given for each record.

PINE, L. G. *The genealogist's encyclopaedia* David and Charles, 1969. op. More a pot-pourri than an encyclopaedia. However, quite useful on Continental Records, and long sections on heraldry, titles, peerage law, orders of chivalry and decorations of honour and the clan system.

*RICHARDSON, J. *The local historian's encyclopedia* Historical pubs., 1974. repr. 1983. Available from Orchard House, 54 Station Rd, New Barnet, Herts.

*RIDEN, P. *Local history: a handbook for beginners* Batsford, 1983. Especially good on maps.

ROGERS, A. *Approaches to local history* 2nd rev. edn of *This was their world* Longman, 1977.

RYE, W. *Records and record searching* G. Allen and Unwin, repr. of 2nd edn (1897), 1969. op.

*SMITH, F. and GARDNER, D. E. *Genealogical research in England and Wales* 3 vols Salt Lake City: Bookcraft, 1956– 59, 1964. A standard work with volumes on 1. Civil registration, census returns, and parish registers. 2. Military and naval records, plus county by county directory to available records. 3. Handwriting guide.

*STEEL, D. J. ed. *National index of parish registers* Society of Genealogists. Vol 1. *Sources for births, marriages and deaths before 1837* 1976. Vol 2. *Sources for Nonconformist genealogy and family history* 1973. Vol 3 *Sources for Roman Catholic and Jewish genealogy and family history* 1974. (Includes combined index to Vols 1–3.) Vol 12 *Sources for Scottish genealogy and family history* 1971. For regional volumes see Parish Registers below.

STEPHENS, W. B. *Sources for English local history: studies in the uses of historical evidence* CUP, 2nd edn, 1981. A very comprehensive guide to sources most of which are equally relevant for family history.

*WEST, J. *Village records* Phillimore, 2nd edn, 1982. (Hereafter cited as *WEST VR) An extremely useful book containing detailed descriptions of sources, together with facsimiles and transcripts of documents. Each section has an extensive bibliography and lists, county by county, records in print. N.B. These bibliographies and lists have not been updated in the 2nd edn. Instead, books and records published *c.* 1961–1981 are listed in an addenda on p. 174.

*WEST. J, *Town records* Phillimore, 1983. (Henceforth cited as *WEST TR) A very welcome addition to the above and equally comprehensive. Sections on borough records, directories, newspapers, census returns, and photographs.

Collections of Articles

BURCHALL. M. J. ed. *Family history annual, 1986* 1985. Publ. by the editor, 3/33 Sussex Square, Brighton, Sussex. A collection of essays by leading British family historians on a wide variety of topics. The date is confusing as it actually appeared in September, 1985. Cited as *BURCHALL, 1986.

CHURCH OF JESUS CHRIST OF LATTER DAY SAINTS *World conference on records,* 13 vols, 1980. A remarkable collection of papers delivered at the second World Conference by experts from all over the world, and not nearly as well known in Britain as it ought to be. Vols 5 and 6 are devoted to British genealogy and family history and vol 2 to family history in general. Cited as *WORLD CONF. 1980.

STEVENSON, N. C. ed. *The genealogial reader* New Orleans: Polyanthos, 1978. Collection of 33 articles on genealogical research.

General Works on Genealogy

CAMP, A. J. *Everyone has roots* Star Books, 1978. op.

STEEL, D. J. 'Genealogy and family history in England', GJ vol 7, nos 2 and 3, June and Sept 1978.

STEEL, D. J. 'Ten years on: a personal view of genealogy and family history in England 1975–1985' in *BURCHALL 1986.

WAGNER, Sir Anthony *English genealogy* Oxford University Press, 2nd rev. edn, 1983. The historical background to English genealogy, with much on the social framework, emigration and the history of genealogy.

WAGNER, Sir Anthony *English ancestry* OUP, 1961. op. A condensed version of the above.

WAGNER, Sir Anthony *Pedigree and progress: essays in the genealogical interpretation of history* Phillimore, 1976.

General Works on Family History

DIXON, J. T. and FLACK, D. D. *Preserving your past: a painless guide to writing your autobiography and family history* New York: Doubleday, 1977. op. A very practical book.

JONES, V. L., EAKLE, A. H. and CHRISTIANSEN, M. H. *Family history for fun and profit* (formerly published as *Genealogical research: a jurisdictional approach*) Salt Lake City: Genealogical Institute, 1972. A guide to systematic searching and the keeping of records, most of which is readily transferable to a British context.

KYVIG, D. E. and MARTY, M. A. *Your family history: a handbook for research and writing* Arlington Heights: Harlington Davidson, 1978. Strong emphasis on the critical analysis and evaluation of sources and the writing of the family history.

LICHTMAN, A. J. *Your family history* New York: Random House, 1978. Another exciting general book on family history as against genealogy. Strong emphasis on oral history, and a useful section on photographs by Joan Challinor.

LICHTMAN, A. J. and FRENCH, V. *Historians and the living past* Arlington Heights: Harlington Davidson, 1978. A useful general book on the critical use of sources, on reconstructing the past and on historical explanation, with a strong emphasis on family, local and oral history.

*STEEL, D. J. and TAYLOR, L. *Family history in schools* Phillimore, 1973. op. A guide primarily intended for the teacher considering introducing family history into the primary or secondary curriculum, but with much of general interest on oral history, family documents, photographs, school records, newspapers and magazines.

Magazines and Journals

Genealogists' Magazine, published quarterly by Society of Genealogists, 14 Charterhouse Buildings, Goswell Rd, London EC1M 7BA. General articles on genealogy, reviews.

Family Tree Magazine, 129 Great Whyte, Ramsey, Huntingdon, Cambs PE17 1HP. A readable bi-monthly magazine. Especially useful for the beginner, since it assumes no prior knowledge of the subject. However its informative articles and its notes and news also serve to keep the more experienced family historian up to date.

Family History News and Digest, published half-yearly by the Federation of Family History Societies, 31 Seven Star Rd, Solihull, West Midlands B91 2BZ. Reports on activities of member societies of the Federation and includes an index to noteworthy articles in their journals. The Society of Genealogists holds a card index of the entries in the digest sections.

Family History, Journal of the Institute of Heraldic and Genealogical Studies, Northgate, Canterbury, Kent. A high proportion of the articles from 1976 to 1980 were lectures delivered at the 13th International Congress of Genealogical and Heraldic Science, Imperial College, London, 1976.

Genealogical Journal, Journal of the Utah Genealogical Association. Quarterly. Not as well-known in this country as it deserves to be, for it carries many first-rate articles of British interest.

Journal of One-name Studies, published quarterly by the Guild of One-Name Studies, Box G, Society of Genealogists, 14 Charterhouse Buildings, Goswell Rd, London EC1M 77BA.

Computers in Genealogy, A quarterly newsletter published by the Society of Genealogists. (For address, see above.)

The Scottish Genealogist, published quarterly by the Scottish Genealogy Society, 21 Howard Place, Edinburgh EH3 5JYY. Often contains articles of general interest, as do the various Irish journals (see p. 191).

Virtually all British Family History societies publish a journal. These will be found listed in the Federation publication *Publications of Member Societies* and articles from nearly all of them are listed in the *Family History News and Digest* above.

Some journals not primarily devoted to family history, but which contain many useful articles are:

Local Historian (formerly called *The Amateur Historian*), published quarterly by the British Association for Local History, The Mill Manager's House, Cromford Mill, Matlock, Derbyshire DE4 3RQ. Contains many very useful articles on sources.

Local Population Studies, published twice yearly by the Local Population Studies Society, Tawney House, Matlock, Derbyshire DE4 3BT. Journal of the amateur demographers. Some articles relevant to the family historian, particularly regarding access to sources.

Local History (1984–), edited by Susan and Robert Howard, 3 Devonshire Promenade, Lenton, Nottingham NG7 2ZS.

Journal of the Society of Archivists (1955–), published biannually, Yorks County Record Office, Elun St, Sheffield S1 4PL.

Archives, Journal of the British Records Association, Master's Court, The Charterhouse, Charterhouse Square, London EC1M 6AU.

A list of older journals, many of them extinct, dealing with genealogy and archives will be found in *STEEL NIPR vol 1, pp. 436–439.

Heraldry

THE HERALDRY SOCIETY (28 Museum St, London WC1A 1LH) publishes *The Coat of Arms*, a quarterly journal, and *The Heraldry Gazette*, a quarterly newsletter.

Genealogical Stationery and Software

The Federation of Family History Societies publishes a pack of forms which will assist the genealogist. These include the ancestry chart partially reproduced on page 113. It also produces D-I-Y Heraldry, a plastic template in a wallet.

THE SOCIETY OF GENEALOGISTS markets an ancestry chart (32″ × 23″ on stout paper for recording eight generations); birth brief form (A3 size suitable for keeping in a spring-back binder, for recording four generations); personal record cards; census record cards; family tree record (for recording all lines of ancestry in book form). In preparation.

LBS ANCESTRAL RECORDS, Hedley House, 39 Hedley St, Maidstone, Kent ME14 5AD (0622 51529). Publishes relationship and pedigree charts, document wallets, workbooks for census reforms etc; also computer software.

ALLEN & TODD, 78 Albert St, Ramsbottom, Bury BL0 9EL, publish packs of forms for recording: 1. baptisms, 2. marriages, 3. Post-1837 marriages, 4. burials, 5. census returns, 6. wills, 7. family groups, 8. personal details, 9. pedigrees, 10. IGI extracts, 11. entries from will indexes, 12. marriage licences, 13. index to births, 14. index to marriages, 15. index to deaths. Form 16 is for census indexing projects.

THE INSTITUTE OF HERALDIC AND GENEALOGICAL STUDIES (see above) publishes *Our Family History*, combining a short guide with blank forms to complete.

B. W. COLE, 44 Landseer Rd, Southwell, Notts. The *'Landseer Chart' Family Tree* is a special kind of chart which indicates both direct ancestry and collaterals.

PHILLIMORE AND CO., Shopwyke Hall, Chichester, Sussex (0243 787636) stock: *Our Family History* (see above); *Family Tree Scroll* (18″ × 23″, First Ave Publishing, Ayr, Scotland); Record your own Family History (blank album on heavy sepia paper, Oxford Illustrated Press); Family Wheel Chart (records ancestry in concentric circles – designed by Hannah Brams).

Research techniques

*SMITH & GARDNER vol 2 has a section on planning research and recording information.

DURTNELL, C. S. 'The fun of the chase', AH vol 3 no 7, Spring 1958. p. 279. Much more than the fun of it. Shows just how much can be obtained from real thoroughness in going through the available evidence, e.g. in examining all available deeds for places associated with the family. Continued into the Middle Ages in 'The quarry in sight', vol 4, Winter 1958-9. (Durtnell's family history is written up in *From an acorn to an oak tree: a study in continuity* Available Durtnell and Sons Ltd, Brasted, Kent, 1976.)

GANDY, M. 'Short cuts in tracing your family history' in *BURCHALL, 1986.

GIBBY, C. W. 'Some difficulties in the use of data required for genealogical research', *Northumberland and Durham Family History Society Journal* vol 1, no 3, Apr 1976. Some practical problems from various records, and some of the solutions.

GIBSON, J. S. W. 'Guiding the Genealogist' in *BURCHALL, 1985 On guides to sources.

Proving a pedigree

STEEL, D. J. 'Proving a pedigree' in R & B vol 9, no 3, 1982. Conference proceedings supplement.

STEVENSON, N. C. *Genealogical evidence* Laguna Hills, Calif., Aegean Park Press, 1979.

Recording

*PELLING has useful advice on recording, including a list of standard abbreviations.

SOCIETY OF GENEALOGISTS Leaflet no 3 *Family records and their layout*.

SOCIETY OF GENEALOGISTS Leaflet no 4 *Note taking and keeping for genealogists*.

PALGRAVE-MOORE, P. *How to record your family tree* Elvery Dowers, 1979.

Computers

Books:

HAWGOOD, D. *Computers for family history* Hawgood, 1985. Available from Hawgood Computing Ltd, 26 Cloister Rd, London W3 0DE. A really basic guide which assumes no prior knowledge of computers. Useful glossary of terms.

STARKS, W. C. 'The Computer and the Genealogist' in EAKLE A. and CERNY, C. *The Source: a guidebook of American genealogy* Salt Lake City: Ancestry, 1984. The most up-to-date summary of the use of the computer in American genealogy. It contains a very extensive bibliography not only of books and articles, but also of buyers' guides, genealogy programs (software) and genealogical databases, on-line information services, on-line databases, genealogical networks and genealogical computer serial publications. Essential reading for anyone wishing to be better informed about the massive American developments in this area.

Periodicals:

Computers in genealogy. ed. D. Hawgood. Quarterly newsletter published by the Society of Genealogists. Nearly all articles in this new magazine are of significance, but have not been listed separately here.

Some articles on genealogy and computers (mainly British) appearing in publications other than *Computers in Genealogy* are:

LAMB, C. 'Computers and genealogy: a survey of the literature'. GJ vol 12, no 4, Winter 1983-4.

REID, A. S. 'Information technology in genealogy', *Scottish Genealogist* vol XXXI, no 4, Dec. 1984. Reviews current developments in the use of computers in searching and indexing Scottish records and looks to the future, e.g. the use of videodisc.

SOCIETY OF GENEALOGISTS Leaflet No 16 *Assessing computer software for genealogical use.*

One-name Studies

GUILD OF ONE-NAME STUDIES *Register of one-name studies* GONS, 1982. Lists 700 families on which members of the Guild are working.

PALGRAVE D. 'One name societies', GM vol 18, no 6, June 1977. p. 296.

PALGRAVE D. A. *Forming a one-name group* FFHS, 2nd edn, 1983.

Many articles on one-name studies will be found in the *Journal of One-name Studies* and also in *Family Tree.*

Publishing

BRITISH STANDARDS No. 5605 *Recommendations for citing publications by bibliographical references* British Standards Institution, 1978. Lays down standards for authors and compilers. Should be acquired by anyone who writes or publishes, as should next item.

BRITISH STANDARDS (vol 6371 *Recommendations for citation of unpublished documents* British Standards Institution, 1983.

DYMOND, D. P. *Writing local history: a practical guide* Bedford Square Press, 1981. Most of the advice is just as relevant to family history.

ELRINGTON, C. R. *Handbook for editors and authors of the Victorian history of the counties of England* Univ. London: Institute of Historical Research, 1969.

SMITH, F. *The lives and times of our English ancestors* vol 2. Logan, Utah: Everton Publishers. 1980. Last chapter sets out a model format for presenting a family history.

Information from relatives and others

*PELLING has a specimen Family Questionnaire Form.

MCLAUGHLIN, E. *Interviewing elderly relatives* FFHS, 2nd edn, 1985. A chatty booklet full of very practical advice.

TAYLOR, L. *Oral evidence and the family historian: a short guide* FFHS, 1984. Deals with kinds of information (genealogical, biographical, historical and topographical), recording and interviewing techniques, processing the information.

THOMPSON, P. and GIRLING, M. 'The interview in social history', *Oral History* no 4, 1972. This issue contains many useful articles on interviewing.

Record Repositories

GIBSON, J. S. W. and PESKETT, P. *Record offices: how to find them* FFHS, 2nd edn, 1982.

ROYAL COMMISSION ON HISTORICAL MANUSCRIPTS *Record repositories in Great Britain* HMSO, 7th edn, 1982, A listing of addresses, hours etc.

CODLIN, E. M. ed. *The Aslib directory.* Vol 2: *Information sources in the social sciences, medicine and the humanities* Aslib, 4th edn, 1980.

EMMISON, F. G. and SMITH, W. J. *Material for theses in local record offices and libraries* Historical Association, 2nd edn, 1979. Useful handlist outlining material in over 100 record repositories.

FOSTER, J. and SHEPPARD, J. *British archives: a guide to archive resources in the United Kingdom* Macmillan, 1984. Outlines the holdings of 708 repositories.

ROBERTS, S. A., COOPER, A. and GILDER, L. *Research libraries and collections in the United Kingdom, a selective inventory and guide* Bingley, 1978.

STOREY, R. L. and MADDEN, L. *Primary sources for Victorian studies* Phillimore, 1977. Information on the Historical Manuscripts Commission and the National Register of Archives, holdings of national and local record repositories, published guides to collections inside and outside Britain. Covers many specialised topics. Most of the information has a relevance beyond the Victorian period.

*IREDALE, D. *Enjoying archives* is excellent on the contents and organisation of county record offices.

Most County Record Offices publish a guide to their holdings. These are listed in Storey and Madden, above. See also GIBSON, J. S. W. *Unpublished personal name indexes in record offices and libraries* FFHS, 1985 (see p. 164).

Civil Registration

The General Register Office indexes use county or regional code numbers (e.g. 1837–1851 IX is Cornwall & Devonshire and X is Devonshire & Somerset; 1852–1946 5b is Devonshire and 5c Cornwall and Somerset). A key to these numbers will be found in *PELLING, and *COLWELL and in *Cornwall Family History Society Journal* no 1, July 1976, p 12, *Hampshire Family History* vol 4, no 1, 1977, p 32 and East Surrey *Family History Society Journal* vol 1, no 3, Sept 1978, p 12. The last-named includes a list of districts before 1851.

*PELLING is good on civil registration and also gives key to code numbers (see above).

*ROGERS deals with a variety of problems in using civil registration.

*SMITH and GARDNER vol 1 is particularly good on the value of approaching local registrars and on causes of difficulty.

MCLAUGHLIN, E. *St Catherine's House: The General Register Office* FFHS, 6th edn, 1985. Chatty style. Excellent on causes of problems.

MAIDBURY, L. 'The General Register of Births, Deaths and Marriages', AH vol 3, no 3, Spring 1957, p 108. Describes causes of problems.

INSTITUTE OF HERALDIC AND GENEALOGICAL STUDIES produce two useful maps of England and Wales: *Registration and census districts. Map 1 1837–1851 Map 2 1852–1946* I.H.G.S., 1979. Both include the county/regional code numbers.

CHAPMAN, C. 'St Catherine's House – inside out' *Bedfordshire Family History Society* vol 4, no 8, Winter 1984. What the GRO contains, rather than how to use it.

CORSER, M. 'Help through New Zealand records', *Cheshire Family Historian* vol 4, no 1, Feb 1977, p 20. Additional information on New Zealand certificates (e.g. parents on death certificates) can help UK searches.

Census Returns

*PELLING is good on census returns.

*SMITH & GARDNER vol 1. A very comprehensive account.

*ROGERS deals with various problems in using census returns.

*WEST TR has a section on the National Censuses 1801–1901. Useful for general historical context, and includes a table giving populations of all towns 1841–1971.

GIBSON, J. S. W. *Census returns on microfilm 1841–1881: a directory to local holdings* FFHS, 4th edn, 1984.

GIBSON, J.S.W. *Marriage, census and other indexes for family historians* FFHS, 1985. Amalgamates two previous Federation guides – Marriage indexes and census returns. Includes Chapman county codes.

MCLAUGHLIN, E. *The censuses 1841–1881* FFHS, 2nd edn, 1985. A practical guide to using the PRO Census Room and its indexes, and interpreting the information.

SOCIETY OF GENEALOGISTS Leaflet No 14. *Census indexes in the library of the Society of Genealogists.*

CAMBRIDGE GROUP FOR THE HISTORY OF POPULATION AND SOCIAL STRUCTURE *Census enumerators' bibliography* A print-out bibliography of analysed census returns (see p. 182).

OFFICE OF POPULATION AND CENSUSES AND THE GENERAL REGISTRY OFFICE, SCOTLAND *Guide to census reports, Great Britain, 1801–1966* HMSO, 1977.

BOREHAM, J. M. *The census and how to use it* Essex Society for Family History, 1983. Available from Soc. Genealogists.

TAYLOR, L. 'The British Census as a source for the family historian' in *WORLD CONF 1980*, vol 5, paper 412. Summarises the history of Censuses and the information they will yield.

Directories, Poll Books and other Name Lists

*WEST VR and TR both have very detailed and useful sections on directories. See also Addenda to VR.

*ROGERS has a useful list of registers and directories of particular trades.

EDWARDS, L.W.L. ed *Catalogue of directories and poll books in the possession of the Society of Genealogists* Soc. Genealogists, 4th edn, 1984.

NORTON, J.E. ed. *Guide to the national and provincial directories of England and Wales, excluding London, published before 1856* Royal Historical Society, 1984.

GOSS, C. W. F. *The London directories 1677-1855* Archer, 1932. op.

GIBSON, J. S. W. *Unpublished personal name indexes in record offices and libraries* FFHS, 1985. County by county, this lists known card indexes, whether general (e.g. the one million cards in the Burnet Morris index in the West-Country Studies Library, Exeter) on a particular place (e.g. West Bromwich inhabitants) or to a particular source (e.g. York Apprenticeship Records).

Return of Owners of Land 1873 2 vols, HMSO, 1875. A printed return of owners of one acre and more of land useful for locating areas where particular surnames are found.

HALCROW, E. M. 'Registration of oaths at Quarter Sessions: a new source for genealogists and ecclesiastical historians', AH vol 2, no 11, Apr-May 1956, p.337. Registers of those taking oaths under the Test Acts, Toleration Act (1688), Act of Association (1696) etc. Lists all relevant acts.

WEBB, C. 'Name and inhabitants lists and the genealogist' in *BURCHALL, 1985.

Parish Registers

HUMPHERY-SMITH, C. R. ed. *The Phillimore Atlas and Index of parish registers* Phillimore, 1984. Compiled by the Institute of Heraldic and Genealogical Studies and incorporating their series of parish maps, this also includes for each ancient English county an 1834 map. It lists all parishes in England and Wales, and indicates the dates of deposited original parish registers, Nonconformist registers at the PRO, the coverage of the IGI (see p 133), copies in the Society of Genealogists, Boyd's Marriage Index (see p 134), the Pallot Marriage Index held by the Institute, local marriage indexes, and parish register copies the Society of Genealogists.

GIBSON, J. and WALCOT, M. *Where to find the International Genealogical Index* FFHS, 1985. Not only a useful guide to where copies of the IGI may be found, but goes way beyond the title with its important articles by Alf Ison (a general guide to using the index), Colin Atkinson (pitfalls for the unwary) and above all Chris Pitt-Lewis (using the IGI for Wales and Monmouthshire). Any IGI user interested in Wales should consult this last article before attempting to use the IGI at all.

STEEL, D. J. et al. eds *National index of parish registers* Soc. Genealogists, 1966–, in progress. Vol 1 STEEL D. J. ed. *Sources of births, marriages and deaths before 1837* 1966, repr. 1976. This has extensive information on the history and content of parish registers. Practical advice and suggestions are given in the sections 'Parish registers and the genealogist' and 'Pitfalls in the use of copies', and there is a quite detailed description of Boyd's Marriage Index and its arrangement. Vol 2 STEEL D. J. ed. *Sources for nonconformist genealogy and family history* 1973. See below. Vol 3 STEEL, D. J. ed. *Sources for Roman Catholic and Jewish Records* 1974. See below. Vol 4 PALGRAVE-MOORE, P. ed. *South-East England: Kent, Surrey and Sussex* 1980. Vol 5 STEEL, D. J. ed. *South Midlands & Welsh Border: Gloucestershire, Herefordshire, Oxfordshire, Shropshire, Warwickshire and Worcestershire* 1976. Vol 6, part 1 PALGRAVE-MOORE, P. ed. *Staffordshire* 1982. Vol 7 PALGRAVE-MOORE, P. ed. *East Anglia: Norfolk, Suffolk, Cambridgeshire* 1983. Vol 11, part 1 NEAT, C. P. comp. *Durham and Northumberland* 2nd edn, 1984. Vol 12 STEEL, D. J. *Sources for Scottish genealogy and family history* 1970.

LOCAL POPULATION STUDIES SOCIETY *Original parish registers in record offices and libraries* LPS Society, 1974 plus suppls 1–4, 1976–82. Available from Tawney House, Matlock, Derbyshire. Lists of deposited registers.

GIBSON, J. S. W. *Bishop's transcripts and marriage licences: a guide to their location and indexes* FFHS 2nd edn, 1985.

GIBSON, J. S. W. *Marriage, census and other indexes for family historians* FFHS, 1985. Amalgamates two previous Federation guides – Marriage indexes and Census indexes.

SOCIETY OF GENEALOGISTS *Parish register copies part 1 Society of Genealogists' collection* Soc. Genealogists, 7th edn, 1985. *Part 2 Other collections* Soc. Genealogists 1974, repr. 1978. An invaluable guide to printed, typescript and manuscript copies. It is important to remember, however, that the second booklet does not include *printed* copies, even though they are very widely available. All those are listed only in Part 1.

MASSEY, R. W. ed. *A list of parishes in Boyd's Marriage Index* Soc. Genealogists, 5th edn, 1984.

GRAHAM, N. H. ed. *Genealogist's consolidated guide to parish register copies and indexes in the inner London area 1538–1837.* Published by the editor, 1983. Available from Soc. Genealogists.

GRAHAM, N. H. ed. *Genealogists's consolidated guide to parish register copies and indexes in the outer London area 1538–1837* Published by the editor, 1977. Suppl. No 1, 1979. Available from Soc. Genealogists.

GUILDHALL LIBRARY *Parish registers: a handlist. Part 1: Registers of the Church of England parishes within the City of London* Guildhall Library, 4th edn, 1979.

PESKETT, H. *Guide to the parish and non-parochial registers of Devon and Cornwall 1538–1837* Devon & Cornwall Record Society, 7 The Close, Exeter, Devon, 1979.

WATTS-WILLIAMS, J. and WILLIAMS, C. *Parish registers of Wales* National Library of Wales In preparation. Guide to parish registers, bishop's transcripts, modern printed, typescript and microfilm copies.

*PELLING is good on parish registers.

*ROGERS deals with various problems in using parish registers.

WALCOT, M. 'Boyd's Marriage Index' *Hampshire Family Historian* vol 1, no 5, 1974, p. 94.

BURN, J. S. *Registrum ecclesiae parochiales: the history of parish registers in England* E.P. Publishing, repr. of 2nd edn (1862), 1976. op.

COX, J. C. *The parish registers of England* E.P. Publishing, repr. of Methuen edn (1910), 1974. op.

WRIGLEY, E. A. 'Parish registers and the historian' in *STEEL NIPR, vol 1.

WALCOT, M. and GIBSON, J. S. W. eds *Marriage indexes: how to find them; how to use them; how to compile one* FFHS, 1979. op. Now largely replaced as a finding aid by GIBSON, J. S. W. *Marriage, Census and Other Indexes* above, but still valid for compiling a marriage index.

Transcribing

*STEEL NIPR vol 1 contains detailed advice on transcription.

Births, Marriages and Deaths Abroad

YEO, G. ed. *The British overseas: a guide to records of their births, baptisms, marriages, deaths and burials, available in the United Kingdom* Guildhall Library, 1984. Available from Soc. Genealogists. An invaluable guide, arranged by country.

Bastardy

MCLAUGHLIN, E. *Illegitimacy* FFHS, 1985. Deals with illegitimacy in parish registers, bastardy bonds. Also adoption etc.

Adoption

*CURRER BRIGGS has a section on 'Adopted and illegitimate children and the law'.

MORDY, I. 'Adopted people', *A.G.R.A. Newsletter* no 15, Jan 1977, p 6. Background notes to the adoption acts and changes in the accessibility of records.

Marriage Licences

*STEEL NIPR vol 1 has a section on marriage licences.

GIBSON, J. S. W. comp. *Bishops' transcripts and marriage licences, bonds and allegations: a guide to their location and indexes* FFHS, 2nd edn, 1985.

COLLINS, L. ed. *Marriage licences: abstracts and indexes in the library of the Society of Genealogists* Soc. Genealogists, 2nd edn, 1983.

Clandestine marriages

*STEEL vol 12 has a substantial section on clandestine marriages, including Fleet marriages; includes a bibliography. (Note that the section on Gretna Green has been superseded by next item.)

*STEEL vol 12 has a section on Gretna Green marriages.

CRIGHTON, G. S. 'Registers of irregular Border marriages' *Scottish Genealogist* vol XXVIII no. 4, Dec 1981.

SOCIETY OF GENEALOGISTS Leaflet No 10. *Irregular Border marriages.*

Other Parish Records

See bibliography in *STEEL NIPR vol 1, pp 402–3, and also the section on the poor.

TATE, W. E. *The parish chest* Phillimore, 2nd edn, 1983.

TUPLING, G. H. Searching the parish records 6 articles in AH (now LH) vol 1, nos. 7–12, Oct-Nov 1953 to June-July 1954, between them cover the whole range of parish records.

*STEEL NIPR vol 1 has a section on the poor.

BURCHALL, M. 'The poor and the poor laws' in *BURCHALL 1986.

*WEST VR is excellent on tithe awards.

Monumental Inscriptions

*STEEL NIPR vol 1 has a section on monumental inscriptions which includes a fuller bibliography than space permits here.

PATTINSON, P. *Recording monumental inscriptions in the UK: a report on current progress* FFHS, 1984.

RAYMENT, J. *Notes on the recording of monumental inscriptions* FFHS, 1981.

WHITE, J. L. *Monuments and their inscriptions: a practical guide* Soc. Genealogists, 1978.

COLLINS, L. ed. *Monumental inscriptions in the library of the Society of Genealogists. Part 1: Southern England* Soc. Genealogists, 1984.

STEWART, F. 'Life and death in an Oxfordshire churchyard', LH vol 13, no 3, August 1978 p 149. This account of a transcription and analysis project is interesting for its detailed account of how to use a mirror to reflect sunlight to recover 'illegible' inscriptions. ('With some persistence we were able to read most of the partially illegible inscriptions, and 30 of the 45 which had appeared completely illegible in 1974.')

JONES, J. *How to record graveyards* Council for British Archaeology, 1979. Written by an archaeologist for archaeologists.

HAMLEY, D. W. 'Monumental inscriptions – recommendations for typing and indexing of manuscript notes,', *Cornwall Family History Society Journal*, Spring 1977, p 13.

LINDSAY, D. T. and J. 'Tombstone photography' GJ Utah Genealogical Association vol 4, no 3, Sept 1975, pp 103–6. Virtually illegible tombstones made readable by flashlight photography.

Roman Catholic, Nonconformist and Jewish Records

Report of Commissioners appointed to enquire into the state of non-parochial registers HMSO, 1859; reprinted by the List and Index Society, 1969. Lists all surrendered non-parochial registers and corrects the many errors in an earlier list published in 1841.

ROMAN CATHOLICS:

*STEEL NIPR vol 3 'Sources for Roman Catholic and Jewish Genealogy and family history'.

WILLIAMS, J. A. 'Sources for recusant history (1559–1791) in English official archives'. Published as vol 16, no 4 of *Recusant History*, 1983.

PRESBYTERIANS, BAPTISTS, CONGREGATIONALISTS:

*STEEL, NIPR vol 2 has a substantial section on the 'Three Denominations'.

QUAKERS:

*STEEL, NIPR vol 2 has nearly 100 pages on Quaker records.

MILLIGAN, E. H. and THOMAS, M. J. *My ancestors were Quakers. How can I find out more about them?* Soc. Genealogists, 1983.

METHODISTS:

*STEEL, NIPR vol 2 includes a section on Methodists.

*PELLING includes a chart showing the divisions of the Methodist Church.

GANDY, M. ed. *My ancestor was a Methodist: how can I find out more about him?* Soc. Genealogists, 1982.

JEWS:

SAMUEL, E. R. 'Jewish births, marriages and deaths' in STEEL, D. J. ed. *National index of parish registers* vol 2. *Sources for Nonconformist genealogy and family history* Soc. Genealogists, 1972.

GANDY, M. ed. *My ancestor was Jewish. How can I find out more about him?* Soc. Genealogists, 1983.

KAGANOFF, B. C. *A dictionary of Jewish names and their history* Routledge and Kegan Paul, 1978. op.

ROTTENBERG, D. *Finding our fathers* New York: Random House, 1977 op. A substantial guide to Jewish genealogy which includes a country by country description of archives and finding aids.

Jewish genealogy has been revolutionised in the last few years (since Rottenberg's book) by the discovery or release of much more German and Polish material than had been known previously to have survived. Much of this has been microfilmed by the Mormons and is available from the Genealogical Library. This material is listed and described in:

CERNY, J. 'Jewish American research' in EAKLE, A. and CERNY, J. eds *The Source: a guidebook of American genealogy*. Salt Lake City: Ancestry, 1984. (Includes 15-page list of German Jewish records on microfilm and a 13-page list of Polish records.)

KURZWEIL, A. *From generation to generation: how to trace your Jewish genealogy and personal history*. New York: Morron, 1980 hdbk; Schocken, 1981 pbk. Emphasis on European Jewish genealogy.

Diocesan and Archdeaconry Records

See bibliography in *STEEL NIPR vol 1, pp 398–400.

*IREDALE, *Enjoying archives* Chapter 4 'Cathedral'.

PURVIS, J. S. *An introduction to ecclesiastical records* St Anthony's Press, 1953. op.

OWEN, D. M. *The records of the established church in England, excluding parochial records* British Records Association, 1970.

Wills

GIBSON, J. S. W. *A simplified guide to probate jurisdictions: where to look for wills* FFHS, 3rd edn, 1985.

MCLAUGHLIN, E. *Somerset House Wills from 1858* FFHS, 3rd edn, 1985. Much useful background information.

CAMP, A. J. *Wills and their whereabouts* The author, 1974. op. A very comprehensive and detailed guide including much general background material.

GIBSON, J. S. W. *Wills and where to find them.* Phillimore, 1974. op. Another comprehensive guide which includes very useful maps showing jurisdictions.

*PELLING is good on wills and on Scottish testaments.

*SMITH and GARDNER vol 2 gives a comprehensive account dealing with many problems.

*UNETT is excellent on wills, particularly on their style over the centuries.

*WILLIS includes a useful key to the Latin of the Act of Probate appended to wills and administrations.

PARKER is good on the light wills throw on our ancestors' way of life. See p 183.

*hamilton-edwards has a good description of the Estate Duty Office wills.

camp, a. j. 'Estate duty office wills' GM vol 15, no 11, September 1967, pp 393–7. Includes a list of volume numbers for each court.

COX, J. *The records of the Prerogative Court of Canterbury and the death duty registers* Public Record Office, HMSO, 1980. This book opened up a vista of additional source material not generally known previously to exist – PCC inventories (card index of 20,000 names at the PRO) and records of litigation and shows how to find the date of death in death duty registers.

PUBLIC RECORD OFFICE, Leaflet No 34. *The death duty registers.*

HOAD, J. 'Death Duty Registers' *North West Kent Family History* vol 3 no 4, Dec 1983. Shows how death duty registers 1799–1903 can be used to supplement information in wills.

Printed indexes to PCC wills are available for the period up to 1700. These are listed in the three works by GIBSON and CAMP above. The period 1750–1800 is currently being published by the Society of Genealogists. To date 3 vols covering A-G have been published:

CAMP, A. J. ed. *An index to wills proved in the Prerogative Court of Canterbury 1750–1800* vol 1 A–Bh, 1976; vol 2 Bi–Ce, 1977; vol 3 Ch–Ci, 1984.

Inventories

*WEST VR has a very substantial section on inventories, including the reconstruction of house interiors, and a list of printed collections. See also addenda.

PARKER has a joyous description of the contents of inventories with much useful guidance on reading between the lines and on the validity of the valuation. See p 183.

moore, j. s. ed. *The goods and chattels of our forefathers* Phillimore, 1976. Very informed introduction. Includes useful glossary compiled by C. J. Spittal.

GIBSON, J. S. W. 'Inventories in the records of the Prerogative Court of Canterbury' LH vol 14, no 4, Nov 1980, p 222. See also letter of D. J. Gerhold in LH vol 15, no 6 May 1983, p 363.

OVERTON, M. *A bibliography of British probate inventories.* Available from Dept of Geography, University of Newcastle-upon-Tyne, 1983. A list of 487 references to published inventories.

STEER, F. W. *Farm and cottage inventories of mid-Essex, 1635–1749* Phillimore, 1969. A very useful book which devotes 68 pages to discussing all the various items found in inventories and their historical significance.

Manorial Records

*WEST VR includes facsimiles and transcripts of documents and lists of published rolls. There is also a useful glossary.

*HOSKINS is very good on the administration of the manor.

STEEL NIPR vol 1 has a section on manorial records. See also the bibliography on p 403.

HARVEY, P. D. A. *Manorial records* (Archives and the User No 5) British Records Association, 1984.

HONE, N. J. *The manor and manorial records* 1925. Kennikat Press, n.i. 1971.

HUMPHERY-SMITH, C. R. 'English manorial records as a source of eighteenth and nineteenth century family history' in *WORLD CONF, 1980. Very clear account with facsimiles.

The National Register of Archives (see p 162) holds a *Manorial Documents Register* – an up-to-date list of known manorial records.

Quarter Sessions

*WEST VR includes examples, and lists printed calendars. See also addenda.

GIBSON, J. S. W. *Quarter sessions records for family historians: a select list* FFHS, 2nd edn, 1985.

Borough, Guild and City Company Records

*WEST TR has much information on borough organisation and records, including lists of publications by local record and other societies.

There are books on many of the Livery companies of London and on provincial guilds and societies, which contain lists of officers, members etc.

PUBLIC RECORD OFFICE Leaflet No 26. *Apprenticeship records.*

Schools, Colleges and Universities

*STEEL and TAYLOR include a section on nineteenth-century school records in their chapter on 'Archive exploration'.

Deeds

*IREDALE *Your family tree* is very helpful.

CORNWALL, J. *How to read old title deeds* Birmingham University, Extra Mural Dept, 1964. op; Pinhorns, n.i. 1971. op.

DIBBEN, A. *Title Deeds* Historical Association, 1968.

EMMISON, F. G. 'Final Concords' LH vol 14, no 7, Aug 1981, p 411.

Public Record Office

*UNETT *Making a pedigree.* Over half of this book is devoted to PRO sources. A very useful practical guide.

*CURRER-BRIGGS lists the classes of records at Chancery Lane and Kew.

COX, J. and PADFIELD, T. *Tracing your ancestors in the Public Record Office* HMSO, 3rd edn, 1984. This includes many bibliographies and lists of published calendars etc.

PUBLIC RECORD OFFICE *Guide to the contents of the Public Record Office* 3 vols, HMSO, 1963–9. Vol 1 *Legal records;* vol 2 *State papers and departmental records;* vol 3 *Accessions 1960–1966.*

LEESON, F. ed. 'How to order by computer at the PRO, Kew' GM vol 19, no 7, Sept 1978, pp 249–50.

At the time of writing, the Public Record Office has published no less than 60 leaflets on sources or topics. Together these constitute a major guide to the resources of the PRO.

Taxes

See substantial bibliography in *STEEL NIPR vol 1, pp 394.

GIBSON, J. S. W. *The Hearth Tax, other later Stuart tax lists and the Association Oath Rolls* FFHS, 1985.

GIBSON, J. S. W. and MILLS, D. eds *Land tax assessments, c. 1690–1950* FFHS, 1984.

*WEST VR has facsimiles and transcriptions of Lay Subsidy Rolls, Hearth Tax and Land Tax and lists of printed returns.

*IREDALE, *Enjoying archives* is excellent on Land Tax.

BECKETT, J. V. *Local taxation: national legislation and the problems of enforcement* Bedford Square Press, 1980. National statutes and the local community.

GLASSCOCK, R. E. ed. *The lay subsidy of 1334* OUP, 1975.

Chancery and other Legal Proceedings

*COLWELL has quite a good general survey.

*UNETT devotes five pages to Chancery proceedings.

GARRETT, R. E. F. 'Chancery and other legal proceedings' *Genealogists' Magazine* vol 15, nos 3 and 4, Sept and Dec 1965. Reprinted as a booklet by Pinhorns, 1968.

HUGHES, M. H. 'Notes on some finding aids to Chancery proceedings in the library of the Society of Genealogists' *Genealogists' Magazine* vol 18, no 3 Sept 1975, p129.

Army and Navy

*HAMILTON-EDWARDS has chapters on 'Naval ancestors' and 'Army records'.

*SMITH and GARDNER vol 2 has a comprehensive section on 'Naval and military records'.

ARMY:

BARNES, D. J. 'Identification and dating: military uniforms' in STEEL, D. J. and TAYLOR, L. eds *Family history in focus* Lutterworth Press, 1984.

BARNES, R. M. *History of the regiments and uniforms of the British army* Seeley Service, 1950. op.

HAMILTON-EDWARDS, G. K. S. *In search of army ancestry* Phillimore, 1977.

HIGHAM, R. ed. *A guide to the sources of British military history* Routledge and Kegan Paul, 1972.

HOLDING, N. H. *World War I army ancestry* FFHS, 1982.

HOLDING, N. H. *The location of British army records: a national directory of World War I sources* FFHS, 1984. Bibliography of lists of men and of First World War bibliographies. Most of the book is devoted to county lists giving regiments, books, regimental and other museums, records in record offices and libraries.

HOLDING, N. H. *More sources for World War I: Army ancestry* In prep. Will probably be published by the FFHS in 1986.

JAMES, E. A. *British regiments 1914–18* Samson Books, 1978. Gives locations.

*MARKWELL and SAUL have a list of units in the British Army with the dates they were raised.

PUBLIC RECORD OFFICE *Records of Officers and soldiers who have served in the British army.* HMSO.

PUBLIC RECORD OFFICE Leaflet No 39. *Prisoners of War: Documents in the PRO.*

PUBLIC RECORD OFFICE Leaflet No 58. *Operational Records of the British Army 1660–1914*

SWINSON, A. *A register of the corps and regiments of the British army* Archive Press, 1972. op.

WATTS, C. T. and WATTS, M. J. 'In search of a soldier ancestor', GM vol 19, no 4, Dec 1977, p 125.

WHITE, A. S. *Bibliography of regimental histories of the British army* F. Edwards, 1965. op.

WICKES, H. L. *Regiments of foot: a historical record of all the foot regiments of the British army* Osprey, 1974. op.

All army officers will be found listed in the Army Lists or the Indian Army Lists.

NAVY:

BROWN, R. Naval records for the family historian, *Bristol and Avon Family History Society Journal* no 8, Summer 1977, p 12.

PUBLIC RECORD OFFICE Leaflet No 18. *Admiralty records.*

SOCIETY OF GENEALOGISTS Leaflet No 12. Army muster and description books.

Musters and militia

*STEEL vol I has a section on muster rolls and there is a bibliography on p 404.

PUBLIC RECORD OFFICE *Militia muster rolls, 1522–1640* PRO, 1984.

Merchant Navy, Customs and Excise

*MANDER gives an outline of available records.

'Index to crew lists and agreements of the British Empire 1863–1913' FHSJ vol 10, no 61/62, n.s. 37/38, July 1977, p 56. Information on what the index covers and how crew lists for 70,000 vessels have been archived.

MATHIAS, P. and PEARSALL, A. W. H. eds *Shipping: a survey of historical records* David and Charles, 2nd edn, 1980. This important survey is in two parts: (1) shipping companies and their record holdings (many include passenger lists), and (2) shipping records in county and other record offices. There is an index of named ships, an index of persons and firms and an index of places and principal trades.

WATTS, C. T. and WATTS, M. J. *My ancestor was a merchant seaman: how can I find out more about him?* Society of Genealogists, 1985.

WATTS, C. T. 'Merchant Navy Records' GM vol 19, no 4, Dec 1977, p 145.

WATTS, C. T. and M. J. 'Unravelling Merchant Seamen's Records' GM vol 19, no 9, March 1979.

PUBLIC RECORD OFFICE, Leaflet No 8 *Records of the Registrar General of Merchant Shipping and Seamen* HMSO.

East India Company

*HAMILTON-EDWARDS has a chapter on this.

Trade, Business and Insurance Records

*COLWELL has quite a good little general survey.

BENNETT, J. and STOREY, R. eds *Trade union and related records.* Univ. of Warwick, 1981.

Most professions produce regular registers of qualified practitioners, e.g. *Crockford's Clerical Directory, Medical Directory*, and many libraries have runs of these sometimes back into the 19th century. The Society of Genealogists has a good collection and the Guildhall Library, London, an even better one. This is often the best way of finding more information on a professional person. In addition, many biographical dictionaries have been published devoted to particular occupations. Some of them are listed in *STEEL NIPR vol I.

Legal records

BLAND, D. S. 'The records of the inns of court: a bibliographical aid' AH vol 5, no 2, 1962.

Medieval Sources (see also Taxes, above)

*UNETT and *WEST are excellent on medieval records.

*STEEL NIPR I has a section on medieval sources consisting of articles on 'Proofs of age' and 'Inquisitions post mortem' contributed by E. Gillett and M. McGuinness.

BLOOM, J. H. 'Genealogical data before the Black Death' GM vol 6 no 10, June 1934, p 471.

CAM, H. 'Pedigrees of villeins and freemen in the 13th century' GM vol 6, Sept 1933, p 299.

CAMPLING, A. 'Sources of genealogical research before 1349' GM vol 7, June 1935, p 61.

DURTNELL, C. S. 'The quarry in sight' AH vol 4, no 2, Winter 1958–9, p 56. A 'how I did it' article on medieval genealogy. (So many genealogists collect hundreds of entries from the registers and then, for lack of an obvious hunting ground, give up the chase in despair. The author shows how he was able to trace his ancestry back to 1180.)

FARADAY, M. and SHEPPARD, W. L. Jr 'Pre Parish register Genealogy' GM vol 19, no 4, Dec 1977, p 129.

HUMPHERY-SMITH, C. R. *An introduction to medieval genealogy.* Part I *Family History* vol 9, pp 3–15, and *Genealogical Journal* vol 3, no 2, June 1974 (also available separately); Part 2 *Bibliography and Glossary* Institute of Heraldic and Genealogical Studies, 1974.

WROTTESLEY, G. *Pedigrees from the Plea Rolls 1200–1500* Harrison, 1905. op.

Note: Calendars to the medieval records in the Public Record Office will be found listed in *MULLINS, *Texts and Calendars* (see p. 187). Much medieval material has been published by local record and other societies. This is listed in *MULLINS, *Hist. and Arch.* (see p 187).

Records of Parliament, including Protestation Returns

BOND, M. F. *Guide to the records of parliament* HMSO, 1971. op.

BOND, M. F. *The Records of Parliament*, 1964. Reprinted from AH. Part I *Acts of Parliament* vol 4, no 6, Winter 1959–60, p 219. Part 2 *Private Bill Records* vol 4, no 7, Spring 1960, p 267. Part 3 *Parliamentary Papers* vol 4, no 8, Summer 1960, p 307. Part 4 *Judicial records and parliamentary debates* vol 4, no 88, Summer 1960, p 354.

SOCIETY OF GENEALOGISTS Leaflet No 8 *Protestation returns of 1641–2: a checklist.* Also printed in GM, vol 19, no 3, Sept 1977, p 84.

RESKERR, F. J. R. Protestation Oaths, AH vol 12, no 8, Oct–Nov 1955, p 25. Gives background and text of the oath.

STOATE. T. L. *The Cornwall Protestation returns, 1641* Available from T. L. Stoate, Lower Court, Almondsbury, Bristol, 1974. Useful introduction.

WEBSTER. W. 'The Protestation returns 1641–2'. *Nottinghamshire Family History Society Journal* vol 2, no 3, March 1977, p 3.

See also *Parliamentary Papers*, below p 165.

The British Library

*WILLIS and TATCHELL have a useful section on 'The British Library Reference Division, formerly called the British Museum Library'.

ESDAILE, A. J. K. *The British Museum Library: a short history and survey* Greenwood Press, 1979.

BRITISH LIBRARY *Catalogue of printed maps, charts and plans in the British Library* British Museum Pubs, 1977.

GILSON, J. P. *A student's guide to the MSS of the British Museum* (Helps for students of history, no. 31) SPCK, 1920.

BRITISH LIBRARY *The British Library: Guide to the catalogues and indexes of the Department of Manuscripts* British Library, 1978.

The College of Arms and Visitations

SOCIETY OF GENEALOGISTS Leaflet No 15. *The right to arms.*

SQUIBB, G. D. *Visitation pedigrees and the genealogist* Pinhorns 1978.

WAGNER, SIR ANTHONY *The records and collections of the College of Arms* Burke's Peerage, 1952, repr. 1974. op.

Other London Repositories

Guide to Genealogical Sources in the Guildhall Library Corporation of London, 2nd edn, 1981.

JONES, P. E. and SMITH, R. *A guide to the records in the Corporation of London Records Office and the Guildhall Library Muniment Room* E.U.P., 1951. op.

RYE, R. A. *Students' guide to the libraries of London:* University of London Press, 3rd edn, 1928. op.

WEBB, C. *Genealogical research in Victorian London* West Surrey Family History Society. Research aid no 6, 1981. Lists roads covered by each registration district.

WEBB, C. 'A genealogical gazetteer of mid-Victorian London' West Surrey Family History Society. Research aid no 9, 1982. An index to London streets in 1875, giving a reference to the parish of each. (To be used in conjunction with *Genealogical research in Victorian London,* above.)

WEBB, C. 'Tracing ancestors in London' R & B vol 11, no 2, Autumn 1984.

Newspapers and Periodicals

*WEST TR has a section on 'Provincial newspapers from 1690' and 'a gazetteer of English and Welsh newspapers 1690–1981'.

GIBSON, J. S. W. and WEST, J. *Local newspapers before 1920.* FFHS, 1985. Based on gazetteer in *WEST TR, but with many additional local holdings shown. Covers England and Wales only.

*STEEL NIPR I has a substantial section on 'Births, marriages and deaths from newspapers' including a bibliography on newspapers up to 1968, and a list of the longer-lived London newspapers before 1837.

'The Times' tercentenary handlist of English and Welsh newspapers, magazines and reviews, 1620–1920 Hodder and Stoughton, 1920. op.

The new Cambridge bibliography of English literature CUP, 5 vols, 1969–77. Vol 2 cols 1313–90; vol 3 cols 1789–1828 and vol 4 cols 1347–1408 list *Restoration and eighteenth, nineteenth* and *twentieth century newspapers* etc respectively.

STOREY, P. J. 'Genealogy from newspapers' *Northumberland and Durham Family History Society Journal* vol 1, no 3, Apr 1976.

FARRAR, R. H. *Index to biographical and* Index Society, *obituary notices in the 'Gentleman's Magazine' 1731–1780* 1891.

FRY, E. A. *Index to marriages in the 'Gentleman's Magazine', 1731–1768* 1922. Supplement to *The Genealogist* N.S. vol 34–38, 1917–22.

Immigrants

NEAGLES, J. C. and L. L. *Locating your immigrant ancestor: a guide to naturalisation records,* 1974.

Huguenots

CURRER-BRIGGS, A. N. and GAMBIER, R. *In search of Huguenot ancestry* Phillimore, 1985.

DELAFORCE, P. *Family History research. Vol I: the French connection* Regency Press, 1983. (Somewhat disorganised book, but does provide a worked example of Huguenot genealogy.

*STEEL NIPR vol 2 has a section on 'Foreign churches' which includes historical background and sources for Huguenots and Walloons, together with appendices on French and Belgian parish and Protestant registers.

Emigrants and Overseas Genealogy

CURRER-BRIGGS, N., *Worldwide family history* Routledge and Kegan Paul, 1982.

*CURRER-BRIGGS There is a sub-section on emigrants in the section 'Sources and their whereabouts in Great Britain' and information on three private indexes formerly federated as the Family History Services *Combined Emigration Index* but now quite separate.

*CURRER-BRIGGS and GAMBIER have a short chapter on emigration.

PUBLIC RECORD OFFICE Leaflet No 7. *Emigrants.*

*COLWELL has quite a good chapter on emigration and travel.

HUMPHERY-SMITH, C. R. 'Genealogy without frontiers' Paper given at *14th International Congress of Genealogy and Heraldic Sciences* Helsinki, 1984. On emigration. Useful table of causes of emigration from Europe.

Palaeography

Review article by Jennifer Thorp on all the main books on palaeography entitled 'Books on palaeography: 16th to 18th century handwriting' in LH vol 16, no 6 May 1985.

*MATTHEWS includes a useful introduction to sixteenth- and seventeenth-century hands.

*IREDALE, D. *Enjoying archives* contains a fuller very practical guide which includes the medieval period.

BUCK, W. S. B. *Examples of handwriting 1550–1650* Society of Genealogists, 1982.

DAWSON, G. E. and KENNEDY-SKIPTON, L. *Elizabethan handwriting 1500–1650* Phillimore, 1981. Includes a large number of examples with transcripts.

DAY, L. F. *Penmanship of the XVI, XVII and XVIII centuries* Batsford, 1978.

EMMISON, F. G. *How to read local archives 1550–1700* (Helps for Students of History No 82) Historical Association, 3rd edn, 1971. An inexpensive little booklet with a representative selection of local documents printed with transcripts and notes. Very useful practice for the beginner.

GRIEVE, H. *Examples of English Handwriting, 1150–1750* Essex Record Office Publications No 21, 1981. Available from Society of Genealogists.

HECTOR, L. C. *The handwriting of English documents* Kohler and Coombes, 1980.

LE HARDY, W. 'How to read 16th and 17th century handwriting' AH vol 1, no 55, Apr-May 1953, p 146. Very useful article, particularly on contractions.

NEWTON, K. C. *Medieval local records: a reading aid* (Helps for students of history No 83) Historical Association, 1971. Reprinted with additional facsimiles of documents from 'Reading medieval local records' AH vol 3, no 2, Winter 1956–7, p 81, repr. AH vol 7, no 3, 1966 p 88. A very useful guide.

RYCRAFT, A. *English medieval handwriting* Borthwick Institute, 2nd edn, 1972. Wallet of documents with transcripts.

RYCRAFT, A. *Sixteenth and seventeenth century handwriting. Series 1 and 2* Borthwick Institute, 3rd edn, 1972. Wallet of documents with transcripts.

RYCRAFT, A. *Sixteenth and seventeenth century wills, inventories and other probate documents* Borthwick Institute, 1973. Wallet of documents with transcripts.

SMITH, D. M. *Medieval Latin documents. Series 1 Diocesan records; Series 2 Probate.* Wallet of documents with transcripts Borthwick Institute, 1984.

*SMITH and GARDNER vol 3 is devoted to 'Old English handwriting, Latin, research standards and procedures'. 1964, rev. edn 1966.

*THOYTS, E. E. *How to read old documents* Elliot Stock, 1893. Repr. Phillimore, 1980.

WHALLEY, J. *English handwriting, 1540–1853* HMSO, 1970.

WRIGHT, A. *Court Hand restored* 10th edn, ed C.T. Martin, 1912.

Graphology (Reading Character from Handwriting)

*CURRER-BRIGGS & GAMBIER include a section on this.

Specialised Terms

*COLWELL, *FITZHUGH, *RICHARDSON and *TATE all include useful lists of unusual words found in documents.

*STEEL NIPR vol 1 has a short section on 'Titles and descriptions'

*MARKWELL & SAUL have a chart to show relationships.

COOK, K. 'The jargon of genealogy' *East Surrey Family History Society Journal* vol 1, no 2 February 1978 pp 24–8. A useful beginners' list.

DU BOULAY, F. R. H. *Handlist of medieval ecclesiastical terms* National Council for Social Service, 1952. op.

HARRIS, P. V. 'Glossary of terms from parochial records' AH vol 1, no 4, Feb–Mar 1953, p 122.

JOHNSON, G. D. 'Legal terms and phrases' AH vol 3, no 6, Winter 1957–8, p 249.

LITTLE, J. E. 'Glossary of Agricultural terms' AH Part 1 vol 4, no 4, Summer 1959, p 152. Part 2 vol 4, no 5, Autumn 1959, p 195. See also correspondence AH vol 4, no 7, Spring 1960, p 291 with supplementary glossary p 293, vol 5, no 1, Autumn 1965, p 29.

PURVIS, J. S. *Dictionary of ecclesiastical terms* 1962.

SIMS, R. *A manual for the genealogist, topographer, antiquary and legal professor* 1888.

THOYTS, above, includes sections on legal technicalities etc.

WRIGHT, J. *The English dialect dictionary* 1898.

WRIGHT, J. *The English dialect grammar* 1905.

The full, multi-volumed *Oxford English Dictionary* is very useful for discovering the various usages of obsolete sixteenth-, seventeenth- and eighteenth-century words or former meanings of current words.

Money values

'HISTORICUS' AH vol 2, no 8, Oct–Nov 1955, p 238. Reference tables on the value of money 1780–1850.

ROGERS, T. *A history of agriculture and prices* pub. 1866–1902 'Medieval prices' AH vol 2, no 9, Dec–Jan 1956, p 271. Table of prices 1261–1582.

Latin

*FITZHUGH includes translations and facsimiles of common documents.

GOODER, E. A. *Latin for local history* Longman, 1978. Intended to be used in conjunction with Kennedy, below.

KENNEDY B. H. *Revised Latin primer* Longman.

LATHAM, R. E. *Revised medieval Latin wordlist* OUP, 1965.

LATHAM, R. E. 'Coping with medieval Latin' and 'A glossary of medieval Latin terms' AH vol 1, no 11, Apr–May 1954, pp 331, 333.

*MARKWELL & SAUL have a glossary of Latin words for relationships and a list of Roman numerals and money abbreviations.

MARTIN, C. T. *The record interpreter* 1892, repr. Phillimore, 1982 with an introduction by David Iredale. Abbreviations of Latin words, abbreviations of French words, glossary of Latin words, Latin names for British and Irish place names, Latin names of bishoprics, Latin forms of English surnames, Latin forms of English Christian names. The glossary has now been superseded by LATHAM, above, but the other lists are still useful.

SIMPSON, E. *Latin word-list for family historians* FFHS, 1985.

*STEEL NIPR vol I has a glossary of Latin words for trades.

Dates

CHENEY, C. R. *Handbook of dates for students of English history* Royal Historical Society, 1970.

CURRER-BRIGGS and GAMBIER have a section on dates before the calendar change in 1752.

EVANS, M. 'A perpetual calendar' R & B vol 2, no 3, Spring 1976, p 114. Ways of working out the days of the week in the past.

MASSEY, R. W. '35 Saints Days and fixed feasts', *Berkshire Family Historical Society Journal* vol 2, no 3, Spring 1977, p 54. Days used in dating documents.

MCKAY, 'The dating of records' AH vol 2, no 6, June–July 1955, p 176.

POWICKE F. M. and FRYDE, E. B. *A handbook of dates for students of British history*, 1970.

ROBINSON, B. 'What day was that?' *Queensland Family History Society Journal* vol 4, Dec 1983 Method of finding the day of the week when someone was born, baptised, married or buried.

WATTS, C. 'Roman dating' *Oxfordshire Family Historian* vol 2, no 4, Spring 1981, p 98. (As found in Mixbury, Oxfordshire, parish registers.)

'Regnal years' will be found in *RICHARDSON, *TATCHELL & WILLIS, *CURRER-BRIGGS and in AH vol 1, no 1, Aug–Sept 1952, p 23, and *Berkshire Family History Society Journal* vol 2, no 4, Summer 1977, p 100.

II HISTORICAL BACKGROUND

General Works

As has been emphasised elsewhere, it is important that the family historian should do background reading in order to set the family in its context. A few works family historians might find of particular interest are:

DYER, C. *Lords and peasants in a changing society* CUP, 1980.

HARRISON, J. *The common people: a history from the Norman Conquest to the present* Fontana, 1984.

HOSKINS, W. G. *Local history in England* Longman, n.e. 1984. Essential reading for family historians. Important chapters on parish, manor and land development and social history of towns, on the landscape, on buildings and on health, disease and population.

LASLETT, P. *The world we have lost* Methuen, 1st edn, 1965; 2nd edn, 1971. 3rd edn, largely rewritten (1983) under the title *The World we have lost further explored*, outlines the main social and demographic features of pre-industrial England and the new edition incorporates the results of the mass of demographic work done in the last 20 years.

MACFARLANE, A. *The origins of English individualism* Blackwell, 1978. Claims that England never had a real peasantry. See review by Alan Rogers LH vol 14, no 2, May 1980, p 105.

SMITH, F. *The lives and times of our English ancestors* Logan, Utah: Everton Publishers, vol 1, 1969. A very basic social history. Vol 2, 1980, includes much on family records and oral evidence and sets out a format for presenting a family history.

THOMAS, K. *Religion and the decline of magic: studies in popular belief in sixteenth and seventeenth century England* Weidenfeld and Nicolson 1971. A massive 700-page book which examines the role of magic, witchcraft etc in people's lives.

TREVELYAN, G. M. *English social history* Longman, 1942; n.e. BBillustrated 1978; Penguin Books, 1970. Now rather dated in its approach but still useful for factual information.

WAGNER, SIR ANTHONY *English genealogy* Phillimore, 2nd edn, 1983. Contains a great deal of useful background information on social history, written with the needs of the genealogist in mind.

Further works published before 1968 will be found listed in *STEEL NIPR vol I, p 407.

Specific Periods

There is a vast range of general histories of particular periods. The following are very readable introductions:

WILLIAMS, P. *Life in Tudor England* Batsford, 1964.

DODD, A. H. *Life in Elizabethan England* Batsford 1961. op.

BYRNE, M. St Clare *Elizabethan life in town and country* Methuen, 1925. op.

ASHLEY, M. *Life in Stuart England* Batsford, 1964.

PARREAUX, A. *Daily life in England in the reign of George III* Allen and Unwin, 1969. op.

MARSHALL, D. *Eighteenth century England* Longman, n.e. 1975.

MARSHALL, D. *Industrial England 1776–1851.* Routledge Band Kegan Paul, 1973.

WILLIAMS, E. N. *Life in Georgian England* Batsford, 1962. op.B

WHITE, R. J. *Life in Regency England* Batsford, 1963. op.

READER, W. J. *Life in Victorian England* Batsford, 1964, op.

CECIL, R. *Life in Edwardian England* Batsford, 1969.

Detailed lists for each period of books published up to 1968 will be fund in *STEEL NIPR vol 1, pp 408–419. A useful review article, mainly devoted to oral history and working-class memoirs is Robin Chaplin's 'Recent Work in Social History', LH vol 12, nos 3 and 4, Nov 1976.

Specific Topics

On topics such as houses, food, education or transport, see the Local History bibliographies listed on p 187.

More Advanced Works

A few more advanced works it would be particularly rewarding for the family historian to study are:

HOSKINS, W. G. *The Midland peasant: the economic and social history of a Leicestershire village* St Martin's Press, 1957; Macmillan paperback 1979. A history of Wigston Magna which illustrates the wealth of documentary material which can be brought to bear in reconstructing the social history of the community. Especially good on medieval genealogical techniques.

SPUFFORD, M. *Contrasting communities: the English villager in the sixteenth and seventeenth centuries* CUP, 1974. 'An attempt to weave together the threads which made up the villager's life in the sixteenth and seventeenth centuries. I have tried to portray the villager in this period not merely as an economic animal, an item on a rent-roll or even a man whose assets were conveniently listed and priced at his death, but also as a sentient human being who could possibly read and even write and who might be expected to have some reactions to the successive changes in his parish church. 'An important book for family historians. See M. Spufford 'The total history of village communities' LH vol 10, no 8, Nov 1973, p 398, and review by L. Munby, LH vol III, no 7, August 1975, p 423.

THIRSK, J. ed. *The agrarian history of England and Wales 1500–1640* vol 4, CUP, 1967. A massive work, very useful as a quarry for background material.

GOUGH, R. *The history of Myddle* Caliban Books, 1979. This remarkable profile of a Shropshire village was written in 1701–1706. 'It is in fact a unique book. It gives us a picture of seventeenth century England in all its wonderful and varied detail such as no other book that I know even remotely approaches' (Hoskins).

HEY, D. *An English rural community: Myddle under the Tudors and Stuarts* Leicester University Press, 1974. Based upon Gough but drawing upon much additional material, this is an invaluable detailed study of the social and economic structure of a rural community, group by group and family by family.

Historical Demography

Some bibliographies are:

MILDEN, J. W. *The family in past time: a guide to the literature* New York: Garland Publishing Inc, 1977. 1300 titles on the family and family life.

A bibliography of historical demography up to 1968 will be found in *STEEL NIPR vol I, pp 420–424, and from about 1966 in the review article by D. M. Palliser 'What to read on population history', LH vol 16, no 4, Nov 1984, p 207. There are useful reviews of important books and articles c. 1970–77 in LPS no 19, Autumn 1977, c. 1977–79 in LPS no 23, Autumn 1979, and c. 1980–83 in LPS 1983.

A printout of a bibliography of census studies undertaken can be obtained from Data Editor, SSRC, Cambridge Group for the History of Population and Social Structure, 27 Trumpington St, Cambridge CB2 1QA. Arranged, by request, by author, county, census date or topic.

Some of the more important general works are:

ANDERSON M. *Approaches to the history of the Western family 1500–1914* Macmillan, 1980.

DOW, F. D. 'The early modern family' *History* vol 63, no 208, June 1978, pp 239–45. A useful synopsis of work on the history of the family.

DRAKE, M. ed. *Population studies from parish registers* LPS, 1982.

HILL, C. 'Household and kinship' *Past and Present* no 88, August 1980. Throws doubts on the conclusions with regard to the prevalance of the nuclear family reached by the Cambridge Group. (But these doubts answered in WRIGLEY and SCHOFIELD, below.)

HOULEBROOKE, R. A. *The English family 1450–1700* Longman, 1984. More balanced across classes than Stone's work (see below).

LASLETT, P. *Family life and illicit love in earlier generation* CUP, 1977.

LASLETT, P. and WALL, R. *Household and family in past time* CUP, 1972. Collection of essays on the history and structure of the family as an institution in western Europe.

PINCHBECK, I. and HEWITT, M. *Children in English society: vol I Tudor times to the 18th century; vol 2 From the 18th century to the Children Act 1948* Routledge and Kegan Paul, 1969, n.i. 1973.

PRIOR, M. ed. *Women in English society 1500–1800* Methuen, 1985.

SHORTER, E. *The making of the modern family* Fontana, 1977. The family in the Western world 1750–1975.

STONE, L. *The family, sex and marriage in England 1500–1800* Weidenfeld and Nicolson, 1977. Abridged paperback edn, Penguin, 1979. A massive work but biased towards upper classes. See review in LH vol 13, no 7, August 1979, p 441.

WALL, P. 'The Age at leaving home' *Journal of Family History* vol 3, no 2, 1978.

WRIGLEY, E. A. and SCHOFIELD, R. S. *The population history of England 1541–1871: a reconstruction* Edward Arnold, 1981. Based on aggregative analysis of 404 parish registers, this 779-page study has largely superseded all previous work. 'The magnum opus on English population history which local historians, and many others, have been eagerly awaiting' D. M. Palliser – see her review in LH vol 15, no 2, May 1982, p 103.

On techniques the best introductions are:

WRIGLEY, E. A. ed. *An introduction to English historical demography,* Weidenfeld and Nicolson, 1966.

DRAKE, M. *Historical demography: problems and projects* Open University, 1974. From Open University course 'Historical data and the social sciences'.

DRAKE, M. *The quantitative analysis of historical data* Open University, 1974.

Local Histories

These should always be sought out and read when doing research on a particular area in order to provide the local context. It is a good idea to read first a general county history before embarking upon the history of a particular place. An excellent series is the Darwen one published by Phillimore which now includes most counties. On the history of the landscape there is the general series *The landscapes of Britain,* edited by R. Millward and A. Roblinson. For reference there is *The Victorian history of the counties of England.* Though started in the late nineteenth century, the series is still incomplete. Most counties have one or more general volumes followed by several volumes of parish histories. For an account of the progress and problems see PUGH, R. B. 'The Victoria county histories' LH vol 13, no 1, Feb 1978.

On local history in general, apart from Hoskins' *Local history in England* and other works cited above, the following are recommended:

RIDEN, P. *Local history: a practical handbook for beginners* Batsford, 1983. Particularly good on maps.

ROGERS, A. *Approaches to local history* Longman, 2nd edition, 1977.

PARKER, R. *The common stream: Foxton* Palladin, 1976. A history of Foxton, Cambridgeshire, which communicates the atmosphere of local history and good detective work with sources. See Parker's article 'I didn't mean to do it' LH vol 12, no 8, Nov 1977, p 391.

Historical Geography

BRIGGS, A. *Victorian cities* Penguin Books, n. edn, 1968.

HOSKINS, W. G. *The making of the English landscape* Hodder and Stoughton 1955; Penguin 1970. The classic work on the history of the landscape. See also TAYLOR, C. 'The making of the English landscape – 25 years on', LH vol 14, no 4, Nov 1980, p 195, and ASTON, M. 'The making of the English landscape – the next 25 years' LH vol 15, no 6, May 1983, p 323.

Gazetteers and maps

*WEST VR has a section on county maps and a useful list of those in print. See also his addenda.

*RIDEN has a good chapter on maps.

DAVID and CHARLES, Newton Abbot, Devon, have published the 1st edition one-inch to the mile ordnance survey maps, surveyed between 1805 and 1873, though with the railways added. Harry Margery, Lympne Castle, Kent are currently publishing the 1st edition maps in 10 volumes. So far published are: vol 1 Kent, Essex, east Sussex and south Suffolk; vol 2 Devon, Cornwall and west Somerset; vol 3 Surrey, west Sussex, Hants, Dorset, east Somerset and south Wilts.

BEECH, G. 'Maps and the Genealogist' in *Summary of Proceedings of 2nd British Family History Conference, Guildford, 1982,* published as a supplement to R & B vol 9, no 3, Dec 1982.

BRITISH LIBRARY *Catalogue of printed maps, charts and plans* British Museum Publications, 1967, 1978.

CHUBB, T. *The printed maps in atlases of Great Britain and Ireland: a bibliography 1579–1870* 1927, repr. William Dawson, 1974.

FALKUS, M. and GILLINGHAM, J. *The historical atlas of Britain* Granada 1981.

HARLEY, J. B. *Maps for the local historian: a guide to British sources* National Council for Social Service, 1972. The basic guide to British maps. Reprinted from a series of articles in AH and LH vol 7, nos 6–8, vol 8, nos 2 and 5, 1967–9. 1. Maps and plans of towns (vol 7, no 6); 2. Estate maps (vol 7, no 7); 3. Enclosure and tithe maps (vol 7, no 8); 4. Maps of communications (vol 8, no 2); 5. Marine charts (vol 8, no 3); 6. County maps (vol 8, no 5).

HARLEY, J. B. and PHILLIPS, C. W. *The historian's guide to Ordnance Survey maps* National Council Social Services, 1965. Reprinted from AH vol 5, nos 5–8, 1962–3. 1. One inch to the mile maps of England and Wales (no 5). 2. The period maps of the O.S. (no 6). 3. Six inch and twenty-five inch (no 7). 4. Town plans and small-scale maps (no 8).

PUBLIC RECORD OFFICE Leaflet No 49 *Maps in the Public Record Office.* HMSO.

PUBLIC RECORD OFFICE *Maps and plans in the Public Record Office: vol 1. British Isles 1410–1860* HMSO, 1967.

RODGER, E. M. *The large-scale county maps of the British Isles 1596–1850: a union list* Bodleian Library Oxford, 1972.

SKELTON, R. A. ed. *County atlases of the British Isles, 1579–1850: a bibliography. Part 1 1579–1703* William Dawson, 1978.

SHIRLEY, R. W. *Early printed maps of the British Isles 1477–1650* Holland Press, 2nd rev edn, 1983.

LEWIS, S. *A topographical dictionary of England* 4 vols, 1831; S. Lewis, 7th edn 1849.

Tithe and Enclosure

*RIDEN is excellent on tithe and enclosure maps and awards.

PUBLIC RECORD OFFICE, Leaflet No 12 *Enclosure Awards* and No 13 *Tithe awards.*

Lists of Inland Revenue Tithe Maps and Apportionments Vol 1 Bedford to Northumberland, vol 2 Nottingham to Yorkshire, Wales, List and Index Society vols 68 and 83.

BREWER, J. G. *Enclosures and the open fields: a bibliography* British Agricultural History Society, 1972.

HARLEY, J. B. *Maps for the Local Historian. Part 3* (see above).

KAIN, R., and PRINCE, H. *The tithe surveys of England and Wales* CUP, 1984.

MARKWELL, F. C. 'English tithe awards and the family historian' GJ vol 7, no 2, June 1978.

TATE, W. E. *The English village community and the enclosure movements* Gollancz, 1967.

TATE, W. E. *A domesday of English enclosure acts and awards* The Library, University of Reading, 1978. Gives details of every enclosure award. See review of TURNER, M. 'A domesday of English enclosure acts and awards 1531–1918 by W. E. Tate', LH vol 10, no 6, p 295.

TURNER, M. *English parliamentary enclosure* Dawson, 1980.

TURNER, M. 'Recent progress in the study of parliamentary enclosure' LH vol 12, no 1, Feb 1976, p 18. Includes a bibliography of publications since 1954.

Biographies

The Dictionary of National Biography 21 vols, 1885–1900. Compact edition of 2 vols, 1975. Biographies of notable persons dying before 1900. A regular series of supplements of recently deceased persons takes it up to 1970.

VENN, J. A. comp. *Alumni Cantabrigienses* 10 vols, 1922–54. Biographical notes on Cambridge graduates to 1900.

FOSTER, J. comp. *Alumni Oxonienses: matriculation registers of the members of the University of Oxford from 1500–1886* 8 vols, 1887–92 (notes on Oxford graduates to 1886).

MATTHEWS, W. comp. *British autobiographies: an annotated bibliography of British autobiographies published or written before 1951* Cambridge University Press, 1956. op; University of California Press, 1984.

There are many specialised biographical dictionaries for particular trades and professions. Some of them are listed in *STEEL, NIPR vol 1. A consolidated index to 350 bio-graphical dictionaries with three million entries is:

HERBERT, M. C. and MCNEIL, B. *Biography and Genealogy Master Index* Detroit, Michigan: Gale Publishing Co. 2nd edn, 1980.

Parliamentary Papers

The many thousands of published volumes of reports by Royal Commissions and by House of Commons and House of Lords Select Committees provide a rich quarry for information on most occupations, industries and areas in the nineteenth century. A complete set is in the State Paper Room of the British Library, and incomplete sets are in university and other major libraries.

The official indexes to House of Commons papers 1696–1899 were reprinted by the Irish University Press in seven volumes, 1968. There is also a *General Index to the Sessional Papers printed by order of the House of Lords.* Three volumes cover 1801–85 and there are annual volumes 1886–1901.

The various select lists such as W. R. Powell's *Local history from blue books* Historical Association, 1962, are not usually very helpful for family history purposes as they list only those papers considered most significant historically. H. V. Jones, ed. *Catalogue of parliamentary papers 1801–1900 with a few of earlier date* P. S. King and Son, n.d. op is far from complete but may give more information than the official indexes.

All the command papers (i.e. those originating by command of the Crown rather than the House of Commons) are included in E. Di Roma and J. A. Rosenthal *A numerical finding list of British command papers* New York Public Libraries, 1967. As the command papers tend to be the ones most likely to be of value to the family historian this finding list can prove useful.

Further information will be found in:

FORD, P. and FORD, G. *A guide to parliamentary papers* Irish University Press, 3rd edn, 1972.

BOND, M. F. *Records of Parliament* (section on parliamentary papers) Phillimore 1964, reprinted from AH, vol 4, no 8, Summer 1960, p 307. Clearly lays out the various kinds of papers.

WALKER, R. S. 'Parliamentary papers – an untapped source?' *Journal of Bristol and Avon FHS* vol 7, Spring 1977, p 15.

Names

*COLWELL, *MATTHEWS and CAMP, A. *Everyone has roots* Star Books, 1978, all have useful chapters on names.

*STEEL NIPR vol 1 has a section on Christian names.

MATTHEWS, C. M. *English surnames* Weidenfeld and Nicolson, 1966. op.

REANEY, P. H. *The origin of English surnames* Routledge and Kegan Paul, n. edn 1980.

BARDSLEY, C. W. *A dictionary of British and Welsh surnames with special American instances* 1901; repr. Baltimore: Genea-logical Publishing, 1980. 30,000 surnames.

HARRISON, H. *Surnames of the United Kingdom* 1912, 1918; repr. Baltimore: Genealogical Publishing, 1969. 25,000 surnames.

REANEY, P. H. *A dictionary of British surnames* Routledge and Kegan Paul, 2nd edn, rev. by R. M. Wilson 1976; corrected repr. 1983. 20,000 surnames.

Note: Bardsley and Harrison are probably two-thirds complete but Reaney only half complete, so all three should be used together with:

HANKS, P. and HODGES, F. *A dictionary of surnames* OUP, 1985.

COTTLE, B. *The Penguin dictionary of surnames* 2nd edn, Penguin, 1978.

DUNKLING, L. *Everyone's dictionary of first names* Dent, 1983. Contains a useful bibliography.

WITHYCOMBE, E. G. ed. *Oxford dictionary of English Christian names* OUP, 1950; 3rd edn 1977.

PUBLIC RECORD OFFICE, Leaflet No 5 *Change of Name* HMSO.

PHILLIMORE, W. P. W. and FRY, E. A. *An index to changes of name 1760–1901* Phillimore, 1905.

PINHORN, M. *Index to changes of name 1901–1915* Unpublished index. To consult contact BCM Pinhorns, London WC1V 6XX.

Pictures

*MANDER includes a chapter on Fashions.

STEEL, D. J. and TAYLOR, L. eds *Family history in focus* Lutterworth Press, 1984. Sections on building up a family photographic archive, copying and restoring; identification and dating – general procedures, costume, military uniforms, photographic processes and papers; picture researching and photographing for future generations.

HIRSCH, J. *Family photos: content, meaning and effect* OUP, 1981.

CHALLINOR, J. 'Family photographs' in LICHTMAN, A. J. *Your Family History* New York: Random House, 1978.

EAKLE, A. *Photographic Analysis* Salt Lake City, Utah: Family History World, 1976.

BARLEY, M. W. *A guide to British topographical collections* Council for British Archaeology, 112 Kennington Rd, London SE1, 1974. Photographs, prints, estate drawings in libraries, museums, record offices, private collections.

EVANS, H. and M. and NELKI, A. eds *The picture researcher's handbook*, Saturday Ventures, 1979. Lists main collections throughout the world.

HUDSON, K. and NICHOLLS, A. *Directory of Museums* Macmillan, 2nd edn 1981.

Museums and art galleries in Great Britain and Ireland, British Leisure Pubs, 1985. Will also assist in locating repositories with pictures.

PUBLIC RECORD OFFICES, Leaflet No 52 *Photographs, microfilms and posters in the Public Record Office* HMSO.

WALL, J. comp. *The dictionary of photographic collections* Heinemann, 1977. Lists 1,580 collections; indexed by subject, owner, location, title and photographer.

Slide-tape, Video and Film

GREEN, H. *Projecting Family history: a guide to audio-visual construction* FFHS, 1982.

STEEL, D. J. and TAYLOR, L. *Family history in focus* (above) includes sections on the use of slide-tape and film in family history and Green's account of the picture researching on which his slide-tape programme was based.

Heraldry

*COLWELL has a good general chapter on heraldry.

*CURRER-BRIGGS and GAMBIER have a chapter on heraldry including a 2-page spread showing at a glance the main divisions of the shield etc.

CAMP, A. *Everyone has roots* has a chapter on 'The right to arms'.

FEARN, J. *Discovering heraldry* Shire Publications, 1980.

HUMPHERY-SMITH, C. R. 'Help with heraldry' LH vol 11, no 8, Nov 1975, p 470. How to identify a coat of arms.

HUMPHERY-SMITH, C. R. *Heraldry* Heraldry Society, 1972. A simple outline of the subject.

HUMPHERY-SMITH, C. R. and LONDON, H. *The right road for the study of heraldry* Heraldry Society, 1968. Guidance on what to read.

HUMPHERY-SMITH, C. R. 'Heraldry for the Genealogist' GM vol 18, no 7, Sept 1976, p 354.

MACKINNON, C. ed *The Observer's book of heraldry* F. Warne, 1975.

MONCREIFFE, Sir I. and POTTINGER, D. *Simple heraldry*, Bartholomew, 2nd edn, 1979. A fun book giving the basics.

Heraldic dictionaries and other works of reference will be found listed in most of the above works.

III BIBLIOGRAPHIES

Genealogical Bibliographies

*HAMILTON-EDWARDS includes a substantial bibliography.

*STEEL vol 1 has a large bibliography which lists works on many historical topics as well as having extensive coverage of genealogy and archives. Note, however, that this volume also contains a number of subsidiary bibliographies scattered throughout the book, and that there are extensive bibliographies on non-conformity in vol 2 and Roman Catholics and Jews in vol 3.

FEDERATION OF FAMILY HISTORY SOCIETIES *Current publications by member societies* FFHS, 2nd edn, 1984.

FILBY, P. W. *American and British genealogy and heraldry* Boston: New England Historical Genealogical Society, 3rd edn, 1983. A massive enlargement of the 2nd edition, with a continental European section as well.

HASLAM, G. E. ed. *Manchester Public Libraries* Reference Library, Subject Catalogue, Section 929, Genealogy (3 parts). Manchester Library Committee, 1956–8.

*HUMPHERY-SMITH, C. R. *A genealogist's bibliography* Phillimore, 2nd edn, 1981. County lists, but biased towards the medieval period. General works difficult to find as listed alphabetically by authors in one indiscriminate list.

KAMINKOW, M. J. *A new bibliography of British genealogy* Baltimore: Magna Carta Book Co., 1965.

KAMINKOW, M. *Genealogical manuscripts in British libraries: a descriptive guide* Baltimore: Magna Carta Book Co., 1967.

ROBERTS, G. B. 'Major genealogical publications of the last two decades: select list' GJ vol 12, no 2 Summer 1983. A world list, though the emphasis is on the United States.

Root and Branch, the journal of the West Surrey Family History Society, has each quarter since Autumn 1975 been abstracting from the *British National Bibliography* new books of interest to the family historian. These include all new books on family history, genealogy and archives, most on social history and all those relating to Surrey.

The Family History News and Digest, published by FFHS, lists with a brief indication of contents, significant articles in journals of member societies. The Society of Genealogists maintains a card index of all entries.

Pedigrees and Family Histories

MARSHALL, G. W. comp. *The genealogist's guide* n.i. of 4th rev. edn, 1903; *Heraldry Today*, 1967. A list of pedigrees in printed sources to 1903.

WHITMORE, J. B. comp. *A genealogical guide: an index to British pedigrees in continuation of Marshall's 'Genealogist's guide'* Society of Genealogists, 1953. A list of pedigrees in printed sources 1900–50.

BARROW, G. B. *The genealogist's guide: an index to printed British pedigrees and family histories 1950–1975, being a supplement to G. W. Marshall's 'Genealogist's guide' and J. B. Whitmore's 'Genealogical guide'* Research Publishing Co., 1977.

THOMSON, T. R. *Catalogue of British family histories* Research Pub. Co., 4th edn, 1980. Covers only published family histories. Unchanged, text from 3rd edn, 1976, but with addenda by C. Barrow covering the period 1976–1980.

BUCK, W. S. B. *A list of names in the document collection of the Society of Genealogists* Society of Genealogists, 1965.

GIBSON, J. S. W. *Unpublished personal name indexes in record offices and libraries: an interim list* FFHS, 1985.

PRYCE, F. R. *A guide to European genealogies exclusive of the British Isles* University Microfilms, 1965.

WALCOT, M. 'Acquiring old published family histories' *Hants Family History* vol 4, no 1, Nov 1977, p 16.

Peerages, Gentry and Royal Descents

Burke's peerage, baronetage and knightage Burke's Peerage, 105th edn, 1975.

Burke's landed gentry 3 vols. Burke's Peerage, n.e. 1969, 1970, 1972.

Burke's family index ed. H. J. Montgomery-Massingberd. Burke's Peerage, 1976. A comprehensive and very useful index to the enormous number of names in *Burke's peerage*, *Burke's landed gentry* and all Burke's other publications.

Burke's dormant and extinct peerages Burke's Peerage, 1883, repr. Baltimore: Genealogical Pubs, 1978.

Burke's extinct and dormant baronetcies Baltimore: Genealogical Pubs, 2nd edn, 1977.

Burke's colonial gentry 1891–95; repr. Heraldry Today, 1970.

Burke's royal families of the world vol 1 Europe and Latin America; vol 2 Africa and the Middle East, Burke's Peerage, 1980.

Note: On the history of Burke's publications and editors, see MONTGOMERY-MASSINGBERD, H. '150 years of Burke' *Family History* vol 9, no 60/NS no 36, Nov 1976, p 13.

COKAYNE, G. E. *The complete peerage of England, Scotland, Ireland, Great Britain and the united Kingdom, extinct or dormant* 1887–98; 6 vols, facs. edn Alan Sutton, Gloucester, 1983.

COKAYNE, G. E. *The complete baronetage* 6 vols, 1900–1909, repr. 1983.

LEESON, F. L. and PARRY, C. J. *A directory of British peerages* Society of Genealogists, 1984. An alphabetical list of titles and surnames showing every title which once existed, first grantee's surname, approximate period of tenure and final fate if not still existing.

PARRY, C. *Catalogue of baronetage creations* Baltimore: Genealogical Pubs, 1970.

MONTAGUE-SMITH, P. ed. *Debrett's peerage and baronetage* 1980. New edn in prep.

PINE, L. G. *New extinct peerages 1884–1971* Heraldry Today, 1972.

RUVIGNY, M. MASSUE, MARQUIS DE *The Jacobite peerage, baronetage, knightage and grants of honour* Skilton, 1974. Genealogies of persons ennobled by the Stuarts and their successors.

SQUIBB, G. D. *Visitation pedigrees and the genealogist* Pinhorns, 1968.

TURTON, W. H. *The Plantagenet Ancestry: showing over 7,000 of the ancestors of Elizabeth, wife of Henry VII* 1928, repr. Phillimore, 1975.

Families Being Researched

Most family history societies produce directories of members' interests, for the most part listed in the FFHS publication *Current Publications of Member Societies* 2nd edn, Spring 1984. Care must be exercised as often only the most recent register is listed, whereas earlier editions often include interests not brought forward. Few societies list interests of deceased or ex-members, as was done in the 1966 *Society of Genealogists' Register and Directory*. yet work done by a person long deceased may be of great value. So all editions of all directories should be searched. Some societies (e.g. Scottish Genealogy Society, Berkshire FHS) list their members' interests in their journal, and nearly all do so for new members, so scan journals published since the last directory. As well as members' interests lists published by societies, current and former editions of the following directories should be scanned:

BURCHALL, M. J. and WARREN, J. eds *National genealogical directory* 1979, 1980, 1982–3, 1984, 1985. Between them these list around 80,000 families which genealogists – mainly British – are researching.

JOHNSON, K. A. and SAINTY, M. R. *Genealogical research directory* Library of Australian History, annual 1981–. Australian in origin, but increasingly international. The 1985 edition alone has over 50,000 entries.

GUILD OF ONE-NAME STUDIES *Register of one-name studies* 4th edn, 1985. Guild members interested in every occurrence of a surname. 800 surnames listed.

STEEL, D. J. ed. *Society of Genealogists: register and directory* Soc. Genealogists, 1966. Includes all entries in the first (1961) register. Supplemented by catalogue of members' interests 1968–71. Both are still useful for locating work previously done. The Society holds a card index covering members' interests from 1971 to date.

Other Overseas Directories

KONRAD, J. ed. *Family associations, societies and reunions: a comprehensive listing* Munroe Falls, Ohio: Summit Publications, 6th edn, 1985.

The LDS Family Registry, Genealogical Library, Salt Lake City, Utah, holds a record of interests of LDS members. Its organisers are currently seeking to extend its coverage to non-Mormons. Available on microfiche.

There are also several American commercial computer indexes of genealogists' interests. These are listed in the notes to STEEL, D. J. 'Genealogy and family history in England: 10 years on' in *BURCHALL 1986.

Published Primary and Secondary Sources

FEDERATION OF FAMILY HISTORY SOCIETIES *Current publications by member societies* FFHS, 2nd edn, 1984.

GOMME, G. L. *Index of archaeological papers 1665–1890.* Congress of Archaeological Socs, 1892–1900.

HUMPHRIES, A. L. *Handbook to county bibliography* 1917; repr. Dawsons of Pall Mall, 1974.

MATTHEWS, W. comp. *British autobiographies: an annotated bibliography of British autobiographies published or written before 1951* Cambridge University Press, 1956, op; Hamden, Conn.: Shoe String Press, 1968.

MATTHEWS, W. *British diaries: an annotated bibliography of British diaries written between 1442 and 1942* Magnolia, Mass.: Peter Smith, 1967.

MORTON, A. and DONALDSON, G. *British national archives and the local historian: a guide to official record publications* Historical Association, 1981.

MULLINS, E. L. C. *Texts and calendars: an analytical guide to serial publications* 2 vols, Royal Historical Society, 1958, 1983. A guide to the publications of source material by the Public Record Office and by record societies.

MULLINS, E. L. C. *A guide to the historical and archaeological publications of societies in England and Wales, 1901–1933* Athlone Press, 1968.

PONSONBY, A. *English diaries from the sixteenth to the twentieth century* Methuen, 1923.

SOMERVILLE, R. *Handlist of record publications* British Records Association, 1951. A list of publications of over sixty English publishing societies.

YOUNG, J. D. *Museum publications in print in the United Kingdom* Mansell, 1978. Includes not only museum publications but also relevant publications of local societies.

The *British humanities index* (Formerly *Subject index to periodicals*) has subject and regional lists of articles in several hundred journals.

See also *Family History News and Digest* under 'Genealogical Bibliographies' above.

The following *Local history handlists* are much more than the titles suggest, listing useful general works on topics such as homes, food or medicine. For recent works, the best source is the current Phillimore bookshop (not publishers') catalogue.

KUHLICKE, F. W. and EMMISON, F. G. eds *English local history handlist* Historical Association, 1969. op. This inexpensive booklet gives a select booklist on various occupations, industries and other social history topics.

STOCKHOLM, P. and ROGERS, J. *British local history: a selected bibliography* Dillon's University Bookshop, 1 Malet St, London WC1. Lists 2,000 works under topics.

Other useful works can be located in libraries using the subject index or just browsing through relevant Dewey numbers on the open shelves. See:

STEEL, D. J. 'The family historian's guide to the Dewey Decimal System' *Journal of the Bristol and Avon FHS* nos 1–6, Autumn 1975–Winter 1976.

County bibliographies are available for most counties, some of them extremely comprehensive. Local histories may also be located by looking up the relevant place in the British Museum's *General catalogue of printed books* (see below).

Bibliography of British history 6 vols Clarendon Press. *To 1485* by C. Gross, ed. by E. B. Graves, 1975. *Tudor period, 1485–1603* ed. by C. Read, 1959. op. *Stuart period, 1603–1714* ed. by G. Davies, rev. by M. F. Keeler, n.e. 1970.
  1789–1851 ed. by L. M. Brown and I. R. Christie, 1977.
  1851–1914 by H. J. Hanham, 1976.
  1714–89 ed. by S. Pargellis and D. J. Medley. Harvester Press, n.e. 1977.

Writings on British history: a bibliography Royal Historical Society, 1901–33; annually 1934–9, Cape; 1940–45, Cape; 1952–4, 1955–7, 1958–9, 1960–1, 1962–4, 1965–6, Institute of Historical Research.

HART, R. E. comp. *Victorian Britain* Library Association, Public Libraries Group, 1976. Bibliography of Britain 1837–1910.

Recent works:

Bibliography of British and Irish history ed. by G. R. Elton. Royal Historical Society. Annually from 1975. Harvester Press, 1976–.

BRITISH MUSEUM (now called the BRITISH LIBRARY) *General catalogue of printed books*. The quickest check on a book when the author is known. Works on local history are also listed under the places they cover, and biographies under the subject of the biography as well as the author. It is important not to overlook the various supplements. A number of subject indexes have also been published covering all books published between certain years.

IV WALES

The vast majority of the works cited in this bibliography so far are applicable to Wales. Some additional works specifically on Wales are:

Genealogical sources

HAMILTON-EDWARDS, G. K. S. *In search of Welsh ancestry* Phillimore, 1986.

SPUFFORD, P. and CAMP, A. J. eds 'Wales' in *Genealogists' Handbook* Society of Genealogists, 1969, pp 36–8. A good outline of the available sources.

BARTRUM, P. C. comp. *Welsh genealogies AD 300–1400* 8 vols, University of Wales, 1974.

COLE, E. J. L. 'Getting down to the Joneses' AH vol 7, no 6, 1967, p 189. Pitfalls in Welsh genealogy.

PITT-LEWIS, C. 'Using the IGI for Wales and Monmouthshire' in GIBSON, J. S. W. and WALCOTT, M. *Where to find the International Genealogical Index* FFHS, 1984. An absolutely indispensable guide to the complexities of using the IGI for Welsh genealogy.

POWELL, A. A. 'South Wales probate records' *Journal of Glamorgan FHS* no 2, Oct 1983.

RAWLINS, B. J. 'Effective use of bishops' transcripts in Wales' GJ vol 7, no 3, Sept 1978.

SOMERVILLE, R. ed. *Handlist of Scottish and Welsh records publications*. British Records Association, 1954.

Historical and Social Background

DAVIES, T. R. *A book of Welsh names* Sheppard Press, 1952.

DODD, A. H. *A short history of Wales* Batsford, 1977.

EGAN, D. 'Record offices and local history in Wales' parts 1, 2 and 3, LH vol 13, nos 6, 7, 8, May, August, November 1979.

EVANS, B. M. 'Sources for the study of Welsh agriculture' AH vol 7, no 5, 1967, p 154. Deals with many problems in using Welsh records.

HOWELLS, B. 'Local history in Wales' LH vol 10, no 8, Nov 1973, p 404.

HOWELLS, B. 'The historical demography of Wales: notes on some sources' LH vol 10, no 6, May 1973, p 291.

JENKINS, J. G. *Life and tradition in rural Wales* Dent, 1976.

JONES, Major F. 'An approach to Welsh genealogy' *Transactions of the Hon Soc of Cymmrodorion* (Session 1948), 1949.

JONES, G. *Modern Wales: a concise history 1485–1979* CUP, 1984.

TURNER, C. B. 'Welsh social history: some 19th century sources' LH vol 11, no 8, Nov 1975, p 449.

JONES, I. C. and WILLIAMS, D. *The religious census of 1851: a calendar of the returns relating to Wales* University of Wales Press, vol 1, South Wales 1976; vol 2 North Wales, 1981.

Biography

LLOYD, Sir J. E. and JENKINS, R. T. eds *Dictionary of Welsh biography down to 1940* Eng. lang. ed. Hon. Soc. Cymmrodorian, 1959.

Note should also be taken of the W. W. Price index at the National Library of Wales. This is a major card index to notable Welshmen of the 19th and 20th centuries.

Atlases and Gazetteers

LEWIS, S. *A topographical dictionary of Wales* 2 vols, S. Lewis, 1833.

REES, W. *An historical atlas of Wales from early to modern times* Faber, repr. 1966.

BRINKLEY, R. 'Welsh topographical literature *c.* 1770 to 1870' LH vol 11, no 1, Feb 1974, p. 7.

Parish Registers

WATTS-WILLIAMS, J. and WILLIAMS, C. *The parish registers of Wales* National Library of Wales, 1986. Lists PR, BT and printed, typescript and microfilm copies.

The Welsh counties are listed in *The Phillimore atlas and index of parish registers* (see p. 173) in three lists – North, Central and South Wales.

V SCOTLAND

Bibliographies

Many of the works listed above include Scotland. In addition there are:

BLACK, G. F. *A list of works relating to Scotland* New York Public Library, 1916. op.

HANCOCK, P. D. comp. *A bibliography of works relating to Scotland, 1916–1950* 2 vols. Edinburgh University Press, 1960. op. Continuation of the above.

FERGUSON, J. P. S. ed. *Scottish family histories held in Scottish libraries* Scottish Central Library, 1960. n.i. 1968. This includes material in manuscript and typescript.

SOMERVILLE, R. ed. *Handlist of Scottish and Welsh records publications* (Pamphlet no 4) British Records Association, 1954.

TERRY, C. S. *A catalogue of the publications of Scottish historical and kindred clubs and societies 1780–1908* Glasgow: J. MacLehose, 1909.

MATHESON, C. ed. *A catalogue of the publications of Scottish historical and kindred clubs and societies and the papers relative to Scottish history, 1908–27* Aberdeen: Milne and Hutchinson, 1928. op.

The bibliographies of Marshall, Whitmore and Barrow (see above p 186) do not include a significant amount of Scottish (or Irish) material.

Peerage and Gentry

Burke's peerage and *Burke's landed gentry* include Scottish families.

PAUL, J. B. *The Scots Peerage* 9 vols. David Douglas, 1904–14.

General Guides

HAMILTON-EDWARDS, G. *In search of Scottish ancestry* Phillimore, 2nd edn 1983.

JAMES, A. *Scottish roots: a step-by-step guide for ancestor hunters in Scotland and overseas* Macdonald, 1981. A chatty introduction, with much good practical advice. Appendix gives a list of professional researchers.

SANDISON, A. *Tracing ancestors in Shetland* T. & J. Manson, 1978.

*STEEL, D. J. *Sources of Scottish genealogy and family history* vol 12 of *National index of parish registers* Society of Genealogists, 1970.

STEEL, D. J. *Genealogical records as family history sources in Scotland: a case study* *WORLD CONF 1980, vol 5, paper 410. A worked example, like that of the Honeycombes, for Scottish sources.

WHYTE, D. *Introducing Scottish genealogical research* Scottish Genealogy Society Library, 9 Union St, Edinburgh EH1 3LT, 5th edn, 1984. An excellent inexpensive booklet for beginners.

BLAKE, T. *MacRoots: how to trace your Scottish ancestors* Edinburgh: MacDonald, 1982.

DONNACHIE, I. 'Sources of archaeology and local history in Scotland' LH vol 12, no 6, May 1977, p 296. Covers maps and plans, printed secondary sources, prints and photographs, estate, legal and business records, oral evidence, some recent publications.

HAMILTON-EDWARDS, G. K. S. 'Some Scottish records' in *BURCHALL 1986.

Family History Journals

The Scottish Genealogist (Scottish Genealogy Society – quarterly); *Highland Family History Society Journal* (quarterly);

Aberdeen and North-East Scotland Family History Society Newsletter (quarterly); Glasgow and West of Scotland Family History Society *(two per year);* Tay Valley Family History Society *(three per year).*

Other Journals

Scottish Studies, published by the School of Scottish Studies, 27 George Sq., University of Edinburgh, Edinburgh EH8 9LD; *Scottish Historical Review*, Dept of Scottish History, University of Glasgow, Glasgow G12 8QQ; *Review of Scottish Culture: A New Journal*, published by the National Museum of Antiquities of Scotland; *Society of West Highland and Island Historical Research, Notes and Queries*, published three times a year – contains much genealogical information.

Other Works on Genealogical Sources

BLOXHAM, V. B. and METCALFE, D. F. *Key to parochial registers of Scotland* Provo, Utah: Brigham Young University Press, 1970.

GIBSON, J. S. W. and WALCOT, M 'Scotland: Old Parochial Register Index' in *Where to find the International Genealogical Index* FFHS, 1984. Reports progress on the comprehensive county by county index to all Scottish registers and where copies of the available parts may be found.

*PELLING has a useful little table showing how under Scottish law an estate could be disposed of.

CADELL, P. 'Scottish estate records as a source for family history' in WORLD CONF 1980 vol 6, paper 442.

MITCHISON, R. 'Sources for Scottish Local History: 2 Kirk sessions registers' LH vol 11, no 4, Nov 1974, p 229.

See also works on irregular border marriages (page 174).

Public Records

LIVINGSTONE, M. *A guide to the public records of Scotland deposited in H. M. General Register House, Edinburgh* G.R.H. 1905. op.

THOMSON, J. M. *The public records of Scotland* Maclehose, 1922.

RODGER, R. G. 'Scottish archives and local government reorganisation' LH vol 14, no 2, May 1980, p 98.

CADELL, P. 'Sources for Scottish Local History: Manuscript Resources in the National Library of Scotland', LH vol 11, no 8, Nov 1975, p 445.

DOPSON, L. 'Scotland's national register of archives', AH vol 1, no 12, June–July 1954, p 374.

Historical and Demographic Background

FLINN, M. W. *Scottish population history from the 17th century to the 1930s.* CUP, 1978.

MACKIE, R. L. *A short history of Scotland.* Rev. edn by G. Donaldson. Mercer Press, 1978.

MARSHALL, R. K. *Women in Scotland, 1660–1780* Trustees of the National Galleries of Scotland, Edinburgh, 1979.

PLANT, M. *The domestic life of Scotland in the eighteenth century* Edinburgh University Press, 1952.

SMOUT, T. C. *A history of the Scottish people, 1560–1830* Fontana, n.e. 1985.

WARRACK, J. *Domestic life in Scotland 1488–1688* Methuen, 1920. op.

Highland Clans

ADAM, F. *The clans, septs and regiments of the Scottish highlands* 1908; Johnston and Bacon, n.e. 1970.

BAIN, R. *The clans and tartans of Scotland* Fontana, 5th edn, 1981.

INNES OF LEARNEY, Sir Thomas *The tartans of the clans and families of Scotland* Johnston and Bacon, n.e. 1971.

MARTINE, R. *Clans and tartans* Spurbooks, 1982.

MONCREIFFE, Sir Iain *The Highland clans* Barrie and Jenkins, 6th edn, 1982.

RENNIE, J. A. *The Scottish people: their clans, families and origins* Hutchinson, 1960. op.

WARNER, G. *Homelands of the clans* Collins, 1980.

Maps and Gazetteers

Parish maps published by Institute of Heraldic and Genealogical Studies, Canterbury, show parish and commissariat boundaries and starting dates of registers.

SMITH, F. *Genealogical atlas of Scotland* Logan, Utah: Everton, 1972.

SMITH, F. *A genealogical gazetteer of Scotland* Logan, Utah: Everton, 1979.

JOHNSTON, W. and A. K. *Gazetteer of Scotland* Johnston and Bacon, 2nd edn. 1958. op.

MONCREIFFE, Sir Iain and POTTINGER, D. *Map of Scotland of old* 1960. Shows areas of distribution of clans and families at the beginning of the seventeenth century.

GROOME, F. H. *The ordnance gazetteer of Scotland* Various edns in 1880s and 1890s. Considerable local detail, particularly on economic and industrial matters.

LEWIS, S. *A topographical dictionary of Scotland* 2 vols. S. Lewis, 2nd edn, 1846.

Surveys

SINCLAIR, Sir John *The statistical account of Scotland drawn up from the communications of the ministers of the different parishes* 21 vols. Edinburgh, 1791–9. Vols 2, 7 11, 12 and 13 available as facsim. edns. Educational Publications, 1974–7.

New statistical account of Scotland by the ministers of the respective parishes 15 vols. Edinburgh, 1845.

Third statistical account of Scotland. Oliver & Boyd, 1951 to date. Published in county volumes and now almost completed.

Newpapers

FERGUSON, JOAN P. S. *Scottish newspapers held in Scottish libraries* Edinburgh: Scottish Central Library, 1956.

Army

BOWLING, A. H. *Scottish regiments and uniforms, 1660–1914* Almark, 1970.

Names

BLACK, G. F. *The surnames of Scotland: their origin, meaning and history* New York Public Library, rev. edn 1984.

DUNKLING, L. *Scottish Christian names* Johnston & Bacon, 1978.

*STEEL, D. J. Sections on surnames and Christian names in *Sources for Scottish genealogy and family history* (see above).

Emigration

DONALDSON, G. *The Scots overseas* Hale, 1966. op.; Greenwood Press, US, n.e. 1976.

WHYTE, D. ed. *A dictionary of Scottish emigrants to the USA* Baltimore: Magna Charta Book Co., 1981.

CARROTHERS, W. A. *Emigration from the British Isles* 1929; F. Cass, n.i. 1965.

HILL, D. *Great emigrations: the Scots to Canada* Gentry Books, no date. op.

WHYTE, D. 'Scottish emigration: A select bibliography' *Scottish Genealogist* vol 21, Edinburgh, 1974.

Pictures

MARSHALL, R. K. 'Sources for Scottish Local History: 3. The Scottish National Portrait Gallery' LH vol 11, no 7 Aug 1975, p 382. Holds 20,000 photographs as well as portraits.

Heraldry

INNES OF LEARNEY, Sir T. *Scots heraldry* Oliver & Boyd, 1956.

GRANT, Sir F. J. *Manual of heraldry* John Grant, 1924.

PAUL, Sir J. Balfour *An ordinary of arms contained in the public register of arms and bearings in Scotland* W. Green, 1893; 2nd edn 1903.

PAUL, Sir J. Balfour *An ordinary of arms contained in the public register of all arms and bearings in Scotland 1902–1973* Edinburgh: Lyon Office, 1977.

VI IRELAND, CHANNEL ISLANDS AND ISLE OF MAN

IRELAND

Bibliographies

DE BREFFNY, B. *Bibliography of Irish genealogy and family history* Cork: Golden Eagle Books, 1974.

EAGER, A. R. ed. *A guide to Irish bibliographical material: a bibliography of Irish bibliographies and sources of information.* Library Association, 1980.

General Guides

There is a useful short summary of sources in SPUFFORD, P. and CAMP, A. J. *Genealogist's handbook* Society of Genealogists, 1969.

BLACK, J. A. *Your Irish ancestors* Paddington Press, 1974.

BEGLEY, D. F. *Handbook on Irish genealogy: how to trace your ancestors and relatives in Ireland* Dublin: Heraldic Artists, 6th edn, 1984. Includes genealogical maps of Ireland.

BEGLEY, D. F. ed. *Irish genealogy: a record finder* Dublin: Heraldic Artists, 1981. A very useful source by source account, with many useful lists of surviving records.

BEGLEY, D. F. *The ancestor trail in Ireland* Dublin: Heraldic Artists, 1982.

CLARE, W. *A simple guide to Irish genealogy* 3rd edn ed. by R. ffolliott. Irish Genealogical Research Society, 1967.

O'LAUGHLIN, M. C. *The complete book for tracing your Irish ancestors.* Privately printed. North Kansas City, Missouri, 1980.

A very detailed work of reference is:

FALLEY, M. C. *Irish and Scotch-Irish ancestral research* 2 vols. Baltimore: Genealogical Pubs, 1984.

Note: The Genealogy Bookshop, 3 Nassau Street, Dublin 2, Ireland offer a special package called *Personal reference library and family tree kit for tracing your Irish ancestors.* This consists of: *The ancestor trail in Ireland: a companion guide* (32pp); *Handbook on Irish genealogy* (160pp); Genealogical and Historical Map of Ireland (map with over 3,000 families in their historical area); *Irish genealogy: a record finder* (a book on sources, 256pp); *The Surnames of Ireland* (over 4,000 names treated, 330pp); Family tree charts. At the time of going to press, this package costs US$20 (US$30 including postage).

Journals

The Irish Genealogist, published by the Irish Genealogical Society of Great Britain (see p 157).

Irish Family Links (formerly called *Family Links, Past and Present*), published by the Irish Genealogical Association (see p 157).

Journal of North of Ireland Family History Society

All Ireland Heritage, available from the Editor, 2255 Cedar Lane, Vienna, Virginia 22180 USA.

Published Pedigrees

MACLYSAGHT, E. *Irish families: their names, arms and origins* Irish Academic Press, 4th rev edn, 1985.

MACLYSAGHT, E. *More Irish Families* Irish Academic Press, 2nd edn 1982.

Burke's Landed Gentry of Ireland, Harrison & Sons, 1899, 1904, 1912, 1958.

MONTGOMERY-MASSINGBERD, H. ed *Burke's Irish family records* 5th edn, Burke's Peerage, 1975–6. The useful introductory section has also been published separately as *Burke's Introduction to Irish Ancestry* Burke's Peerage, 1976.

Names

MACLYSAGHT, E A. E. *The surnames of Ireland* Irish Academic Press, 6th edn 1985.

MATHERSON, Sir R. E. *Irish surnames.* Lists all surnames which have at least 5 entries in the birth registrations for 1890, and gives information on the distribution of the name and variant spellings.

WOULFE, P. *Irish names and surnames* Dublin: Gill, 1906. Returns of owners of land of one acre and upwards, 1876. Useful for relating surnames to particular areas.

Maps and Gazetteers

HERALDIC ARTISTS LTD, *Genealogical and Historical Map of Ireland* Heraldic Artists Ltd, Dublin, 1979.

LEWIS, S. *A topographical dictionary of Ireland* Facs. 1837 edn, Kennikat Press, 1970.

SMITH, F. and GARDNER, D. E. *Genealogical atlas of Ireland* Logan, Utah: Everton: 1972.

ISLE OF MAN

*SMITH and GARDNER vol 2, p 252 have a useful summary of Manx records, most still valid.

MOORE, A. W. *Manx names* Elliot Stock, 1903. op.

CHANNEL ISLANDS

BURNESS, L. R. 'Genealogical research in the Channel Islands' GM vol 19, March 1978.

BALLEINE, G. R. *A biographical dictionary of Jersey* Staples Press, 1948.

LANGTON, C. 'Records and record searching in Jersey, GM vol 5, June 1931, p 314.

PAYNE, J. B. *An armorial of Jersey being an account, heraldic and antiquarian of its chief native families with pedigrees, biographical notices* Jersey, 1859–65.

Index